CONFIDENTIAL RELATIONSHIPS

Psychoanalytic, Ethical, and Legal Contexts

VIBS

Volume 141

a volume in
Philosophy and Psychology
PAP
Jon Mills, Editor

CONFIDENTIAL RELATIONSHIPS

Psychoanalytic, Ethical, and Legal Contexts

Edited by

Christine M. Koggel,
Allannah Furlong
and
Charles Levin

Rodopi

Amsterdam - New York, NY 2003

The paper on which this book is printed meets the requirements of "ISO 9706:1994, Information and documentation - Paper for documents - Requirements for permanence".

ISBN: 90-420-0835-0

Printed in the Netherlands

CONTENTS

Part Three

ETHICS

Part Four

LAW

EDITORIAL FOREWORD

Editors Christine M. Koggel,Charles Levin, and Allannah Furlong have compiled an extraordinarily timely and monumental contribution to the problem of confidential relationships within contemporary society. Focusing on psychoanalytic, ethical, and legal perspectives situated within the ongoing challenges posed by the privacy debate, these essays offer illuminating inquiries into the conundrums of confidentiality each of us potentially face.

The nature of confidential relationships in the clinical consulting room is as much a sacred relationship as the Catholic confessional and lawyer-client privilege. Until now, relatively little has been said on the value, meaning, and primacy of professional confidentiality and its ramifications for public and private life with such clarity, substance, and cogency as do the essays assembled here.

The contributors in this volume call attention to the need for ethical, legal, and clinical reform within psychotherapeutic practice and persuasively argue for increased research, dialogue, and practical cooperation among the disparate fields of mental health, law, philosophy, public and social policy, the behavioral sciences, moral theory, information technology, mass media, economics, gender and cultural studies, and human relations within our liberal democracy.

Nowhere do we find such outstanding contributions with potentially viable solutions to the dilemmas of context as set forth in this volume. This book is destined to revolutionize the way we conceptualize and broach the question of confidentiality within professional and private space.

Jon Mills
Editor, PAP

PREFACE

The idea for this volume emerged in the aftermath of the international conference, "Confidentiality & Society: Psychotherapy, Ethics and the Law: Social, Philosophical and Psychoanalytic Perspectives," held in Montreal in October 2000. At this conference, researchers from the three main areas of psychoanalysis, philosophy, and law began the work of examining the concepts, principles, therapeutic processes, court cases, and legislation relevant to confidentiality both inside and outside the liberal democratic context. The conference opened up a forum for interdisciplinary dialogue that is continued in this collection that brings together the work of some of the most prominent psychoanalysts, philosophers, and legal theorists on the topic of confidentiality.

Confidentiality as examined at the Conference and in this volume is a concept reserved for the therapeutic context. While the concept of confidentiality is closely related to that of privacy, the latter is a broader concept covering a diverse set of legal and philosophical issues ranging from the debate on abortion to issues raised in the modern day context of electronic surveillance and the suspension of rights when terrorists strike. Unlike privacy, confidentiality is not usefully conceived as a general concept inviting "application across the board." Instead, it functions in specific social practices and pertains to particular kinds of relationships that are highly context-dependent and context-sensitive. Confidentiality thus generates extremely interesting and often conflicting accounts of the values of privacy, secrecy, and individuality; particularly with regard to the functions of information and "truth" in relationships.

Professional, psychological, ethical, and legal perspectives on the consequences of, and justifications for, breaching confidentiality often diverge radically. For these reasons, our subject shares the topicality but not the broadness of the contemporary privacy debate. Confidentiality usefully reframes many of the basic philosophical and social policy questions related to privacy and autonomy because it poses them directly in terms of well-defined relationships governed by explicit codes of professional conduct.

Finding solutions to the problem of confidentiality is vital for several reasons. It illuminates the overlap in ethical preoccupations shared by the research community and front line professionals in psychotherapy and the law. There are, for example, important links to be made between the scientific principles upon which clinical practice is based and new philosophical work that critically analyzes traditional liberal democratic values of privacy, autonomy, and individual rights. Second, identifying the areas of disagreement and tension opens the way to understanding, if not resolving, the different concerns of all those interested in balancing the relevant interests and values at stake in the debate on confidentiality. At this intersection where ethical, legal, and clinical issues collide, timely and important interdisciplinary contributions can be made.

This volume addresses the need for research and dialogue by focusing the collective attention of psychotherapists, the legal community, public policy experts, social scientists, and ethicists on the moral, social, and clinical problems of confidentiality in psychotherapeutic practice. Of critical significance, in our view, is the opportunity for an exchange between forms of discourse rooted in sometimes inherently different principles and practical aims. What are the practical and theoretical issues relevant to the different stakeholders on the topic of confidentiality? What effects does the modern day proliferation of information technology and mass media have on our understanding of confidentiality? Does common ground exist among the methods and concepts of "truth" proper to therapeutic, legal, and academic contexts of meaning and professional practice? Can the ethical disjunctions arising from these different contexts be respected and harmonized at the level of public policy? How can these competing perspectives be weighed in the balance of the larger public interest? Do changes to social practices or particular political contexts affect the meaning of confidentiality and what happens then in the therapeutic context? What impact does the law or the therapeutic process have on members of disadvantaged groups and is this relevant to the discussion of confidentiality? Is an analysis of the role and function of relationships useful in discussions of the therapeutic, moral, and legal aspects of confidentiality? If so, does this area of convergence hold promise for the possibility of devising solutions to a problem that continues to be vexing for theorists and policy makers? In preparing this collection, the editors have been concerned about the need to determine the relevance of confidentiality in ethics and the law, not only for government, science, and the professions, but for all persons who rely on these institutions for appropriate use and well-being.

Christine M. Koggel
Charles Levin
Allannah Furlong

ACKNOWLEDGMENTS

This book would not have been possible without the hard work of the contributors. For most of them, their work began with the presentation of papers at the "Confidentiality & Society" conference in Montreal in October 2000. Our contributors proved to be unfailing in their efforts, often in the face of numerous suggestions for revisions and last minute requests during the editorial process. We would like to thank them for their commitment to issues of confidentiality and to this project.

We are grateful to Carleton University and, in particular, Aviva Freedman, Dean of Arts and Social Sciences, and Jay Drydyk, Chair of Department of Philosophy, for awarding a grant toward the cost of the editorial work. We would also like to thank the Quebec English Branch of the Canadian Psychoanalytic Society and the Canadian Psychoanalytic Society for their support, both financial and moral.

A number of people were involved in preparing the manuscript. Lorraine Kirschner and Jodi Jacoby could be counted on for advice about the mysteries of Word and various Editors at Rodopi have been particularly helpful in the tasks related to production. A special thanks goes to Richard Hull, who prepared the manuscript and the index. Richard worked with a tight schedule and made the pressure filled final stages of preparing the manuscript manageable. It was a pleasure to work with him. We would also like to thank our Series Editor, Jon Mills. His support of this project from the very early stages of its conception made all the difference to our goal of maintaining high standards.

Last, but far from least, all three editors express heartfelt gratitude to their respective spouses who have been exceptionally patient about the time and attention required for this endeavor.

We hope that psychoanalysts, psychotherapists, social workers, philosophers, ethicists, legal theorists, lawyers, and the general public will find the book useful in the theoretical and practical work they do on confidentiality and for the confidential relationships they are in.

Part One

INTRODUCTION

One

QUESTIONS AND THEMES

Charles Levin, Christine M. Koggel, and Allannah Furlong

Though it is not likely to determine the outcome of any general elections, the problem of confidentiality in psychotherapy has developed so many complex policy ramifications in the last few decades that it may now be considered a political bell-weather issue. As the chapters in this book will demonstrate, it is no longer possible to think deeply about confidentiality in purely formal or exclusively professional terms as exemplified in the discourse of constitutional rights or administrative guidelines. Confidentiality has become an important interdisciplinary and multidisciplinary problem. It is the focus of intense dialogue among psychotherapists, social scientists, philosophers, and legal theorists regarding central questions in contemporary culture: the nature of psychoanalytic psychotherapy; the meaning and value of confidentiality and the related concept of privacy; the nature of law's impact on professional relationships; the relationship between mental health and law; the political and cultural effects of mass media and information technology; the current crisis of professional authority; differential treatment on the basis of factors such as gender and race; the distinction between the private and the public spheres (or between private life, civil society, and the state); the meaning and scope of constitutional rights; as well as the "balance" between different kinds of rights. To ask questions about confidentiality is to ask about democratic culture itself and the form we would like it to take.

The Hippocratic Oath is in many ways a prototypical condensation of the kinds of social process that have informed and shaped the social practices of confidentiality as we understand it today. Apart from the confessional booth, it is probably the most widely recognized symbol of a confidential relationship in our culture. The Hippocratic Oath conveys the vague but inspiring idea that certain individuals, by virtue of their special status in an indistinct hierarchy of knowledge, wisdom, and expertise, actually take an oath in which they swear themselves to secrecy. Why this should be so is usually left unclear; but there is something compelling about the idea of a "sacred vow," of someone making what is in effect a spiritual commitment on our behalf, a solemn undertaking to protect and to serve our intimate being, our health, our body, our soul. What could be more romantic, more seductive, more conducive of trust? Remnants of the mythology and metaphysics of the sacred pact of secrecy and confidence still thrive in contemporary social life, notably in religious sectarianism, politics, and organized crime. They linger on as well in the rhetoric of rights and duties that inspire national covenants, institutional charters, and professional codes of conduct. The ideal of a sacred vow is still present as an image, but it is pushed into the background in contemporary liberal democracies and replaced by the rational-discursive construct of confidentiality as a particular instance of the general concept of privacy, usually conceived as an inherent right of the individual citizen.

In medicine, appeals to the Hippocratic Oath have played an important rhetorical role in advancing the notion of confidentiality as a mysterious and inviolable ethical absolute. Yet scrutiny of the actual oath suggests that physicians have always been more like pragmatic communicators than spiritual leaders or ethical idealists: "Whatever in connection with my professional practice or not in connection with it I may see or hear in the lives of my patients which ought not be spoken abroad, I will not divulge, reckoning that all such should be kept secret." Like the lawyer, the physician historically has turned out to be a mundane specialist whose practical consciousness is oriented toward the social and technical *uses* of information, not its sacred character or its safekeeping. In order to achieve his or her purposes, the healer requires access to personal information not usually sought and not normally disseminated. As part of the *modus operandi*, he or she must be mindful of the way in which context changes the information received. For professional reasons, the healer will certainly share a great deal of what he or she sees and hears in the course of treatment with fellow practitioners, who are also bound by the oath. And the healer may require that members of the patient's family, or even of the community, who can play a critical role in the healing process, be selectively informed.

The conclusion that the notion of confidentiality in the helping profession has its roots in pragmatic considerations about the requirements of professional practice and treatment is inescapable. The fundamental issue appears to be not patients' privacy or a sacred oath of secrecy; rather, it is the built in need for the individual patient's *cooperation* in order for treatment to work. The work of the healer simply cannot be accomplished without free access to information that individuals, even in primitive and collectivist societies, do not spontaneously divulge. This is a far cry from a sacred vow. The point and purpose of confidential relationships in the healing profession, sketched here and by the authors in Part Two, is also a far cry from how they tend to be viewed and have been treated by the law and society in general.

While privacy is central to contemporary debates about confidentiality, the meaning and status of this principle are highly contested in the professional, political, and legal realms of policy formation and legislation today. If, as already suggested, psychotherapy is sensitive to nuances in the social environment, the practice of law, in so far as it seeks to establish itself on universal principles and repeatable practices, is prone in the opposite direction, to oversimplification and misapplication in the specific and vulnerable context of the healing profession that we have been examining. The demand for justice might entail, for example, that a defendant in a sexual assault case be granted access to a confidential psychiatric file in order to satisfy his right to "full answer and defense." The public demand for safety might require that the identities of potentially dangerous individuals in treatment be made known and that their potential victims be warned. Society may require that professions be held to strict standards of conduct and that they be made accountable through investigation and quality control of professional practice. And finally, the marketplace of public and private insurers may demand third-party access to clinical files and control over information about individual cases.

The clash between professional practice and the public interest, and the values defended on each side, are so complex that many questions related to the meaning of confidentiality and its practical social implications remain not only unanswered, but virtually unexamined. The central aims of this book are to outline some of the terms of the current debate, to examine the practical and the moral implications, and to begin to provide answers to questions about the problem of confidentiality in the modern day context. Two key strategies are used to achieve these aims. First, Parts Two through Four present a range of perspectives by psychoanalysts, ethicists, and legal theorists on the meaning and value of confidentiality to individuals, specific relationships, and the state. These parts identify the issues at stake in the debate and allow the disagreements and differences of perspectives within and across the disciplines to emerge. What also emerges, however, is a sketch of the intersections and commonalities not only within each part, but also among them. This feature of the book as a whole introduces the second strategy. Bringing together detailed exchanges across the disciplines centrally related to confidentiality allows us to explore convergences in the perspectives and among the disciplines, some of which we outline at the end of this introduction. First, however, we want to draw out the various connections within and across the disciplines to highlight features of the contemporary context that have shaped the debate on confidentiality. Then we draw attention to some underlying and unifying ideas in order to begin the task of providing insights into the problem and its solutions.

Confidentiality has become controversial in recent years in part because the psychotherapeutic relationship it is designed to protect has been affected by various changes to social practices and the political context. As Paul Mosher recounts in his masterful review of the last half-century of American jurisprudence on the question of privilege, psychotherapy as a profession has undergone a massive process of expansion and diversification in recent years. This has had a profound impact not only on the way psychotherapy is offered and consumed, but also on the larger culture in which it is embedded. The contribution of Michael Yeo and Andrew Brook details this point from a social, economic, and technological perspective. They identify both a significant shift in the status and role of the helping professions in the modern "post-industrial" world of information technology and a silent revolution in the moral framework within which psychotherapy is practiced. In a parallel exploration of the confluence of consumerism, commodification, and the therapeutic culture, Charles Levin and Christine Ury examine a similar transformation of moral framework in the psychological and cultural domains, showing how the traditional inward orientation of psychoanalytic psychotherapy has been superceded in part by a culture of transparency in which the public confession, as exemplified in modern day television talk shows, has begun to replace the private confidence as a therapeutic modality.

As the personal has become increasingly public and political, psychotherapy itself has evolved and proliferated into a variety of activist statements about political issues, social values, and alternative lifestyles. For example, confidentiality in the context of professional and administrative practice has become an important concern for women and for minority and disadvantaged groups generally. Feminists point out that because women and other disadvantaged groups continue to suffer from discriminatory practices, they tend to be more affected by confidentiality issues in general whenever legal proceedings, third-party payers, or any other practice involving the transmission of clinical information, are involved. Work in the chapters by Karen Busby, Sue Campbell, Margaret Denike, Christine Koggel, and Nathalie Des Rosiers offer feminist perspectives on the problems of confidentiality, ones that cross the traditional boundaries of psychoanalysis, philosophy, and legal theory by examining the discriminatory impact of legislation and court decisions on clients, patients, and therapists. The impact of this analysis and the controversy it has generated is reflected in the turmoil generated in the courts and in changes to the legal process itself.

Spectacular trials involving real and imagined atrocities discovered or reconstructed in therapy hurled the psychotherapy profession onto the witness stand and into the political process. Suddenly, psychotherapists were being seen as important sources of information and leadership in the struggle against crime and social injustice. In Canada, this led to a striking series of court decisions involving compelled disclosure of personal files on evidentiary grounds, notably the Supreme Court decisions in *Osolin*, *O'Connor*, *Carosella*, and *Mills*. The extraordinary implications of these legal developments for the privacy and confidentiality of ordinary citizens (particularly women) is the subject of detailed exploration in chapters by Busby, Campbell, and Denike. They apply their analyses to specific issues that have loosened restrictions in court proceedings and created what many would describe as a "crisis of confidentiality."

Busby's contribution focuses directly on the havoc created in the psychotherapeutic world by this "crisis of confidentiality." No longer able to assure the security of their professional services, therapists and counselors, particularly those working with sexual assault victims, have been forced to reconsider basic practices, even the details of clinical record keeping. Urgently required psychological treatment is often deterred or refused for fear that therapists and their files will be subpoenaed. Even personal diaries are at risk. Busby discusses what counselors and social workers may need to do to prevent the disclosure of the personal records of their clients in contexts in which confidentiality is not protected by legislation. In a related investigation, Campbell discusses the politicization of memory research in court testimony questioning the reliability of witnesses. She argues that the controversy over recovered memory in recent decades has further encouraged a long-standing practice of undue intrusiveness into the lives of complainants in assault cases. The process of memory is abstracted from its social context and hypostatized as a fragile entity, always subject to gender related doubt and skepticism. Campbell demystifies the role of memory by arguing that suggestibility is a feature of the lives of all of us since we are all affected and shaped by the relationships we are in. In similar fashion, Denike shows how the hypostatization of individual rights serves to obscure the unequal social context in which intrusive manipulations of legal process have been occurring. Behind the judicial claim to be "balancing rights," Denike argues, a long history of gender stereotyping and social myth has been silently tipping the balance in favor of disclosure of personal records. An important aspect of her analysis, which we return to later, is her critique of liberal conceptions of individual rights that fail to capture inequalities in public and private relationships.

The social consequences of these developments cannot be isolated from the fact that psychotherapy is itself an extremely sensitive process, more than usually vulnerable to social, political, and legal pressures. The result has been that confidentiality, formerly taken for granted as a moral precept, has been transformed into a self-conscious ethical practice contested from within the profession of psychotherapy itself on matters such as informed consent, the prioritization of public safety concerns over individual mental health, and clinical reporting. R. D. Hinshelwood uses his chapter to illustrate the inseparability of clinical and ethical reflection in contemporary psychoanalytic clinical practice. Through several detailed case examples, he illustrates the intricate way in which social and ethical conflicts become intertwined with the unconscious transference and countertransference dynamic in the therapeutic process. Like Hinshelwood, Allannah Furlong also argues that confidentiality is a highly context-specific relationship. Her investigation identifies a fundamental incommensurability between the context of psychotherapeutic discourse and the context of legal reasoning: "In court, a witness is sworn to 'tell the truth, the whole truth and nothing but the truth.' What the psychoanalyst asks of patients is radically different, that is, to suspend their rational, moral, or social inhibitions so as to say whatever comes to mind, be it true or false, silly or serious, lurid or laudable. Within the limits of the therapeutic hour, [psychoanalysts] promote irresponsibility in speech, the very opposite of what is demanded on the witness stand" (this volume, p. 13). Not only does this lead to an important reconsideration of the concept of "truth" in psychotherapy; it also reveals the incompatibility of statements generated in the psycho-therapeutic process and the specific criteria of the truth-seeking process in law, which employs very different standards and methodologies.

The surprising depth at which ethical issues involving confidentiality inform the transference-countertransference relationship is further explored in Jacques Mauger's reflections on the transindividual unconscious significance of what cannot be revealed in the dyadic relationship. Taking his departure from Freud's late metapsychological research, Mauger shows how the transindividual dimension of unconscious mental life has been ignored in the confidentiality debate. The analyst is ethically bound to maintain the privacy of the individual; yet much of what both analyst and patient encounter in the therapeutic process expresses a collective (if unconscious) history and experience not reducible to the isolated history of the individual. The analyst inevitably communicates more than he or she intends. In raising the question whether it is even desirable for the analyst to remain silent about the transindividual dimensions of human suffering, Mauger raises fundamental doubts about the very nature of the distinction between the private/individual and the public/collective spheres of psychological life.

The classic liberal private/public dichotomy with its corresponding defense of non interference by the state in the private lives of individuals has already been brought sharply into question by Denike, Campbell, and Busby. Yet this liberal framework is of fundamental historical importance in the analysis of the current crisis of confidentiality, as Yeo and Brook and Levin and Ury also contend. Denike, Des Rosiers, and Koggel respond to the current crisis by providing critical analyses of liberal individualism, offering new conceptions and preconceptions of equality and the law, and drawing out the implications of this for moral and political theory and the courts. Des Rosiers calls for a thoroughgoing re-examination of legal approaches to privacy and confidentiality. Citing the 1997 mandate of the Law Commission of Canada "to develop a multidisciplinary approach informed by analysis of the context in which the law is lived and applied," (this volume, p. 230) she argues that the Law Reform process, in order to fulfill this mandate, needs to adopt a *relational* approach to the problem of confidentiality.

Relational approaches have roots in many intellectual traditions, none predominant, and thus serve as an excellent meeting point for interdisciplinary dialogue. Among these source traditions, the developing theory of restorative justice, relational thinking in linguistic philosophy and ethics, neo-liberal and feminist theories of social equality, and various kinds of relational theory in psychoanalysis have proved particularly important. It can be said that a key insight emerging from the exploration of different views thus far is the interdisciplinary work of theorists who are placing an analysis of relationships in the forefront of discussions of confidentiality. Koggel's contribution to this volume represents a seminal statement on the contours of a relational theory of confidentiality. She uses relational insights to challenge traditional liberal understandings of individual rights and individuality. Specifically, she reconceives the paradigmatic individual right to freedom of speech in relational terms and thereby shifts the focus to an analysis of relationships that can either help or harm moral development and human flourishing. Relational theory may, therefore, signal a potential convergence of disciplines and new approaches, if not solutions, to the problem of confidentiality.

When attention is paid to relationships and the function and purpose of confidentiality within them, then processes of our socialization into particular kinds of relationships and the relevance of these to an account of confidentiality become apparent. The most basic of these processes can be found in any society whatsoever: the experience of intimate interpersonal relationships, in which one learns about the differential exchange and flow of communication within the social group; for example, the complex psychological and social dynamics of gossip or the making, keeping, and breaking of secrets. The second source is more specific (though not exclusive) to contemporary Western society. It involves a complex initiation into the labyrinth of specialized modern services, expert practices, and vested authorities that characterize the work world of the nation state: medicine, religion, education, law, business, and government. In other words, it involves the general structure of institutions in which one learns to negotiate the implicit and explicit norms, customs, and ideals of the professional and public milieu.

Of these broad cultural inputs, the first may be only tacit and rather obscure in its meaning and influence; it has to do with intuitions and feelings about the internal worlds of others, the ways in which personal and social boundaries are experienced and manipulated for any number of motives. It has to do with the ways in which both personal and public relationships shape our lives and our very ability to develop as moral agents. Psychoanalytic theory shows that much of this relational interplay is internalized at an early age and experienced unconsciously. The second social input that constitutes the norms of confidentiality is, by contrast, usually overt and declarative, easily lending itself to efforts of simplification and formulaic articulation, such as logical formalization and codification. It has to do with political ideologies, constitutions, and codes of ethics. The public profile of confidentiality is largely determined by this more explicit dimension of confidentiality as a social institution. The actual meaning and practice of confidentiality, however, remain embedded in the shadowy politics of the interpersonal world. Both the private-interpersonal and public-collective dimensions of confidentiality are continuously intertwined; and both implicate confidentiality in complex relationships of desire and power at the levels of both the personal and public.

Bill Fulford has argued that we need to question "the belief that ethical issues of professional confidentiality would be resolved if only we had a sufficiently clear and comprehensive set of rules. ...[W]e need to widen the agenda of bioethics. Instead of continuing to chase after ever more detailed criteria of confidentiality, we should look rather to the *processes* by which, drawing on implicit knowledge, professional judgments of confidentiality are actually made" (Fulford, 2001, p. 13). A relational approach, with its attention to the specificity of context and practices, captures this shift in perspective, a shift that has several important consequences for the issue of confidentiality. The first is that confidentiality no longer appears as a uniform concept, a specific instance of a general idea, which can be deduced and analyzed in the abstract. Instead, confidentiality is reconfigured as a highly context-dependent and heterogeneous form of activity, with meanings and protocols different in psychoanalysis from general medicine or social work or law or religion. The second important consequence is that the relationship between confidentiality, now conceived as a practice, and democratic legal principles needs to be reconsidered. If confidentiality is no longer simply an instantiation of abstract principles like privacy, then it no longer makes quite so much sense to think in terms of "balancing" it against other instances of such principles or trying to get it to weigh more than them. Confidentiality may still be defended on the grounds that it implies or embodies certain fundamental rights, but the main argument will shift onto the ground of its pragmatic meaning and, therefore, toward the nature of psychotherapy itself as one of many different contexts generating a specific form of confidentiality which may warrant a precise legal understanding in our context and for our time.

That the grounding of confidentiality may turn out to be context and practice dependent does not at all suggest that it has been severed from its ethical moorings in liberal democratic theory and cast adrift in a relativistic sea of shifting political currents and special interests. On the contrary, the debates and struggles around confidentiality can themselves be viewed as instances of good democratic practice, and the latter itself may be understood in much the same way as confidentiality is theorized in this book. In attempting to move beyond traditional liberal democratic conceptions of equality and rights, what emerges from the discussions of confidentiality offered here may be a relational theory of liberal democracy itself. According to this way of seeing things, the principles and practices of democratic life are not applications of abstract and universal ideas to political and social life. They are a complex arrangement of evolving activities that have emerged only gradually, and by no means always in harmony with each other. Freedom of speech, the concept of moral autonomy, the value of individuality, the pursuit of equality, or the confidentiality of psychotherapy—all may be part of the same democratic political totality, but they by no means represent a homogeneous and integrated culture. They are practices generating experiences that sometimes lead to insights suggesting better or fairer or more inclusive or more productive ways of arranging social relationships. The insights upon which they are based come partly through the trial and error of political life and it takes many generations to establish them, remember them, and develop them.

Works Cited

Fulford, Bill (K.W.M.). (2000) "The Paradoxes of Confidentiality: A Philosophical Introduction," in *Confidentiality & Mental Health*, edited by Christopher Cordess. London: Jessica Kingsley, pp. 7–23.

Part Two

PSYCHOANALYSIS

Two

THE QUESTIONABLE CONTRIBUTION OF PSYCHOTHERAPEUTIC AND PSYCHOANALYTIC RECORDS TO THE TRUTH-SEEKING PROCESS

Allannah Furlong

"As Sherlock Homes remarked on more than one occasion, evidence which seems to point unerringly in one direction, may, in fact, if viewed from a slightly altered perspective, admit of precisely the opposite interpretation."

(Meyer, 1974, p. 6)

1. The Cross-Purpose of Cross-Examination of Psychotherapy Evidence

In court, a witness is sworn to "tell the truth, the whole truth and nothing but the truth". What the psychoanalyst asks of patients is radically different, that is, to suspend their rational, moral, or social inhibitions so as to say whatever comes to mind, be it true or false, silly or serious, lurid, or laudable. Within the limits of the therapeutic hour, we promote irresponsibility in speech, the very opposite of what is exhorted on the witness stand. Patients are encouraged to engage in experimental thought and to postpone critical judgment. By this stratagem, the murky and poorly understood parts of our inner life eventually find expression in words allowing them to be contended with.

To delimit my analysis of the contribution of psychotherapeutic and psychoanalytic records to the law's truth-seeking process, I must revisit and insist upon the crucial distinction between expertise and the treatment situation. I see no valid reason why the courts should want to deprive themselves of a prudent and informed awareness of current cognitive and neuropsychological findings by calling upon expert witnesses who have no ongoing professional relationship to the parties before the bench. However, it is a different matter altogether for the court to seek evidence from the psychotherapeutic or psychoanalytic treatment relationship because of the nature of the emotional/psychological bond between therapist and patient. What makes material from "dynamic" forms of psychotherapy of questionable value to the courts are the very same elements that account for its sensitivity to disruption from outside forces.

One way to convey to non-psychotherapists the problematic value of psychotherapy records in the truth-seeking process is by dissecting an actual court case. I will take as an example the Supreme Court decision of *R. v. Osolin* [1993] in which a rape conviction was overturned by the appellate court because the trial judge had denied the accused an opportunity for cross-examination of the alleged victim regarding a remark her psychiatrist had noted in her dossier. The seventeen-year old had been under psychiatric treatment for depression and anxiety. "She is concerned that her attitude and behavior may have influenced the man to some extent and is having second thoughts about the entire case" (*R. v. Osolin* [1993], p. 661).

It is fascinating to note that although the court acknowledged the potentially misleading impact of this material, nonetheless, relevance was more or less taken for granted. Without access to the tool of cross-examination, the court reasoned, it was impossible "to determine whether there was evidence to support a defense of honest but mistaken belief [in consent] or evidence to support an allegation of fabrication" (*R. v. Osolin* [1993], p. 601).

Unfortunately, established legal avenues for determining relevance and probative value are unsuitable when applied to psychotherapeutic or psychoanalytic documents. The yield is bound to be misleading, unreliable, and prejudicial. The error is akin to one of de-contextualization, of lack of appreciation of the nature of the therapeutic relationship from which the information has been culled. In the *Osolin* decision, the court was quite willing to acknowledge the complainant's interests in privacy with her psychiatrist, as well as recognizing that she could be re-traumatized if forced into a cross-examination of remarks made in the context of her psychotherapy. However, in doing so the court was really only acknowledging the sensitive nature of the subject matter rather than appreciating the uniqueness of her rapport with a psychiatrist. Similar sensitive information could just as easily have been revealed in the secrecy of a personal diary or in confidence to a trusted friend. What the court does not fully comprehend is that when such a statement occurs within a psychotherapeutic relationship, our capacity to investigate it outside of the treatment situation is radically curtailed. The quantum leap has to do with the special nature of the psychotherapeutic interaction and the regressive emotional patterns and fantasies which surface within it.

When the aim of a professional relationship is self-knowledge and personal growth, as is the case in most forms of dynamic psychotherapy, a series of special considerations must guide the outsider's appreciation of confidentiality. These elements characterize the founding principles in psychoanalytic treatment, and, to a greater or lesser extent, other forms of psychotherapy and counseling.

2. Aspects of Psychotherapeutic and Psychoanalytic Treatment which Militate Against the Truth-Seeking Process of the Court

A. Division in the Patient-Subject: Who is Speaking to Whom?

It is well known that psychoanalysis presupposes that human beings are divided from parts of their own psychic life by internal repressive forces. No person finds it easy to accept awareness of parts of self that do not coincide with personal or social ideals. These parts may be leftovers from earlier experiences in which unwanted identifications have taken place with negative adult models or they may derive from unconscious compliance with parental expectations. Though the adult subject may explicitly disavow them, these split-off parts of self continue to influence attitudes and behavior

When a patient says something in therapy, the therapist must be curious about whom, in the internal psychological sense, he or she is actually speaking and to whom, as an unconsciously targeted listener, the statement is being made. Is it a child confessing to a parent? Is it a little boy trying to hit back at a primitive and persecutory mother figure? The patient may not be fully aware of the hidden reverberations, present and past, of interactions with the therapist. The adolescent complainant in the *Osolin* trial had been having a lot of difficulties with her parents in the months prior to her turbulent encounter with the defendant. We can wonder what aspects of her conflicts over sex and authority were triggered in her psychotherapy whenever references to the alleged traumatic events came up.

Psychotherapists are trained to listen for unacknowledged turmoil in the human heart and to realize that more often than not patients are speaking to them with richly forked tongues—that is addressing them as unconscious stand-ins for other significant individuals in the patient's current life or history. In fact, the bread-and-butter, as it were, of therapeutic work counts on the ambiguity of address in speech, an ambiguity that exists in non-therapeutic situations as well but which is fostered and deepened by the particular framework of the psychoanalytic situation. It is unwise of courts to wade into this marshy territory of latent meaning in efforts to second-guess the credibility or memory of witnesses. For instance, whether or not a man was browbeaten by his mother should not alter the court's assessment of the factual question of his having committed rape. Yet such a history, perhaps forgotten or denied, might be an important topic in psychotherapy as a crucial element undermining his interactions with women. If, for the sake of argument and as a fictitious example, we imagine him as having confided to his psychiatrist that the woman was "forcing him to have sex with her," cross-examination on such a remark (and the family history behind it) would only muddle all our traditional and necessary assumptions about legal responsibility and free action.

B. Transference and Counter-Transference: The "Relativity" of Meaning

In psychotherapy and psychoanalysis, speech is not a simple descriptive communication. Speech is understood as communication related to the wish by one human being to be recognized and validated by another. Speech is not just about something. It is *addressed to someone* about something. We referred earlier to parallel psychological processes which "double" or "shadow" the professional encounter with conscious and unconscious personal meaning. These meanings may derive from earlier relationships or present-day fantasies of the patient and, we must underline this, they are activated on both sides of the professional relationship. Typically, they are not integrated by the conscious self, and are often repudiated. Technically, they are known as "transferences" when they occur in the patient and "counter-transferences" when they occur in the doctor or analyst.

The most important difference between the medical and psychotherapeutic relationship lies in the way these transference and counter-transference processes are handled. In the doctor-patient relationship, transference may play a secondary role of some importance, but outside of the controversial placebo effect, it has no recognized medical involvement. The diagnosis and treatment of organic pathology requires no exploration of the relationship between doctor and patient and is normally conducted without reference to the meaning, for the patient or the doctor, of the patient's symptoms or the therapeutic relationship itself.

In sharp contrast, psychotherapeutic treatment largely consists of attention to transference and counter-transference phenomena. The invitation to identify and put into words the experience of transference feelings and behaviors brings old or chronic conflicts into the therapist's office. In this way, psychotherapy avoids becoming a purely intellectual exercise. One of the distinguishing features of psychoanalytic and dynamic therapies is this mobilization and exploration of traumatic patterns within the therapeutic relationship.

It is common nowadays for analysts to conceive of treatment as a "two-person" process. Subtle interpersonal pressures brought to bear by the personality and subjectivity of the healer must be taken into consideration in assessing the patient's behavior in the consulting room. Working from an independent paradigm, the philosopher Ian Hacking has referred to this inter-subjective dialectic as a "looping effect" specific to human beings by which they react to and integrate, in more or less conscious ways, what is mirrored back to them from others (Hacking, 1999, p. 34). In fact, contemporary cognitive science research converges with psychoanalysis in the view that all human memory is a dynamic retrospective narrative constantly being rearranged according to categories which are shaped in part by interpersonal forces in the present (Schacter, 1996). Human beings are not indifferent to the feedback they get from others and can, in some cases, adjust their self-image instantaneously and unconsciously.

> I do suggest that a cardinal difference between the traditional natural and social sciences is that the classifications employed in the natural sciences are indifferent kinds, while those employed in the social sciences are mostly interactive kinds. The targets of the natural sciences are stationary. Because of looping effects the targets of the social sciences are on the move (Hacking, 1999, p. 108).

Mutual suggestion, conscious and unconscious, between patient and therapist is an unavoidable and completely necessary part of the work they do together. It follows that the therapist is always, inevitably, and necessarily, a stimulating factor, a contaminant, in treatment. The whole nightmare of false allegations of sexual abuse based on memories recovered in therapy illustrates both how this can happen and why this material should never be exported outside of the treatment situation. As with other ideas, defenses against memory arise because of the current meanings of those memories. For contemporary analysts, it is as important to ask what role a reported memory or feeling plays in the current interaction of analyst and patient as it is to puzzle out its impact on the person's development.

To illustrate the point, let us imagine, among other possibilities, one scenario between the *Osolin* complainant and her psychiatrist. The complainant's remark to her psychiatrist in the *Osolin* trial might plausibly have been unconsciously determined by transference feelings towards her psychiatrist who was male, an authority figure, and perhaps a paternal substitute. In voicing her doubts about the trial, the victim could have been simultaneously expressing, and displacing onto the male therapist, similar feelings about her father, perhaps wishing to placate the latter or please him by appearing to exculpate her alleged assailant. However, such unconscious attitudes would not be accessible to direct questioning, and no amount of cross-examination could hope to elucidate them without in the process setting up another spiral of expectation and submission on the part of the witness. It is only within the special parameters of the treatment setting, in a private relationship of one-on-one, that such underlying attitudes can be teased out in a subjectively convincing fashion. The stance of "benevolent neutrality" and relative "anonymity" of the psychoanalytic practitioner constitutes a prime technical device for the observation of the patient's personal, historically determined, "looping process" and for the arrest of further spirals of this inter-subjective process. Since clinical material is inextricably welded to the interpersonal dynamic activated in treatment, it is quite simply fallacious to consider it pertinent to the fact-finding task of the court.

During oral argument of the *Jaffee v. Redmond* case, Justice David Souter pointed out how untenable the usual distinctions between objective and subjective are when sought-for evidence derives from psychotherapy or psychoanalysis. "What if a patient says [to the psychotherapist], 'I feel bad about killing someone.' Is that a statement of fact or feeling?" Justice Souter asked the plaintiff's lawyer.[1] Impossible in the legal setting for Justice Souter to have asked is the very question the psychotherapist or psychoanalyst must ponder in her consulting room: "And to whom (really) was the patient expressing this 'bad' feeling?"

C. Therapy as a Thought Experiment or Deliberative Process

The human being is the only animal that cannot function effectively and authentically without a personal theory of his or her existence and mind, a personal theory repetitively jostled by the fortunes and misfortunes of a lifetime. In order to allow our patients to delve into themselves, to critically examine their hopes and fears, their memories and their identities, we ask them—*for the time of the psychotherapeutic or psychoanalytic session*—to suspend conventional, learned, and expected ways of speaking, and to voice whatever comes into mind without censorship. It is only in this way that previously disowned ideas, prejudices, and impulses can break the surface of the stable self-narratives with which patients enter treatment. The object is not just to permit the patient to unburden him- or herself of socially unacceptable thoughts, whether it be, for example, that of a man's wish to violently possess a woman, or a woman's wish to be violently possessed. The object is also to permit for the first time a space and a time for thinking these thoughts out loud and exploring their significance and signification for self-concept and self-esteem.

These thoughts, it must be pointed out for the reasons given above, are not necessarily taken at face value by the therapist. In fact, it is assumed that there are latent meanings that will only emerge in the uncensored, neutrally empathetic, atmosphere encouraged in the treatment. When we speak about a *transitional space* (Winnicott, 1978), we mean that in the treatment session, a cigar does not necessarily mean a cigar, and that the wish to murder someone might paradoxically express feelings of impotence, depressive despair, or a wish for magical possession, to name just a few of the possibilities.

Defense lawyers and some judges are perfectly willing to grant the subjective and unreliable nature of communication in psychotherapy. They merely insist upon the right to use acceptable legal methods to tease out the relevant nuggets of fact suitable for the court. The tentative, experimental, nature of patients' communications within the emotional lines of force of an intense rapport with a psychotherapist is simply not grasped. In the Supreme Court's *Osolin* decision, Judge Cory expressed it this way:

> what the complainant said to her counselor ... could well reflect a victim's unfortunate and unwarranted feelings of guilt and shame for actions and events that were in no way her fault. If this is indeed the basis for her statement to the counselor, then they could not in any way lend an air of reality to the accused's proposed defense of mistaken belief in the complainant's consent. However, in the absence of cross-examination it is impossible to know what the result might have been (*R. v. Osolin* [1993], p. 525).

Following common law method, the proper thing to do, as asserted by the Canadian Council of Criminal Defence Lawyers' (CCCDL) factum in another sexual assault case, is to "put the statement to the witness so that its significance can be tested in a meaningful fashion" (Response of the Intervener of The Canadian Council of Criminal Defence Lawyers (CCCDL) to the Factum of the Intervener Canadian Psychiatric Association, *R. v. Mills* [1999], point 11). The CCCDL added, "As always, an actual, contextual, examination is preferable in the search for the truth" (point 12). What these advocates for relevance have failed to realize is that a mutually suggestive interpersonal field is a technical necessity in treatment and that it is this real "context" that should militate for its exclusion from searches for legal truth. One can only wonder if in large part their miscomprehension stems from the failure of mental health professionals to undertake a sustained campaign to explain our work to other disciplines.

Contrasting metaphors come to mind which illustrate differences in understanding. The CCCDL's perspective invokes the ancient task of threshing in which wheat is separated from chaff. The patient's doubts, fantasies, and rehashing of the alleged events, as expressed in psychotherapy sessions, are tossed into the cross-examination threshing machine, in the mistaken belief that judge and jury can pick out kernels of wheat-truth without denaturing the healing relationship. A metaphor more respectful of the psychoanalytic point of view is a special-effects image from the film, *The Abyss*. On the ocean floor, a stranded group of deep-sea oceanographers experience close encounters with other worldly beings who take shape from the water itself. At once astonishing, enchanting and eerie, humanoid faces gracefully coalesce, solidify, glide about, and then dissipate in the ambient water. This film image is more faithful to the delicate inter-subjective tissue of the psychotherapeutic dialogue than that of the robust thresher. The alien, other worldly faces are inherent in the water just as the patient's words are inherent, immanent, in the "other-dimension" emotional dynamic of the treatment relationship and cannot be teased apart in the outside world of the courtroom. Peter Brooks' conclusions on, as he puts it, the "difficulties of passing confessional discourse of the psychotherapeutic sort through the eye of the legal needle" (Brooks, 2000, p. 129) are entirely consistent with mine. For instance, commenting on the use, in court, of evidence of recovered memory in therapy, he avers: "The problem I detect here is the court's bland assertion that memory, as a concept, can be separated from its content, and that judgment of that content—its credibility—can go forward without establishment of the validity of the memory as recall. There appears to be here a collision of psychotherapeutic and legal understandings" (Brooks, 2000, p. 123).

A legal avenue already exists which appears to dovetail with many of the arguments advanced in this paper and that thus might be extended to encompass a strong protection for the psychotherapeutic and psychoanalytic relationship. The reasoning behind what is known as the privilege of the deliberative process (Morissette, 1994) has the potential of providing an entirely appropriate legal shield. To my knowledge, it has never been asserted in this fashion. Covered by this privilege are cabinet meetings, certain phases of labor arbitration and mediation proceedings, and judges' personal trial notes. This concept has the heuristic value of offering an alternative platform to other utilitarian-based professional privileges that assert confidentiality as a basis of client "trust." The deliberative process privilege offers a separate ground of public interest: that of sheltering a creative trial-and-error speech or thought in certain professional relationships. Confidentiality of the psychoanalytic or psychotherapeutic relationship would thus join the specific areas demarcated by common law where frank discussion, experimental thinking, and speculation can occur without the risk of disclosure or repetition out of context. It should be emphasized that traditional applications of the deliberative process all relate to governance or to the legal system itself. Yet we may ask, is there any logical, moral, or philosophical impediment preventing the extension of this privilege to the self-and-other deliberative function of psychotherapy?

D. The Neutrality of the Therapist

In scientific studies, double blinds and random assignment are designed to limit the influence on results of both experimenter bias and subject expectation. A plethora of research in a number of inter-related fields has amply demonstrated the need to control for powerful suggestive forces. It should surprise no one then to learn that the presence of external pressures, such as parental or spousal wishes for the patient to behave in a certain way or work-related deadlines or financial compensation that is linked to disability status can seriously obstruct the spirit of open self-inquiry which is essential in meaningful treatment. In order for psychoanalytic therapy to work properly, the therapist must not ally with one part of his patient's mind, with a specific expectation or basic assumption, against other parts of it.

Even in psychotherapy with sexual assault victims, a psychotherapist should avoid pronouncing for or against recourse to the courts, for or against any particular aspect of the victim's "story," in order to hear in more depth about the subjective repercussion of the assault in the context of other relationships and experiences. If the psychiatrist in *Osolin* had testified before the court about his patient's doubts about the trial or if he had allowed his dossier to be handed over to the court as evidence, he might well have been reinforcing self-punitive and authority-pleasing aspects of his patient's personality. Having a conscience is not always an indication of personal maturity and independence. In fact, it can be just the opposite, acting as an internal slave driver, harsh and primitive, in its evaluation of good and evil.

Not only would any co-operation by the treating psychiatrist in *Osolin* with the court's use of his work as evidence have automatically forfeited his neutrality vis-à-vis his patient's internal conflicts, he would have been simultaneously altering his status as an object of transference. The knowledge that patients attribute to their psychotherapists, in contrast to other medical and academic disciplines, should remain for the most part virtual, a much needed fantasy on the part of the patient that justifies and strengthens his or her optimal trust and capacity to "let go." When, however, the analyst or therapist is requested to share his or her "observations" of the patient in court, this imaginary differential is suddenly transformed into a very concrete legal reality. Though the law may differentiate witnesses of fact from expert witnesses, such niceties are lost on the patient for whom any public utterance about his or her psychological condition is necessarily heard as an expression of the therapist's "expert" perspective. Whether what the patient hears confirms or shatters the previous perception of the therapist makes little difference insofar as either occurrence can be expected to disrupt the natural course of their relationship.

Since most patients begin treatment expecting their therapists to act as expert witnesses to their lives, it can appear a small step for them to consent to the subpoenaing of their therapists. Patients often beg their therapists to tell them what to do, to make pronouncements about their personalities, to take sides in their disputes. They often ask their therapists to tell them if a memory actually happened or if they have done the right thing or made the correct choice. It is part of the therapeutic process for the therapist to sidestep these requests until he or she can offer insight into the internal forces underlying the patient's indecisiveness. An analogy with certain principles in particle physics is possible. Just as any attempt to measure the position of the electron alters the indeterminacy of its path, so too will any attempt to "measure" the evidentiary value of psychotherapy material alter the quality of that relationship. And just as light behaves as a wave until, encountering an obstacle, it displays particle-like properties, so too does the nature of the psychotherapy relationship, when drawn into considerations extraneous to therapy, mutate from an enterprise of self-knowledge to an adversarial agenda with respect to the outside world. The professional ethic must be, claims Allen Dyer, "defined by the needs of those who come for help, not by the rival interests of society" (Dyer, 1988, p. 12). In a dispute with the provincial government over the quality of care patients receive in emergency rooms, Dr. André Green, spokesperson for the *Quebec College of Physicians and Surgeons,* made a similar distinction: "By tradition and history in countries around the world, our code of ethics makes a doctor responsible to his patient, not to the people" (quoted in the *Montreal Gazette*, 25 July 2002, p. A–4).

3. The Truth-Seeking Process

I hope that you can now appreciate why the usual justifications for accessing psychotherapeutic material as evidence betray a lack of comprehension of the therapeutic process. The most common reasons for requesting disclosure are based either on this misapprehension or on the following questionable assertions related to it.

(1) To avoid the conviction of innocent people. There is to my knowledge no empirical evidence justifying such a fear. Known cases of wrongful conviction have occurred for reasons other than lack of access to confidential psychotherapy files. The three main causes in cases of wrongful convictions have been: mistaken eyewitness identification, improper police interrogation, and sloppy investigative work (Dwyer, Neufeld & Scheck, 2000). While no one should make light of the need to safeguard against the jailing of innocent persons, this risk must be empirically confirmed rather than merely asserted. In my limited reading, I have come across only one criminal case in which access to confidential psychiatric records—though pertaining to a hospitalization not to a psychotherapy—avoided a wrongful conviction (*R. v. Kliman* [1994]). On the other hand, there are many documented cases, such as those involving memories of sexual abuse recovered in therapy (see for example *Ramona v. Ramona* [1994], and *Johnston* [1997]), in which evidence from psychotherapy led astray the truth-seeking process.

(2) To seek an alternate version of the alleged events. The court is trying to have its cake and eat it too. Any discussion about the likely relevance of this material sidesteps the crucial question from the therapeutic point of view; that irrespective of mental status, mental illness, or specific diagnosis, psychotherapy and psychoanalysis encourage patients to "think" about their lives. A basic premise of our legal system is the expectation that citizens behave responsibly and that they assume responsibility for their actions. The irony of the *Osolin* case is that whereas the alleged assailant admitted several times during proceedings

that, “I just wasn’t thinking” as the events unfolded which culminated in his sexual encounter with the complainant, his conviction was overturned by the Supreme Court so that the “thinking” of the complainant to her psychiatrist could be cross-examined. Surely, it is unreasonable of courts to delve into the very private space where a witness (or a defendant for that matter) can examine her or his own conscience and motives, a necessary prelude to taking “responsibility” for her or his role in the affair? In the dissent he penned in the United States Supreme Court decision of *Jaffee v. Redmond* ([1996], p. 3 of Scalia dissent), Justice Antonin Scalia wondered why the law should allow a witness protection when confessing a crime to a therapist and not when confessing a crime to his or her mother. Scalia too misses the fundamental difference between speaking to a professional therapist and speaking to a family member or friend. Speech in the former relationship aims not only to obtain relief in a confessional catharsis of painful secrets but also, and more importantly, to bring about a change in the patient, a psychic change, through the process of thinking about self and others without external or self-censorship.

(3) To establish the credibility of a witness or to have information on his or her mental status at the time of the event or of the complaint. This apparently rational assertion of grounds for likely relevance also loses solidity when deconstructed with respect to a true appreciation of the psychotherapeutic process. If, for the sake of argument, an alleged victim in a sexual assault trial has begun proceedings with a deliberate falsehood, she is far more liable to eventually deliver reliable testimony if the privacy of her psychotherapy remains respected. In her psychotherapy, she will have the freedom to question her motives, as well as the freedom to investigate their emotional roots, and to hear her therapist’s interpretations of them. Moreover, if she believes herself to be telling the truth, an undisrupted psychotherapeutic relationship will counteract the traumatic impact of testifying before the court and by virtue of the benefit of a confidential unburdening of her doubts, fears, and misgivings, strengthen the reliability of her court testimony. Neither patient nor psychotherapist can be expected to sustain an unbiased examination of emotional and imaginary features connected with the events in question or, for that matter, with the decision to initiate and continue court proceedings, if their work together will become, or might become, subject to an eventual review (even in *huit clos*) by that court or by the opposing party and legal representation.

(4) To determine whether the therapeutic relationship has been a factor in the complaint. Even if a complainant's allegations might have been consciously or unconsciously influenced by the therapeutic interaction, it remains prudent for courts to base their decision on other sources of evidence so as to leave patient and therapist to work this out in the therapy. It is an ironic sequel to the recovered memory debate that requests for production of psychotherapy files before the courts are increasingly couched in the need to assess whether treatment has contaminated complainants' allegations. On the contrary, it is precisely because of the inherently and necessarily affect-laden quality of these relationships that they should be carefully excluded from the legal arena, and this is true whether requests come from the Crown or the defense. As argued earlier, the court's assumption that it possesses truth-finding techniques that can be legitimately applied to the psychotherapeutic interaction is erroneous. Unless there is good reason to doubt the competency of the mental health professional involved, the court must acknowledge the limitations of its methodology by "leaving unto Caesar that which is Caesar's," and confining its investigation to evidence drawn from outside this relationship.

(5) Because the sheer number of decisions in which psychotherapy evidence has been produced supports their potential relevance. There is little doubt that mental health professionals are partially responsible for the increase in records production, as they have sometimes allowed themselves to be drawn into an active form of "helping" under pressure from their patients, as well as from the pressure of their own wishes to be useful in furthering their patient's presumed best interests. It is, nevertheless, misguided for psychotherapists to become patient advocates before the courts. Increasingly, experts have argued for the complete exclusion of the treating psychotherapist from court proceedings (Shuman, Greenberg, Heibrun & Foote, 1998).

In summary, witness credibility, in the overwhelming majority of cases, can only be enhanced by the protection of the psychotherapeutic relationship.

The former president of the Law Commission of Canada, Roderick Macdonald, has asked "[h]ow willing are we to jettison the beliefs that the state has a monopoly on law-making and that courts are indispensable to solving human conflict?" (Macdonald, 1999, p. 5). The legal profession has failed to notice that safeguarded psychotherapeutic relationships constitute multiple, miniature, sites favoring what Macdonald has called a "more just living law" (Macdonald, 1999, p.5). Psychotherapy certainly counts among the institutions of civil society that "are better attuned to preventative law and to transformative justice than are courts" (Macdonald, 1999, p. 6, note 9). Revisited and revamped within the confines of these specialized therapeutic relationships, in the space and time of their individual needs, a more authentic, personal, and diversified response can be anticipated from citizens interacting with official legal bodies.

4. Privilege and Admissibility

If courts continue to insist on basing their determinations of access to psychotherapeutic documents on the grounds of relevance, psychotherapists will be facing an impossibly slippery slope. Given what the court requires, it is logically impossible to refute the "likely" relevance of this material. If we were to exclude from the therapeutic consulting room discussions about the dramatic, conflicted, and often traumatic events prompting claims before the court, psychotherapy would become a meaningless exercise. Justice Doherty came to a similar finding in the Ontario Court of Appeal hearing of *R. v. Batte*:

> If the likely relevance bar is that low, it serves no purpose where the records relate to counseling or treatment connected to allegations of sexual abuse. It is impossible to imagine that such records would not contain references to the alleged abuse or matters that could affect the credibility of the complainants' allegation of abuse. ...[T]he mere fact that a complainant has spoken to a counselor or doctor about the abuse or matters touching on the abuse does not make a record of those conversations likely relevant to a fact in issue or to a complainant's credibility (*R. v. Batte* [2000], p. 449, para. 71).

In my opinion, we are lead to the conclusion that determinations must be made, not on assessments of likely relevance, but rather on the intertwined and double grounds: 1) of inadmissibility as evidence because of the potential for leading astray the court's search for truth and, 2) on the grounds of privilege as a protection for the integrity of the therapeutic endeavor.

Justice L'Heureux-Dubé has reminded us of the contrast between privilege and other rules of exclusion:

> It is important to remember that the rationale underlying resort to privilege and privacy rights is diametrically opposed to that underlying most ordinary evidentiary rules of exclusion. Privilege and privacy interests would exclude evidence despite the fact that such evidence might further the truth-seeking process. On the other hand, ordinary rules of exclusion are generally motivated by the desire to further the truth-seeking process, in that they tend to exclude evidence which might be unreliable, which might

> mislead or prejudice the trier of fact, or which might otherwise prejudice the fairness of the trial (*R. v. O'Connor* [1995], p. 170, para. 147).

I hope I have succeeded in communicating the wisdom of excluding evidence from psychotherapy or psychoanalysis *on both of these usually oppositely affirmed grounds*. In the first place, regardless of any potential usefulness to the courts, this "evidence" should be excluded on the basis of privilege in order to protect the integrity of the professional relationship of psychotherapy or psychoanalysis. In the second place, this "evidence" should be just as vigorously excluded as inadmissible because of its enormous potential for leading astray the pursuit of justice. Cross-examination for "probative value" of phrases, ideas, or perceptions exported from a psychotherapy relationship is like poring over the entrails of a bullock for guidance in major decisions. Not only is the estimate of dubious scientific value, but the poor bullock is an appropriate parallel for the evisceration of the therapeutic relationship as this prognostication is taking place! Moreover, it can be said that the contents of entrails (read evidence culled from psychotherapy) are more instructive of the bullock's relationship with the human who was responsible for his last meal (read the patient's relationship with the psychotherapist) than of the unknowable future.

The legal profession has acknowledged the need for fundamental principles that could inform judicial determination about requests for access to confidential documents. In the last decade, the Supreme Court of Canada has made several attempts at agreeing on such a set of principles, the most recent example is *R. v. Mills* [1999]. In determining whether to order disclosure of the records by the person in possession of them, the judge must now consider the factors set out in section 278.5(2) of the *Criminal Code*, and confirmed in *R. v. Mills* [1999], which read as follows:

> (*a*) the extent to which the record is necessary for the accused to make a full answer and defence;
> (*b*) the probative value of the record;
> (*c*) the nature and extent of the reasonable expectation of privacy with respect to the record;
> (*d*) whether production of the record is based on a discriminatory belief or bias;
> (*e*) the potential prejudice to the personal dignity and right to privacy of any person to whom the record relates;
> (*f*) society's interest in encouraging the reporting of sexual offences;
> (*g*) society's interest in encouraging the obtaining of treatment by complainants of sexual offences; and
> (*h*) the effect of the determination on the integrity of the trial process.

To allow for a separate assessment of confidentiality issues on its own specific grounds, I would propose two additional factors to the eight already enunciated above, which the judge should take into account:

i) *the effect of the determination on the integrity of the professional relationship and on the quality (the deliberative process) of treatment,*
j) *whether the information available in the files, or from the therapist, would be prejudicial or misleading when exported outside that professional relationship.*

The guidelines in *Mills* allow an intensive analysis of privacy interests in sexual assault cases. Whereas privacy is a factor contributing to the integrity of the individual, I have tried to show how confidentiality of the professional relationship, among other things, reinforces the integrity of treatment.

5. Conclusion

Evidence based on material drawn from psychotherapeutic treatment situations has a high potential for leading astray the court's search for truth and justice. This assertion applies specifically to psychotherapy and psychoanalysis understood as treatments by which individual healing and self-understanding are found within specialized professional relationships of completely uncensored speech. A "self-deliberative" process is set in motion in these circumstances by which the troubled person can review his or her life in a spirit of open-ended inquiry without distortion or pressure from outside interests. The common motives for production requests must be critically examined in light of the inevitable distortion that occurs when clinical material is taken out of context. It is argued that witness credibility will be enhanced by the protection of the psychotherapeutic relationship where self-doubts, exaggerated urges for vengeance, possibly distorted perceptions, conflicting memories, and so on can first be examined by the witness herself in a nonjudgmental and neutral atmosphere before the decision to seek redress is taken.

While capable of acknowledging the subjective and unreliable nature of communication in psychotherapy, defense lawyers and some judges, nevertheless, insist upon the right to use acceptable legal methods to tease out relevant facts. This emphasis on relevance belies appreciation of the tentative, experimental nature of patients' thoughts and speech and the inevitable coloring of this material by the emotional lines of force of the intense rapport with a psychotherapist. Advocates for relevance have failed to realize that a mutually suggestive interpersonal field is a technical necessity in treatment. The "self-deliberative" nature of this process cannot, therefore, remain internally unbiased and honest if threatened with the risk of becoming potential evidence before the courts.

We hold that integrity, not obligation, is the hallmark of psychotherapeutic and psychoanalytic work. As the British psychoanalyst, Anne Hayman, wrote some years ago, "In principle, there may be less conflict between our moral obligations to the law and the rules of professional conduct than would appear at first sight. Justice as well as our ethic, is likely to be served best by silence" (Hayman, 1965, p. 785).

Note

[1] Referred to by Barry Landau in "Confidentiality Considerations in Regard to 'Documentation of Psychotherapy' in the Light of the Supreme Court *Jaffee v. Redmond* Decision." Discussion at the American Psychiatric Association Meetings, Chicago, Thursday, 18 May 2000. Available on the American Psychoanalytic Association website: http://apsa.org/pubinfo/redmond.htm.

Works Cited

Brooks, Peter. (2000) *Troubling Confessions: Speaking Guilt in Law and Literature*. Chicago: University of Chicago Press.

Dwyer, Jim, Peter Neufeld, and Barry Scheck. (2000) *Actual Innocence: Five Days to Execution and Other Dispatches from the Wrongly Convicted.* New York: Doubleday.

Dyer, Allen. (1998) *Ethics and Psychiatry: Toward Professional Definition*. Washington, D. C.: American Psychiatric Press.

Hacking, Ian. (1999) *The Social Construction of What?* Cambridge: Harvard University Press.

Hayman, Anne. (1965) "Psychoanalyst Subpoenaed," *Lancet*, 16 October: pp. 785–786.

Jaffee v. Redmond. [1996] 518 U. S. 1.

Johnston, Moira. (1997) *Spectral Evidence: The Ramona Case: Incest, Memory and Truth on Trial in Napa Valley.* Boston: Houghton Mifflin.

Macdonald, Roderick. (1999) "Law, Justice and Community: The Way Ahead." From an address delivered 17 April 1999 at the Symposium: *Law, Justice and Community* held at the Faculty of Law of Dalhousie University, Halifax, Nova Scotia. Available on the Law Commission of Canada's Web site: http://www.lcc.gc.ca/en/pc/speeches.

Meyer, Nicholas. (1974) *The Seven-Per-Cent Solution*. New York: Ballantine.

Morissette, Y.-M. (1994) "Review of Administrative Record," Paper presented to the Centre for Trade Policy and Law Workshop, in Ottawa, 22 November.

R. v. Batte. [2000] 145 C.C.C. (3d) 449.

R. v. Kliman. [1994] BC W. L. D. 587.

R. v. Mills. [1999] SCC. Court File No. 26358.

R. v. O'Connor. [1995] S. C. C. No. 24114.

R. v. Osolin, [1993] S.C.C. No. 22826.

Ramona. v. Ramona. [1994] Napa Cty Super Ct. No. 61898.

Response of the Intervener of The Canadian Council of Criminal Defence Lawyers (CCCDL) to the Factum of the Intervener Canadian Psychiatric Association. *R. v. Mills* [1999] SCC. Court File No. 26358.

Schacter, Daniel L. (1996) *Searching for Memory: The Brain, the Mind, and the Past.* New York: Basic Books.

Shuman, Daniel, S. Greenberg, K. Heibrun, and W. Foote. (1998) "An Immodest Proposal: Should Treating Mental Health Professionals Be Barred From Testifying About Their Patients?" *Behavioural Science Law,* 16: pp. 509–523.

Winnicott, D. W. (1978) "Transitional Objects and Transitional Phenomena." In *Through Paediatrics to Psycho-Analysis*. London: Hogarth Press, pp. 229–242.

Three

A PSYCHOANALYTIC PERSPECTIVE ON CONFIDENTIALITY: THE DIVIDED MIND IN TREATMENT

R. D. Hinshelwood

The legal process is hindered if potential witnesses are protected with immunity from divulging their confidential professional notes; and the patient in psychoanalysis is inhibited if confidentiality cannot be honored. We are in a cleft stick. On the surface the principles seem absolute: to protect the legal process or to protect the analytic process.

In this article I shall argue that the conflict between the social good that comes from the need of the legal process to know and the psychoanalytic need for privacy is not as stark as it at first appears. A psychoanalytic understanding does not necessarily make the issues easier, but it does open up a space for thinking and maybe for maneuver. However, to follow my argument will involve some understanding of certain psychoanalytic concepts such as splitting, projection, and introjection, and I will explicate these. My psychoanalytic understanding of these problems follows from an examination, reported elsewhere (Hinshelwood 1997), of the unexpected complications that a consideration of the unconscious introduces into the ordinary ethical principles involved in consent for medical treatment.

In the first part of this article I shall necessarily touch on this psychoanalytic examination of consent for treatment as I extend the argument to the issues of confidentiality. Then in the second part I shall deal particularly with dangerous patient warnings, subpoenaed notes, and briefly some points concerning relations between the medical/psychoanalytic and the legal professions.

A counter-intuitive example: I shall introduce my point of view with an initial example. Though this is not from a classic psychoanalytic setting, it presents the crucial paradox that is central to my argument. The patient was seen in a psychiatrist's out-patient session and reported how relieved she was to be treated as a danger, indicating a curious inner conflict in the patient, which psychoanalysis is adept at understanding.

> A woman of forty four with a moderate paranoid personality described to her psychiatrist how independent she was, how alert to instances of injustice she felt, and how she got embroiled in retaliatory retribution. She talked of a recent enduring rage against the neighbors of her elderly father. The

> neighbors had been rowdy, insulting, and threatening him. The patient was protective of her father to the point of being equally insulting and threatening to the neighbors. But she went further, buying a baseball bat and making a phone-call to the neighbors with a murder threat. This threat was made with such intensity and apparent conviction that the police, already involved in the dispute with the neighbors, were called to deal with the patient. They arrested her at home and took her off in the cage in the back of their van and confined her at the police station until the officer in charge gave her a formal warning in a gruff and humiliating way.

To the psychiatrist's surprise the patient did not react with violent indignation. Instead she told the story with an excited relief, adding that she had complimented the police on how excellently they had handled her!

The psychiatrist was perplexed by her enthusiasm, as if she were on the side of the police. At the time she spoke to the psychiatrist, she no longer seemed a potential perpetrator of a crime—or rather, she was allied with the police in wanting to control the perpetrator in her.

It would seem that this patient did have a powerful knowledge of the need to control her aggression. However, she could not always retain that knowledge. At times, a murderous side of her became liberated and quite without restraint. At other times, she became completely overtaken by a self-restraining side of herself that policed and caged her murderousness into non-existence. In the latter frame of mind, she relied (with relief) on the police to know it for her. The police had in effect taken over her own self-restraint—with her approval, and relief!

This patient was not a psychoanalytic one, and the reasons for her paradoxical relief cannot be explored in detail. However it leads us to ask certain questions: how is it that a potentially aggressive person is relieved to be controlled by others? It implies that there is some aspect of her that wishes a control over her aggression. She was at war with herself, as it were; and we need to consider her state of mind as being plural—both murderous and at the same time a fear and regret at that aggressiveness in herself. But such a war failed to happen properly. The patient became aligned with one side only or the other.

Such an "internal" war has implications for confidentiality; but first I must describe some psychoanalytic discoveries that serve as initial assumptions for my argument.

1. The Divided Mind: Psychoanalytic Background

Psychoanalysis has shown that the human mind does not always function as a unitary entity. Particularly in states of anxiety a person will have opposing currents in him or herself which cannot be adequately brought together. Such conflict states may be resolved by one side of the conflict being relegated (repressed) to an unconscious zone of the mind. In *Therapy or Coercion* (Hinshelwood 1997), I described many of these implications and dwelt especially on the consequences for medical and general ethics. Though I focused there on "informed consent," some of the conclusions in that book apply to the present discussion. In particular when unconscious motives conflict with conscious ones, consent to medical treatment can become ambiguous; and I shall argue that such conflicts in the mind make the issues of confidentiality equally complex.

Repression: Freud initially found that in the condition of hysteria, insoluble conflicts were resolved by one side of the conflict being relegated to the unconscious through the process of repression. There is then a resistance to that unconscious content becoming conscious again. For instance, in the following not uncommon occurrence, a patient early in his analysis clearly resisted knowing unconscious meaning in the dream he had reported:

> I asked my patient to tell me what a figure in the dream reminded him of. He said "Nothing. He reminds me of no one at all." And, he promptly went off to sleep for some minutes until I said something and he woke with a start and some embarrassment having forgotten my question and his answer.

His unconscious resisted its contents being examined in this instance. Clearly the patient resisted the co-operation normally expected, maintaining unconsciousness by literally going to sleep. The resistance to conscious knowledge of this meaning is the result of the mechanism of repression.

Interesting questions arise in this case. At that moment the patient had decisively withdrawn his unconscious consent to continue treatment, consent to a treatment which consisted of understanding himself. What should the analyst do, ethically at that point? As analysts, we know that unconsciously the patient has withdrawn his consent. And this may occur while he is still willingly coming for analysis, and even trying to work in the analysis, as for instance with regard to his intellectualizing defenses. This is a frequent occurrence. Do we take the conscious consent or the unconscious withdrawal of consent as the ethical imperative? In fact, the analyst in practice does something altogether different—he neither abides by the consent nor does he honor the withdrawal of it. Rather, he analyzes the resistance. You could say that this amounts to accepting the conscious consent and going on analyzing. But that is only the appearance. In fact, the analyst analyzes the divergence in the patient—the repression exerted by the unconscious, but also the conflicting conscious wishes. In a way the analyst stands "above the battle," and attempts to bring the two parties into some better communication with each other resulting in a more fruitful use of the unconscious, more adaptive ego defenses, and so on.

There are other and more radical processes that defend against conscious knowing.

Splitting of the ego: A more drastic defense measure is the process by which the mind becomes divided, not between conscious and unconscious, but with a split in which there is no communication between the separated parts. This kind of division literally causes a division in the identity of the person (ego). A patient of Melanie Klein's reported very strong feelings of frustration, envy, and grievance.

> [When] I interpreted … that these feelings were directed against the analyst and that he wanted to destroy me, his mood changed abruptly. The tone of his voice became flat, he spoke in a slow expressionless way, and he said that he felt detached (Klein, 1946, p. 19).

So when the analyst drew attention to the patient's aggression and the danger he put her under, the patient reacted dramatically. Something of him disappeared altogether, and he was left with a flat, blank lack of feeling or interest. She said, "He added that my interpretation seemed correct, but that it did not matter." Klein emphasized:

> The patient split off those parts of himself, *i.e.* of his ego which he felt to be dangerous and hostile towards his analyst. He turned his destructive impulses from his object *towards his ego*. With the result that parts of his ego temporarily went out of existence. In unconscious phantasy this amounted to annihilation of part of his personality… [and] kept his anxiety in a latent state (Klein, 1946, p. 19).

The splitting process deprived him of his feelings of frustration, envy, and grievance. They were no longer represented in any form; there was no substitute idea as might occur in a dream. He was left in a blank state as if something had gone missing, the energy had gone out of life at that moment.

However, the loss of a part of the mind is reversible. Klein's patient recovered his lost feelings:

> My next interpretations centered on the causes for this change of mood. I suggested that at the moment of my interpretation the danger of destroying me had become very real to him and the immediate consequence was the fear of losing me. Instead of feeling guilt and depression, which at certain stages of his analysis followed such interpretations, he now attempted to deal with these dangers by a particular method of splitting. … My interpretation of these processes had the effect of again altering the patient's mood. He became emotional, said he felt like crying, was depressed, but felt more integrated; then he also expressed a feeling of hunger (Klein, 1946, pp. 19–20).

The annihilation, as Klein called it, was strictly in terms of what happened in his own mind. It was as if that part had gone somewhere else, but was available to return and once more be a part of him and his experience. Klein emphasized that the hunger he felt was an expression, at the bodily level, of the internalization of his emotional self once again, back into some more integrated state within him. About another patient Klein said, "It was not only that parts of her personality did not co-operate with me; they did not seem to co-operate with each other" (Klein, 1946, p. 17).

This kind of occurrence implies that in certain people parts of their experience, and in fact of their "selves," can become detached and to all intents and purposes go out of existence. In this case it was the patient's aggression that he wished to disown, and literally did so. This process "annihilated" the patient's wishes, and annihilated his knowing his own wishes, and it would have prevented others from knowing his wishes. This is important for the ethics of consent, since the wish for treatment (the motivation) may be annihilated in this way. We will see the importance of splitting for confidentiality later when odd things may happen to the wish for privacy.

Projection and introjection of parts of the self: The annihilation of a part of the patient is only true from the patient's point of view. If it does return, as it did in Klein's example, one can ask, where has it been? In the next brief illustration, the annihilated wish appears to be relocated into another mind, the mind of the analyst. We shall see that the part of the self that disappears (or rather is relocated) is the patient's motivation for treatment. The psychoanalysis came to be structured so that the patient's motivation disappeared and the analyst remained as the one who wanted the patient to get better; the patient obligingly continued to turn up to her appointments but was impervious to real understanding about herself.

> A patient came to analysis for understanding her problems with men. During the earlier part of the analysis she met and eventually married a man who made no sexual demands on her. She embarked on a virtually celibate marriage. The patient had a senior academic job and was clever and productive in her work. She was equally clever and thoughtful in her analysis, often taking away with her the interpretations of her lack of sexuality, and thinking hard about them between her sessions. Yet her complaint about her symptom had vanished quickly. The problem was that her hard thinking did not change her problem. Instead of the analysis changing her relation to her body and her feelings, it seemed that the analysis itself was changed into one that was as sterile as her marriage. In the process the psychoanalyst had to endure being the only one who wished to bring her sexuality to life. Much of the analyst's task was to control his

own frustration and his strong wish to push the patient into a more emotional awareness.

In this very brief description we can see two things. First, the patient's wish to improve her sexual relationships with men disappeared quickly; and she institutionalized in marriage a non-sexual relationship. In a way the problem was solved. But she continued with her analysis *as if* she were still consenting to a self-questioning about her lack of sexuality. The second thing is that the wish for the analysis to progress and for her to change did not in fact disappear completely. We had arrived at a state of affairs in which the patient no longer appeared to want to progress, instead the analyst wanted her to! The patient's approval of analysis (shown by her persistence in coming to sessions) is in the category of the approval given by the murderous woman to the police in my first illustration. Someone else is mobilized to perform a function the person has radically disowned.

A complex set of processes was occurring here. First the patient had split herself, her motivation for change coming adrift and to all intents and purposes annihilated from herself. However it was not fully annihilated; it simply resided elsewhere. The patient can be said to have projected that part of herself into her psychoanalyst, who had introjected it. For the patient a major revision of her identity had occurred and she had lost a vital part of it—her motivation. She was no longer a patient seeking an analysis. By the same token there was an alteration (a minor one) in the identity of the analyst. He had his own motivation to conduct an analysis of this patient, but this had been supercharged by the addition of the patient's motivation so that the analyst's motivation had intensified and he had suffered an equally intensified frustration brought on by the projection which created the impasse.

One might ask, why does the patient continue to come in this case? The answer is complicated. It would seem that part of the answer is that such a patient *needs* the analyst as a vessel to project into, and does so in order to prevent the disturbance she might get from having a wish to know and to change. In addition, with this patient, it became clear that there was a gratifying transference in which my interest in pursuing her analysis was felt by the patient in a different way—it was my special interest in her which I displayed by "my" wish to continue seeing her. This was the gratification of a narcissistic wish.

The idea that a part of the self resides inside the analyst is strange and counter-intuitive. Nevertheless it is an important realization in contemporary psychoanalysis, and it has clinically useful consequences. The changes the analyst can feel in his own set of attitudes, and in his changed identity in relation to the patient (known technically as "countertransference"), are a crucial source in helping him to recognize the unconscious interaction between his mind and his patient's mind (Hinshelwood, 1995).

Many ordinary non-clinical situations can be understood in terms of one person giving over personal responsibility for aspects of their personality to another. For instance, a situation in which a teenager says "Dad, I'm going to stay out till two o'clock tomorrow morning. And I'm going to that disco, the one which was busted for drugs," and then waits, apparently innocently unaware of the provocation in this statement, for Dad to say something. But, her announcement is likely to have made Dad pretty anxious. Dad, having his child's best interest at heart, will dutifully get worried and tend to admonish and advise good sense about getting home early, what company to keep, and so on. The teenager has blissfully shed her own capacity to assess the risks for herself. She has engaged with a specific part of her father that she knows will respond in a certain worried way; this is the responsible and protective father in him. It is not that she is unable to judge the risks involved in her plan for the evening. In fact the opposite is true; it is because she "knows" the risks, that she has a way of engaging her father in worry. But she seems to have chosen to create the worries *in him*, rather than suffer them *in herself.* It is common enough that adolescents, poised between childhood protection and adult responsibility, find it difficult at first to carry the worries that adult independence throws up. In this illustration the parent is functioning to hold or "contain" the adolescent's anxiety for her. We can see there is a defensive quality for the adolescent in projecting her worry into her father and leaving him to suffer it instead of herself. She is defending herself against a worry that she fears could be too great for her. But the consequence is that she loses a significant part of herself, the emerging adult capacity to judge and to worry about her judgements. This process of one person *containing* a part of another is now familiar to psychoanalysts.

Michael Conran (1985) illustrated the same process of putting certain aspects of one's own ego into someone else's hands (mind) when a patient consults a doctor. As an example of the loss of the capacity to make judgements for oneself, Conran described the admission to hospital of a surgical patient with appendicitis. Having fallen ill, the man gave up certain responsible aspects of himself when he progressed beyond a certain point of pain and anxiety. He simply gave up his work activities and responsibility and went home, took himself to bed, asked his wife to call the doctor, and left the doctor to decide what should be done. This patient had passed his anxiety to his wife and then to the doctor, and the doctor passed it on to the hospital surgeon. With this relocation (projection) of his anxiety "has gone also the capacity to look after himself and take decisions about himself" (Conran, 1985 p. 33). It was an enormous relief, in these circumstances, for a quite normal person to give up his own capacity for decision-making and taking care of himself. The patient was enabled to regress to a state of immature helplessness, which though it depleted his personality, relieved him of anxiety. That is to say, he regressed to a use of his objects—wife and doctor—to carry his anxiety and to make judgements for him. He had relocated a significant part of his adult identity outside himself. Once his physical health was regained, this surgical patient could regain "governance of himself."

We can also revisit the example at the beginning of the woman who praised the police for controlling her. We can see the division in her mind, in which her self-control was projected into the police who responded in the manner demanded by this projection of the patient.

Indeed, to what degree do the police exist precisely to act as the receptacles for the split-off parts of certain people? In a recent television documentary about the *Jerry Springer Show*, the senior security guard was interviewed about his experience of the sometime violent encounters on the show. He described his intuition that it was precisely *because* of the presence of guards that the participants felt "safe" to express their aggression in the most physical manner. In this instance, people can "lose" their inhibitions because others, the security guards, can be counted upon to inhibit them. Self-restraint can be disowned (split off) and projected into the guards. Though this guard's remarks draw attention to a mundane and familiar kind of occurrence, it points to an underlying level of interaction that affects personal identity.

2. Confidential Psychoanalysis

I will now consider how the phenomena of splitting and projection give us a new appreciation of some aspects of confidentiality.

Because of the analyst's countertransference, he must consider how much his own feelings and intentions reflect his patient's feelings and intentions and might in fact be imported by him from the patient. Thus the analyst's thoughts, feelings, and actions have to be considered in terms of those of the patient; and the analyst has to appraise carefully his own experiences in the light of what he may glean in this way of the patient's unconscious processes. There is of course no straight correspondence between the analyst's reactions and the patient's. The analyst may find himself anxious and driven to telling some outside agency about the patient's impulses, and this may be acting upon an impulse the patient has split off and projected into the analyst. However, it may also be the case that the analyst is getting very anxious on his own account, feeling the need for some support for himself—perhaps even a wish on his part to off-load responsibility. Analyzing the dynamic process of transference and countertransference helps the analyst to work out when he is acting on his patient's behalf and when merely on his own.

In this section, I propose to address three situations that illustrate psychodynamic aspects of confidentiality related to psychoanalytic unconscious processes. The situations are dangerous patient warnings, subpoenaed clinical notes, and relations with lawyers.

1. Dangerous Patient Warnings

When a psychoanalyst has a patient he fears is potentially dangerous, the analyst needs to consider his own reactions. Such reactions include the felt danger threat; his impulse to call for others to help (such as reporting to the police); his anxiety regarding his responsibility in being privy to confidential information; and so on. In all these cases the analyst needs to think out as best he can how much of his experience comes from his own disturbed feelings, and how much he is the recipient of some disturbing parts of his patient. I shall discuss three main possibilities (and give brief clinical examples of each):

> (1) *The analyst as the patient's self-control.* In this case, the patient projects his own split off self-control into the analyst who then feels a double pressure—his own anxiety plus his patient's.
>
> (2) *The analyst overcome by a projection.* In this second case, the patient's projection into the analyst renders the latter so anxious that the analyst himself represses or splits off these feelings.
>
> (3) *The over-anxious analysis*. The third case occurs when the analyst feels anxious about a patient's behavior for reasons related to his own internal world, although the patient is *not* in fact trying to project the need for control into the analyst.

i. The Analyst as the Patient's Self-Control

In the example that follows, the patient seriously worried the analyst about the risk of violent behavior. The psychoanalyst was able to understand the complexity of the unconscious communications from the patient and was able to use it for therapeutic benefit.

> A young man in his twenties, in once-a-week psychotherapy, told me of some exploits with friends that involved breaking into cars. His problem was an enduring adolescent one, arising from his relationship with an erratically violent father who had also loved him. The transference in this psychotherapy was difficult because I seemed inconsistent (present for him only once a week)—and this touched his memories of his father, as well as those of his alcoholic mother. One day he mentioned, in a passing way, that some friends had been involved in a minor criminal incident, which had escalated into severe violence, leaving a victim who was thought to be dead. My patient, who was not directly involved on that occasion, treated it with an indifferent bravado, and seemed to invite me to enjoy the humor

of these school boy pranks. I found my reaction was not in the least humorous, and I felt very concerned that my patient could have been involved with his friends in a murder or, if not so this time, might be on another occasion. He was even now harboring information on the identity of the perpetrators needed by the police in their investigation, but was adamant he would not inform on his mates. Strictly speaking, I too had become implicated in the investigation, as I now had the information that could lead the police to the lads, if I took action. My alarm at my patient's predicament (and my own) rose in proportion to his attitude of casual unconcern. And I had to consider if I was receiving his own alarm, split off from him and projected into me, leaving him depleted of his own capacity to feel due alarm and concern.

In fact I did not take action and inform the authorities that week. And in the next session I learned that the victim had fortunately not died and that the police had discovered the culprits. My patient seemed to insist more than ever that the whole incident was "just a laugh"! I was still not amused and he conveyed I was seriously over-reacting. I did not agree and found myself pushing towards a debate or confrontation on this. However, I was aware of the father's easy temper; and then interpreted that he feared me over-reacting, that it could become accusation and recrimination against him, and even end in violence as his father's reactions did. He said, "You bet!" I then said I thought he wondered whether, if he had been present at the incident, he might have become murderous himself, and that he was worried he might be like his father. I said he tried to cope with that worry with humor, but then became afraid I would worry on his behalf, and over-react to the worry that now seemed so minor to him.

I was saying, in summary, that he had projected his worry about himself, and his father's violence, into me, becoming afraid of me over-reacting with worry about him. In this way a part of his own experience (his worry about his own violence) had vanished, and accumulated in me.

He was quiet for a moment and then said more sincerely (I thought) that he saw exactly what I meant—"You mean I am more worried than I think." I said, "It's possible," and he said with some seriousness, "It's possible. Maybe I should go to the police." At this point the patient seemed to acknowledge for himself a concern about his impulses. So, it seemed very clear to me, and eventually to my patient, that I was carrying the worry of his father-like behavior, the worry that could end in murderous violence. Had I actually informed the police, I don't think that all would have been lost in this case. The patient was working, unconsciously, with the question

> whether I would over-react murderously towards him, like his father. And my breaking confidentiality could not have been considered in that category of reaction. It would, however, have entailed working through the same interpretations that I made. I suspect it might have taken us a good deal longer. I had been filled by the impulse that we both had to get police help, but I was working on it on my own without my patient. In fact, I was containing that part of himself that he had disowned; and so there was no pressure in him to work on it with me. Hence progress might have been slower if I had reported.

The illustration shows how complex the situation can be because the psychoanalyst needs to analyze his own reactions that are prompting him to want to report a dangerous patient. He needs to know to what extent he is acting *instead of* getting his patient to think about some unconscious problem that the patient needs to address for himself.

Of course this situation cannot always be resolved, and sometimes it is necessary to alert the authorities. Another situation, in a non-analytic setting, illustrates how necessary it may be to invoke restraint.

ii. The Analyst Overcome by a Projection

The next illustration (summarized from the case described by Richard Davies (1996) for purposes of this paper) is not from a psychoanalysis or psychotherapy, but it conveys graphically how the authorities can become apparently (and defensively) bemused by a patient's projection, and then *fail* to act appropriately. The carers neglected the risk of danger communicated by the patient and became dysfunctional in their practice. Consequently the patient had to provoke more and more desperately to get them to accept (introject) worry about his sexual violence.

> A man who had been convicted of serious sexual assaults on women was released from prison although he begged to remain there! The prison did not respond and he was placed in a hostel, where he was accepted, though it was known how dangerous he was. The hostel staff formed a plan that he would be "monitored" by the two senior men on the staff and that female workers would have minimal contact with him. His previous failure in group treatments indicated he needed supportive management and not counseling.
>
> Unexpectedly, due to sickness, the two men left the scene. All other workers were female. He was seen outside a school watching children go home, and was reprimanded. Then a female worker became involved in

> working with him, often staying late in the evening, and trying to support his confidence by telling him he was "sexy"! She later realized she had "forgotten" his crime was rape. This man's history was difficult to keep in mind because of the psychological disturbance it must have created in the caregivers.
>
> The probation officer (a woman) began to work more seriously with him—but again seeing him at night. He expressed fears of his compulsion to rape, and was thus, again, trying to get his worries into the mind of the authorities. At the same time, a prison visitor (another woman), who he had known previously, resumed contact. On one occasion at her house he hit her and then begged her to phone the police. He ran to the Samaritans telling them what he had done, but they did not report him to the police as he requested. He then took an overdose, and was diagnosed by the hospital as extremely depressed, but was nevertheless subsequently discharged. Finally, the probation officer referred the patient to a forensic psychiatry unit where he was—at last—admitted to a secure environment.

This man appears to have engaged in implicit and explicit behavior designed to get professional people to worry about him and about his lack of control over his violent sexuality. In terms of the processes of splitting and projection, this man was continually attempting to project his concern into others so that they would be provoked to control him. In this case it was a long time before the professional authorities finally responded as he needed by admitting him to a secure environment, the forensic psychiatric ward. The professionals caring for him seemed too disturbed by the case to be able to act on behalf of the patient's projected need for self-restraint; for instance, the female worker "forgot" he was a rapist. He was in urgent need of actual external restraint, and somehow knew it, as it was he who, implicitly, gave a number of dangerous patient warnings.

iii. The Over-Anxious Analyst

Another illustration shows a third possibility, one in which the analyst's impulse to report is not engendered by the patient:

> A woman of forty-three had recently delivered a healthy male child, now six weeks old. The pregnancy had been completely unexpected by herself and her husband, and had caused considerable friction between them. She had come for treatment (a second treatment, as she had had an analysis more than fifteen years before) partly because her husband wanted her to sort out her feelings about the baby and about him.

There was a sort of indifference in her manner with the analyst, and I often felt she must be very hostile behind that. It turned out that she thought her husband was very suspicious that the baby was not his. I was never told categorically who fathered the baby, but the patient gave me evidence to believe she had had affairs usually when she was displeased with her husband about something. She also feared for a long time that he had been having affairs behind her back. It seemed a love-less marriage, and there was a bleak affectionless air in the analysis.

I often felt bored, and a little irritated that she seemed a wealthy and privileged woman who contributed nothing back to life. I found myself quite censorious, and became concerned that she was not looking after the baby well. The bleak atmosphere made me think she was failing the baby, having little warmth or affection to give, and relying only on a mechanical form of mothering, feeding, and cleaning. I told her my thought that she might be frightened she was not mothering her baby as she would wish; to which she responded with some defiance, that she was perfectly capable and told me of many people who commended her. She then described the technical procedures she employed in her baby care, though they were carried out mechanically. She had methods of dealing with his crying, methods of dealing with him not sleeping, and methods of dealing with his excited states. I was not reassured, in fact less and less so. It encouraged me to try to help her with this excessively mechanical mothering—based partly on my sense of irritation at her lack of giving.

This approach did not progress well, but I pursued it for a while, whilst her coldness towards the baby increasingly worried me. There began to be hints that the husband was assaulting her, and that the baby might be in danger from him. For instance she told me of a friend's husband who had hit his own baby some years ago, followed by remarks about her husband's brief career as a boxer. I could recognize the transference aspects of this and indeed interpreted her feeling I was assaulting her, which in a sense I was. But I continued to feel strongly the need to take seriously the extra-transference situation at home in which there might really be a baby at risk. I took some advice from a social work colleague about reporting a suspicion of abuse. I did not report my suspicions for a week or so, since that step seemed to be such a grave one, even though the analysis was not progressing well. Her bleakness and feeling of assault held me back, while I concentrated on her experience of me as abusing her—and for a while I left the "abuse" of her baby. I gradually became aware of a new tone in the bleakness. It was a hint of mockery at my efforts.

> This became clear in a dream she soon had. She was with her husband watching a street performer trying to juggle, but one of the balls was a large piece of rock, too big and heavy for him to lift and throw properly. She told the husband to go and help, and they both laughed at the juggler's efforts. She mentioned then, in a cold way, that she and her husband often discussed my interpretations, and she generally referred to them contemptuously as "balls." It seemed I was the juggler who was burdened with something too much to handle, and whom she watched with laughter. When I said this, she agreed in an amused way that I didn't seem much use in helping her to be a better mother. I said the dream was in fact a wish to help me, but it got overwhelmed with making fun of me. A moment or two later she suddenly seemed sad, rather than contemptuous. She admitted that she had often tried to worry me quite deliberately, but she realized it was not helping her.

So the upshot was that this woman had *not* disowned her anxiety about mothering—rather she had tried to deal with her anxiety in a different way. Her way was to mock me and wind me up, deliberately, and in a sense let me know the despair she was still feeling. Unconsciously, she was still aware that she needed my efforts (and represented that need in the dream). It was not the case that she had split off her anxiety and feeling of inadequacy. She did know about help with a burden and could represent that in the dream. It was still available to her and represented in her mind in a dream-like form. To be sure she had made *me* feel inadequate, and then mocked me rather cruelly. But she had not in the process lost touch with her anxiety, on which any help or improvement in her mothering would eventually depend. Her strategy was more an attempt to let me know about the heavy burden of feeling inadequate, rather than off-loading it into me to take in her place.

Although stirring me to the threshold of reporting her potential "abuse" of her baby, this woman was not losing sight of her own problem—and shortly this emerged in the sessions without too much resistance. She would subsequently begin to give me a different picture of her feelings about her baby. She did know she worried about the baby and was not as cold as she presented herself to be. And when this became apparent, she was able to restore a different relationship in the psychoanalysis and began to gain some real help from me.

In my view it could have been a serious mistake to have reported this woman. But this could only have been known through unraveling the transference relationship she had developed. The psychoanalyst had to make these discriminations in order to understand the relational process going on between him and his patient (that was his job). He needed to understand how much the woman actually wanted to be controlled, for the baby's sake, and how much there was a pressure to make the analyst aware of her despair and inadequacy.

To understand this interaction was not just therapeutic but, in this case, contributed significantly to informing the psychoanalyst of the way the patient actively and deliberately worried him for other reasons as well. He could understand how she wished more to communicate to him her despair and inadequacy, rather then to off-load her responsibility for her baby whilst retaining her anxiety that remained with her to the extent that it could be expressed in dream form.

These three cases illustrate how varied are the unconscious meanings that a break in confidentiality can have for a patient. Psychoanalytically speaking, these meanings inform us of the delicate and complex issues involved in confidentiality. However they remain foreign territory for lawyers as we shall see below.

B. Subpoenaed Notes

A court has the right to see the case notes of a patient. The psychoanalyst may comply and produce confidential material or may risk being in contempt of court. At times a court may have very considerate views on the confidentiality of psychoanalytic notes; and, at other times, it may not.

To view this psychoanalytically, we need to recall that this legal procedure too, will have resonances with unconscious psychodynamic roots as well as the conscious legal and contractual ones. A third party becomes incorporated into the unconscious and current dynamic process of the ongoing analysis. The processes of splitting and projection of the kind we have been considering can embroil the judicial system in the role of a punitive, restraining influence upon the patient. A psychoanalyst should consider to what degree the judicial authorities have become part of a patient's unconscious system of projective processes, which requires of him that he submit to his own projected restraint in a form that has been re-located in the court.

Naturally, psychoanalysts may, and frequently do, fear the legal system as an extraneous influence that interferes uncomprehendingly in their difficult work. However, analysts need to be aware that the judicial system may be an important and complex part of a patient's relational psychodynamics that they need the analyst to comprehend. If an analyst fails to understand the wider range of psychodynamics that may be involved in the legal process, then he or she is likely to respond to the court order in an adversarial manner—viewing the court as merely interfering. Subsequently, the analyst may feel forced to give in to the greater power of the courts. If, on the contrary, the psychoanalyst continues to uncover the psychodynamic processes at play then he or she stands a better chance of enlightening the patient about these processes. In the latter event at least, regardless of what the analyst decides to do, patients have a fuller knowledge of what is happening to them, and how they have got themselves into the situation and the analyst into this dilemma—self-knowledge being the prime aim of our treatments. Once the patient has understood his or her own experience of the legal process, then there will be more of a chance that the patient will appreciate the analyst's actions with respect to cooperation with the court procedure—even though the patient might not wholly like them. A telling instance of the importance of analyzing the unconscious meaning a patient gives to the legal process is the following:

> A sexually promiscuous man in his thirties was accused of rape by one of his contacts. He was very frightened and he expected that his psychoanalytic notes would be exposed to public view in court. He wanted my guarantee not to produce his notes for lawyers. Analysis of the situation with me indicated that his promiscuity had many causative factors. One of the unconscious imperatives driving him was his need to display his penis to as many girls as possible, and to solicit their admiration for it and his use of it with them. But that drive was as much for reassurance about his sexual anatomy and physiology as it was about direct sexual gratification.
>
> His fear of exposure through his notes appeared to derive from the underlying insecurity about what would be exposed; not least, certain violent thoughts towards the girls he used. Fortunately legal proceedings take a long time and we were able to work over some of the unconscious issues, including his need for me to collude with hiding his worries about himself; and this was exacerbated by a fear (equally hidden) that I had sexual equipment which was greatly superior to his. It did seem likely that his pursuit of girls and his provocative exploitation of them (leading to the charge of rape) was an attempt to have someone call a halt to this activity, and particularly to understand his sexual insecurity. The legal process set in motion by his behavior, together with my anticipated surrender of his notes, became a split-off need for us to understand. He was able in the time available to understand this need. His attitude towards the question of my compliance with the court changed a lot and he was able to understand that if I chose to comply I was acting, at least partly, in line with some wish (or need) in him.
>
> In fact the case never came to court; so in the end I did not have to make a decision about whether to surrender the notes. Nevertheless, it had served to give a profound push to the progress of the analysis—and had shown me how complex were his feelings about the court's demand to produce his notes. In this case, the answer was that both the court and he were behind this wish. To the degree that this was true, the dilemma for me was reduced by the same degree.

This illustration has a further aspect. The notes were not very full ones and I might not have had to worry about revealing too much, and nor would the patient. However, I found myself thinking I might be judged on the adequacy of my note-keeping. This was hardly a matter that in a reasonable way should disturb me, as I had clear reasons in my own mind for not writing too profusely about my patients. Yet, I did worry about the reaction of my patient, when he would see how much (little) I wrote about him. I predicted intuitively that he would be disappointed with me, perhaps angry and rebuffed that I did not devote more of my time and interest to documenting the work with him. This I realized was an element of narcissism in my patient – his wish to be shown as somehow special – which touched an element on my side that was my reluctance to expose myself in such a way as to have him critical of me.

Publishing papers. A related issue is when a psychoanalyst deliberately publishes case material in a professional paper. Often we assume that publishing details of patients is going against the contract of confidentiality and will interfere with the analysis because the patient's trust will collapse. It is as if we assume that the patient will be confronted with a judging and judgmental third party, just like a law court. In the case of published case-histories, the "third party" that intrudes into the psychoanalysis is no longer the law-courts; instead it is the readership, more like a theater audience. The latter is potentially fantasized as a more benign intruder, fascinated by the patient, although exposure can also mobilize the fear of a hostile audience.

However, this may not be the patient's reaction. In fact, in my experience the relational issues again are more complex. The patient does not just feel that his or her trust has been let down. In many cases, he or she is also extremely curious to get, as it were, inside the analyst's head and see what thoughts the analyst really thinks about them. There is the narcissistic hope that the analyst has done a great deal more thinking, has devoted a great deal more time and interest, and has specifically chosen him or her to write about.

At a surface level, the patient may be grateful to the psychoanalyst and may want out of gratitude to allow him or her to write the paper. Or, often, the patient will assume that the analyst's paper is an expression of the analyst's own narcissism. The patient may not be at all wrong, and the patient can then react with resentment claiming exploitation of the self and his or her case. In the last illustration of the case of the promiscuous young man, there was such a reaction, and it could be seen that he believed me to be boosting my ego exactly as he felt when he conquered a new girl. He had used my self-interest to project his own into; and then he could observe the quality of exploitative narcissism in me that he was then innocently free of.

C. Relations Between Psychoanalysts and the Legal Profession

It is clear that psychoanalysts are not the only persons to collaborate in processes of splitting and projection. Some of the earlier examples in this paper demonstrated how the police and the mental health services can also be used in this way, to harbor condemnation which the patient can exploit for projective purposes. It is not that the involvement of controlling figures is necessarily a bad thing, since in certain cases an external restraining influence needs to be exerted. However, when the patient uses someone other than the analyst in this way, that third party may with the best of intentions become an interference in the analytic process.

The court may be party, as in the example of the man accused of rape, to the question of exposing criminal actions; and unwittingly, lawyers and the judicial system may become implicated in the unconscious processes which unfortunately only the psychoanalyst can have access to. The privileged position of the analyst in this respect often feels matched by the analyst's helplessness to use such knowledge on behalf of either the patient or the judicial process. The problem of making apparently incomprehensible unconscious processes understandable to patients, who resist awareness of these processes, is redoubled by trying to make these processes understandable to other professionals. However, the analyst's privileged position provokes another specific problem that may frequently become a source of unconscious friction in relations with the legal profession.

The primal scene: A third party who has dealings with a psychoanalytic treatment is likely to have their own unconscious reaction of fascination, exclusion, hostility, idealization, and so on. Psychoanalysts recognize that a protected space like the analytic setting always rouses fantasies and feelings about the "primal scene." According to psychoanalytic theory the Oedipus complex is at the heart of the psychology of each and every one of us. From early in infancy there is an awareness of parents forming an exclusive couple, a couple from which the infant is excluded. Freud called this the "primal scene" when he found the infant's feeling of exclusion to be so significant in his analysis of the Wolfman case (Freud, 1918). The sense of exclusion leads to the powerful aggressive and murderous feelings of the Oedipus complex. Fantasies of this scene, as well as the feelings it evokes, are aroused in the unconscious part of the mind of most people when confronted with an exclusive couple. We need to remind ourselves that in our work, as an analyst with a patient, we are an exclusive couple. We maintain the integrity of the psychoanalytic couple in its setting with great rigor, but this can easily trigger unconscious primal scene fantasies and feelings in others.

Thus when we assert the exclusiveness of the psychoanalytic setting, we need to bear in mind that fantasies of the primal scene will come into play at an unconscious and primitive level. Persons outside the psychoanalytic setting will feel envious and excluded, driven by an equally primitive urge to intrude into the scene. Those who have dealings with us—in the case in point it will be lawyers—will be affected by this complex of fantasies and feelings, even though they are implicit and concealed.

At the same time, for us within the setting we will be driven by equally primitive fantasies and feelings aimed at protecting the boundaries of our setting as if they were the taboos surrounding the parental bedroom and the intercourse that takes place there.

Clearly there is no obvious, explicit way of handling this fantasy issue with our colleagues from other professions. Nevertheless, we have to understand that these potentially explosive feelings can creep into any discussion of the topic. Since this unconscious subtext can lead to a degree of obstruction to any reconciliation between the psychoanalytic and the legal parties, we should be aware of these hidden potentialities. An insight into these professional dynamics can give a measure of protection against blindly following them, and creating more obstruction.

The conflict between the law and psychoanalysis over confidentiality can get heated. In a session on confidentiality at a recent International Psychoanalytical Association congress (at Nice in 2001) there was a surprising amount of bad feeling, and indeed heckling, occurring in response to a paper by a lawyer. Though he seemed to take it in good part, the tension and fraught feeling is itself of interest and can be understood psychoanalytically as a defense of the privileged space of psychoanalysis which might be under attack. These powerful and primitive sources of affect form one hurdle to calm discussion, and we need to be aware that it can occur on both sides: within us, as well as within those outside psychoanalysis.

3. Conclusions

The impact of breaking confidentiality goes way beyond the surface and impacts upon the dream-life of the unconscious, with the result that we can find ourselves and colleagues succumbing to unconsciously-driven decisions and behavior. These unconscious impacts can be disastrous to the successful progress of a psychoanalysis, but it is not necessarily so. The very unconscious meanings that confidentiality has, and the breaches of it, also provide a road into the unconscious life of patients which we are continually exploring in psychoanalysis.

In this paper, I have concentrated on certain defensive processes: splitting, projection and introjection. These result in major deficits to the personality and identity. However they solve problems in ways which, albeit maladaptive, are serviceable. So often the end result of splitting and projection is that an internal struggle between opposing currents in the individual is converted into an external struggle between the patient and the analyst (or a third party). The two people come to represent and enact the separate sides of the individual's conflict—the intrapsychic struggle of the patient becoming an interpersonal struggle with his or her analyst.

And this is true also of third parties, who may unwittingly come to play a part in someone's internal struggle. The psychoanalyst however, is both obliged and trained to make discriminations regarding what the patient is projecting into him or her. Understanding this relational process going on between the analyst and patient is the analyst's job; but it is not just therapeutic, it can contribute significantly to informing the analyst of the real need to report a dangerous patient or not. He or she must weigh the real need for actual external restraint, as a solution to an insoluble inner conflict, versus the pressure to engage the analyst in a scene that is not present but a repetition of the past.

I do not wish in my conclusions to elaborate much on the nature of repetitions in the transference relationship with the analyst, but a brief further note on the woman who appeared to me to be abusing her baby is illustrative of the way the patient used the analyst quite differently from the splitting and projection I have stressed throughout the chapter.

> When it appeared that I might report her to the social work authorities, she experienced me as making a violating intrusion into her and her life. My intentions were unconsciously felt by her as abusive ones. What transpired later in the psychoanalysis was that there had been incidents in her childhood when she was interfered with sexually, though without full penetration, by an older brother. The psychoanalysis became for a while an arena for re-enacting in represented form, some aspects of her abuse, the exposure, the intrusion, the sense of inadequacy and guilt. Although the psychoanalyst had become a *representation* of the abuser, the experience felt completely real to the patient, and the analyst seemed to be the violator of her childhood who had to be kept out at all costs.

In this instance the patient had not relocated a part of herself in the analyst. Instead she had seen the analyst as representing—or from her point of view, actually being—a figure from the past. This is a very different use of the analyst by the patient. And it is this discrimination (whether he allies with and takes on a disowned part of the patient or represents a quite separate figure from the patient whom the patient has cause to fear) that is important. Where breach of confidentiality has happened or is likely, it is always wise for the analyst to seek out evidence about whether the patient feels abuse in the therapeutic relations—violatingly exposed. In that case, the dynamic of the therapeutic interaction may be enacting an early trauma rather then being used for the purposes of splitting and projection.

It seems to me that some of these unconscious issues should be more fully acknowledged by psychoanalysts. Then if the efforts of the legal profession and the judicial process seem intrusive (in whatever form), they can be assessed for their unconscious psychodynamic power, as well as their disruption of the psychoanalytic setting. And on occasion they can even be turned to the advantage of the analytic process.

Confidentiality is a crucial aspect of the psychoanalytic setting. It has unconscious meanings for the patient and is not just a technical feature of the method we use. Therefore breaking confidentiality is not just a technical obstruction to our method. It produces violent feelings, and overwhelming experiences for our patients; as well as for us as analysts and for third parties. The impact of breaking confidentiality goes way beyond the surface and impacts upon the dream-life of the unconscious, with the result that we can find ourselves and colleagues succumbing to unconsciously-driven decisions and behavior. Analysts are trained to keep a grasp of unconscious levels of interaction that other professionals might only at best dimly perceive.

Works Cited

Conran, Michael. (1985) "The Patient in Hospital," *Psychoanalytic Psychotherapy*, 1: pp. 31–43.

Davies, Richard. (1995) "The Interdisciplinary Network and the Internal World of the Offender." In *Forensic Psychotherapy: Crime Psychodynamics and the Offender Patient*, eds. Chris Cordess and Murray Cox. London: Jessica Kingsley.

———. (1996). *Psychodynamics and the Offender Patient*. London: Jessica Kingsley.

Freud, Sigmund. (1918) *From the History of an Infantile Neurosis*. In *The Standard Edition of the Complete Works of Sigmund Freud,* 17. London: Hogarth.

Hinshelwood, R. D. (1995) "The Social Relocation of Personal Identity," *Philosophy, Psychology, Psychiatry,* 2: 185–204.

———. (1997) *Therapy or Coercion: Does Psychoanalysis Differ from Brainwashing?* London: Karnac.

Klein, Melanie. (1946) "Notes on Some Schizoid Mechanisms," *International Journal of Psycho-Analysis*, 27: pp. 99-110. Republished in 1975 *The Writings of Melanie Klein*, vol. 3. London: Hogarth, pp. 1-24.

Four

PUBLIC, PRIVATE . . .

Jacques Mauger

"Individual and universal beginnings are perpetual continuations— movements, rather than contents, a permanent recurring of prehistory in history."

Moscovici (1989) (Translated from French.)

Since the publication of a few papers of mine more than ten years ago, in which I clearly describe various moments of transference deadlock between patient and analyst, I have been unable to find a comfortable way of including further "demonstration pieces" in my writings. No doubt, I have been held back by my awareness of the confidentiality issue, a particularly disturbing debate as its scope widens. However, these days, I find myself wondering. We always say more than we intend. The same goes for what we read or hear. When making a public statement, does not the analyst betray—while trying to convey an essentially private relationship—by revealing something of his/her own transference which the patient, as a potential reader or listener, may perceive as "confidential"? We must therefore consider the inevitable overflow of transference in any statement, both on the part of the speaker and of the listener as a primary issue. As Allannah Furlong argues, the interpretation that the analyst chooses to make of a given analytical situation, whether in writing or orally, is not only a question of the "violence" and "seduction" of the portrait that the patient may recognise as his/her own. There is the added stimulation of what may seem to him/her enigmatic about his/her analyst's need to report on their relationship. Both these levels of new meaning, conveyed in the patient's encounter with a "public" account of his/her analysis, may precipitate a need to re-evaluate his/her own version of the analysis, whether it is still underway or completed (Furlong, 2002).

Yet is not our so-called counter-transference, our own transference that comes into play in its most unconscious aspects, also the source of our thinking, speaking, and writing endeavors? We may readily agree. But then how do we determine, when such endeavors transcend the bounds of privacy, what will be acceptable first to our patients, but equally to our colleagues, and to our audience? The transference forces nurtured by the individualizing framework within which we retire with our patients has an impact on us as analysts, which can make us lose sight of other factors at work in this setting. These other factors cannot be reduced to the inter-individual level, since they constitute an undifferentiating, impersonal impact on us that calls out for no less of a recognition and transmission to others.

1. "The Reporting Analyst"

In attempting to justify the nature and the boundaries of his/her clinical account, the analyst wavers between two imperatives: to say the least possible in order to protect the secrecy of what is revealed to him/her by the individual patient, and to say more, in order to comply with the requirements of a collegial overview of his/her practice. Though recently, the issue of confidentiality is evolving in a different direction—as the objective value of clinical "facts" is questioned—the difficulty remains of how, and how much, to report in public and to the public, without altering the basic nature of a process that can only develop in private. Furthermore, how does one translate this experience in a way that is respectful of the nature of the interaction between patient and analyst (Levin, 2001), without necessarily reducing the situation to its inter-individual dimension?

We may have forsaken too soon an old debate among psychoanalysts, which may once again become relevant in the context of our present discussion. The issue at stake was the relative priority of allegiance between the secrecy owed to a patient-candidate and the analyst's responsibility to act as a *reporting analyst* on behalf of his/her society and institute. Should the training analyst report to his/her colleagues on the evolution of the candidate's personal analysis? It would no longer occur to us to challenge what has become for a great majority of us a principle of abstention by virtue of which any request to breach the secrecy of a personal analysis for a collective interest would be considered inappropriate. However, in adopting this principle, have we renounced sharing that which cannot be reduced to the individual level in a personal analysis? Since we have agreed that no word should transpire from the personal analysis of a candidate, have we given up discussing "impersonal" issues? For instance, what is and what becomes of the analyst's ability to care for the patient in a process which puts in doubt the usual "therapeutic aim" in favor of the "analytic" one? The matter of a specific kind of care-taking is at the heart of what particularly traverses the analysis of future colleagues, and therefore should, at a number of levels, be of interest to the society they wish to join.

However, since psychoanalysis is primarily considered to be an individual undertaking, it has always seemed self-evident to apply our ethical rules only to what concerns the individuals involved in the process. Similar thinking has permeated the debate on confidentiality. As a result, the matter of respecting or breaching confidentiality has tended to be viewed as restricted to individuals in their singularity. We have tended to dismiss too soon, I believe, the ways in which these relationships and their outcomes are not also obligated to a compelling *beyond*. We will come back to this.

2. Too Much and Too Little

Let us take another tack. But first another question: Why are some analysts inclined to disclose more details than necessary for the purposes of a presentation, thereby revealing "too much" about the patient and thus, too much about themselves? The complementary inquiry, or the hidden face of the first, would be to ask why the majority of analysts remain silent—or say too little— about how they cope with the impact day after day of the experience entrusted to them?

In attempting to answer these questions, we generally refer to the fate of the impact on each patient and each analyst of their combined transference forces, in explaining both the too much revealing, and the not daring to reveal, of clinical reporting. This reference to singularity seems obvious. Yet how difficult it is to distinguish it from another factor, non-individual and common to all colleagues. In this common factor do we not find an unconfessed and unconfessable need to share something of the polymorphous transference charge placed on the analyst day after day? Whether from the ethical point of view or from the strictly clinical/psychoanalytic point of view, this need seems to elude an acceptable rendering. It is all very well to state that it is up to each individual to discretely find private channels through which he/she can share transference overflow—personal analysis, professional supervision, or exchange with one or more colleagues. It all appears insufficient. Regardless of the confidential information one analyst may reveal to another about an individual treatment, is there not something of the deep transference which analyst and patient experience individually in the privacy of the consulting room, which remains unarticulated and unrecognized? In any case, the traditional avenues of sharing in inter-analytic space barely expand the limits of what we are expected to keep to ourselves.

To better illustrate what I mean, I will enlist my experience as "reporter" at the sixtieth conference of French-speaking psychoanalysts held in Montreal in June 2000. This conference is a three-day discussion forum, focusing on two major presentations (reports) based on the conference's general theme. Six months prior to the conference, the first version of these two "reports" is sent to all registered participants, who are invited to comment in writing. The most relevant commentaries are immediately published and sent to all participants prior to the conference. Following the conference, a final version of the reports, including the discussions they raised, is published in the *Revue française de psychanalyse*. The theme in 2000 was "L'idéal transmis" ("the transmitted ideal"). Together with my colleague Lise Monette, I presented a paper entitled "Pure Culture" (Mauger and Monette, 2000).

Our text focused on various forms of resistance to the psychoanalytic process experienced by the analyst: the melancholic side of the psychoanalytical vocation; the analyst's unconscious hatred of transference; the idealizing elevation of any form of technical purity; the couch as the common bed of the "shrink species"; the discrete *entre-nous* (amongst ourselves) of our professional territory; the elusive resistance of the natural flow to what is familiar; and the "discontent" in contemporary psychoanalytical culture.

Since our presentation did not include any case study, the issue of confidentiality, in its usual sense, did not seem to be an issue. Little did we know!

Personally—and here, I only speak for myself—I felt that this *exposé* could not have more closely reflected the impact on me of the daily routine of psychoanalytic practice I have undertaken for more than twenty five years. In more than one way, this text had been penned under the influence of multiple transferences. It was meant as a reflection on the impasses many of us face in our practice, and which transform occasionally, depending on the situation, into physical, psychological, or ethical "suffering."

Above all, in trying to speak from the perspective of what touches those who are the most involved in this work, and who are most active in the life of the institutions that determine its course, I found that my "confiding" ran into an ambiguous reception. I was taxed with having said too much, and this particular aspect of my attempted communication was the most misunderstood. What I had been trying to convey was the immoderation of psychoanalytical practice that I believed, and still believe, to be a condition also experienced by my colleagues.

However, our audience obviously did not understand it that way, quite the contrary. "Keep this to yourself! What you are exposing is your own business. Come to terms with it! Are not training analysts the most privileged in the profession, the guardians of traditional practice?" This is the feedback that, more often than not, I received.

Was the *reporting analyst* attempting to resurface?

What to make of this uproar in response to our "report"?

The issue of transferences, those projected onto us as an object, and those we initiate as subject, is inevitably at the heart of the confidentiality issue in its dual meaning: that which pushes us to confide and that which invites us to hold back.

Isolated in bearing the cumulative impact of the transferences that traverse him/her, and deprived of a place to safely deposit what has been confided in him/her, the psychoanalyst suffers from adverse effects, though he/she may not realize it. Typically, as the years go by, the longer that he/she is exposed, the less the "experienced" analyst is inclined to discuss this issue. He/she will find every excuse to keep quiet, as more and more of his/her patients are fellow analysts, others similar to him/her. He/she even ends up believing that in order to comply with the conditions of his/her practice this asceticism is the only acceptable behavior.

These observations show how much the call to confidentiality can be misunderstood, since we all need to share the transference charges which never fail to get through to us and "beyond" us. I doubt that it is sufficient to invite the analyst who wants to relate what goes on during a session to simply more clearly define that part of his/her unconscious desires—inherent in his/her transference onto the patient referred to—that might transpire through his/her description. It is not merely a question of lack of attention to these matters or even of a carelessness that is relatively easy to remedy. I would propose that on the contrary, in the majority of cases, what is at stake is a veritable impulse to say more than is usually considered necessary, to say more than others are prepared to hear. Acknowledging such a fact does not imply that there are not problems associated with it.

The analyst's need to convey to others what he/she experiences during a session, beyond the generally recognized basic facts, remains enigmatic in many ways. The fact that such a counter-transference enigma may have effects on the patient informed of it—which Furlong (2002) invites us to take into account—seems self-evident. Yet even more troubling is to think that the "excessiveness" of such a disclosure, understood now as a necessity and therefore not reducible to the analyst's capacity to keep clinical material private (whether alone or with a colleague), stems from the unbearable nature of what is confided to us. Here, I am referring less to individual experiences on a case-by-case basis than to the cumulative effect of the transferences in which we take part day after day. At stake is not so much the impact of each patient's history, however burdensome and traumatic it may be, as the impossibility of containing—or, for some analysts, the excessive containment of—this compulsive dimension of human experience which repetitively permeates individual conflict. Too often, the analyst becomes absorbed exclusively in the latter dimension, neglecting to report on what lies "beyond" the individual. This "beyond" alludes to the concept of the compulsive return and actualization in transference introduced by Freud in 1920 in *Beyond the Pleasure Principle* to distinguish it from individual repression. This "beyond" forms a part of memory that though not unique to the individual is, nevertheless, a condition of the individual's psychic constitution. In the same way, Freud referred in other places to what he called variously the "originary," "phylogenesis," and sometimes "historical truth." Not that these notions are equivalent; however, they are all different approaches to a "beyond" the individually repressed unconscious, a beyond fugitively exposing the two protagonists of the psychoanalytical situation to the conditions of their common human existence, to a shared founding identification of their humanity. Does not the ongoing debate about the modalities of the transmission of phylogenetic inheritance, often reducing the issue to its biological aspects, reveal a resistance to this portion of "beyond" that lies at the heart of the ego of the two *persons* in the analytic situation?

Thus, when an analyst publicly trespasses the limits of what seems acceptable, is he/she perhaps trying, unbeknownst to him/herself, to convey the remnants of a *transindividual* experience languishing for want of "delivery" outside the narrow privacy of sessions?

This question reminds me of the work of psychic transformation, explored by Nathalie Zaltzman under the theme, borrowed from Freud, of *kulturarbeit*, "considering the constitutive mutual dependencies between the individual and the human species" (Zaltzman, 1998, p. 14). She develops this theme partly on the basis of stories from survivors of concentration camps, where exactly this condition of mutuality was no longer respected, where "the totalitarian organization has dismissed from its common goals the concern for the material and moral conservation of the individual" (Zaltzman, 1998, p. 15). Under such conditions, these exceptional narratives are by their very existence testimonials *in extremis* to the individual's unconscious and indestructible sense of belonging to human reality, which has been kept alive through the impersonal function of language.

Furthermore, this process of psychic transformation, dramatically illustrated in and by the work of survivors, may also be accessible, though differently, through the psychoanalytical experience. Consider what Freud wrote in *Moses and Monotheism*, about the psyche, "This content of the unconscious, indeed, is in any case a collective, universal property of mankind" (Freud, 1920, p. 132). The unconscious is to begin with an impersonal reality that materializes in the individual. Consequently, does not the history of humanity lie within each human being, and is not the "prehistory" of each one to be credited to a founding identification shared by all, in which they never cease to seek recognition? The psychoanalytical experience is often too exclusively centered on the individual, and any account of it occults, most of the time, the constitutive mutual relationship between the individual and the human race.

3. Public, Private . . .

Recourse to the public, "our fellow men and women," is thus not really a "release valve" of transference overflow. It is rather a "return to sender" of information that by its nature transcends individual existence, passing through it, leaving deposits, even burrowing within the inevitable transference repetitions of an enacted and actualized memory. It is to this memory that Freud refers, especially in *Beyond the Pleasure Principle* (1920), as a memory existing beyond the patient's and the analyst's egos. Thus returned to the public is an "excess" that is not a version of ill-contained privacy and that is not synonymous with the return of the repressed in search of a new venue.

I am hereby dismissing both the professional ethics of confidentiality towards the individual patient and the legal obligation to disclose, in certain cases, the subject matter of the confidence. As long as individual privacy remains the only focus of confidentiality, whether it is in justifying secrecy, or whether, on the contrary, it is in justifying a needed lack of it in court, is not the unconscious transindividual content, of which we are equally the keepers, left "outstanding"? This veiled content is often unknowingly doomed to lead to a deadlock in treatment, which will eventually become a symptom of the lack of *kulturarbeit*, underlying both the silence of the ones who do not dare speak and the too much talking of the others.

Both the reader-listener of the voluntary confiding/sharing of the analyst, and the judge who orders its disclosure, are generally uniquely interested in one person's story at a time, as if the confidentiality issue can only be posed on an individual basis.

Could it be that the inner recesses of the most unconscious part of reporting—and of the confidentiality related to it—are not confined to the inter-individual register? Could it be that our grossly macroscopic consciousness readily recasts this material within the scope of the more familiar dimensions of an ego governed by the principle of pleasure-displeasure, neglecting to account for what lies "beyond"?

No doubt, we are justified in stressing the potential "violence" to which the patient who is the subject of an oral or written disclosure is exposed. However, as Piera Aulagnier points out (1975), which is the share of necessary violence compared to abusive violence in our clinical reporting? The line cannot be so easily drawn if we do not first consent to the violence of expanding our usual categories. Could it be that, sometimes, part of what is conceived as abusive from the point of view of a given individual, is, nevertheless, necessary?

This necessary violence originates from the ongoing sources of what unceasingly founds each individual's history. It stems from the perpetual recurring of the prehistory of the human species, where in the beginning there was the incestuous and murderous act that continues with each repetition to dismantle what is created. Do we not have here a violence that both delimits and exceeds, in the analytical situation, the uniqueness and coherence of the individual human being?

Might the need to publicly reveal something of this transindividual unconscious, in some cases, unavoidably take the form of an individual "breach of confidence"? In the best of cases, it may be possible only in an *après-coup* reflection to think about differentiating this abuse from a "breach of confidentiality." In other words, the transmission of the content of an impasse might only be achieved by means of an impasse in the transmission process (of clinical reporting), whereby either too much or too little is conveyed.

Transmission of an impasse and impasse in the transmission process. Absorbed in his/her *compulsion to represent* (Rolland, 1998) a privacy he/she claims to be the custodian of, should not the *reporting analyst* acknowledge that he/she is just as strongly bound to *present* the human reality which lies *beyond* individuality?

Acknowledgments

This chapter has been translated from the original French by Yolande Amzallag. Thanks to her and also to Allannah Furlong and Charles Levin for their work on this chapter.

Works Cited

Aulagnier, Piera. (1975) *La violence de l'interprétation*. Paris: Presses Universitaires de France.

Freud, Sigmund. (1939) *Moses and Monotheism*. Standard Edition, 23: pp. 7–137.

———. (1920) *Beyond the Pleasure Principle*. Standard Edition, 18: pp. 7–64.

Furlong, Allannah. (2002) "Potential Violence of Interpretation and Implantation in Clinical Writing," Presentation made to the Canadian Psychoanalytic Society (English Branch), Montreal, 21 March.

Levin, Charles. (2001) "The Siege of Psychotherapeutic Space: Psychoanalysis in the Age of Transparency," *Canadian Journal of Psychoanalysis*, 9: pp. 187–215.

Moscovici, Marie. (1989) *Il est arrivé quelque chose*. Paris: Petite Bibliothèque Payot.

Mauger, Jacques, and Lise Monette. (2000) << Pure culture . . . >> *Revue française de psychanalyse,* 64: pp. 13–77.

Rolland, J. C. (1998) *Guérir du mal d'aimer*. Paris: Gallimard.

Zaltzman, Nathalie. (1998) *De la guérison psychanalytique*. Paris: Presses Universitaires de France.

Five

WELCOMING BIG BROTHER: THE MALAISE OF CONFIDENTIALITY IN THE THERAPEUTIC CULTURE

Charles Levin and Christine Ury

1. Introduction

In his never-completed *History of Sexuality*, Michel Foucault famously denied the Freudian thesis of repression, arguing instead that in the Judeo-Christian world sexuality had become part of a prodigious culture of confession. From this perspective, Foucault was able to argue that psychoanalysis itself is part of a normalizing "production" of discourse in which even the "liberation" of sexuality and the freeing of the unconscious functions as a form of regimentation and social control.

> Western man has become a confessing animal. ... The obligation to confess is now ... so deeply ingrained in us that we no longer perceive it as the effect of a power that constrains us. ... One has to be completely taken in by this internal ruse of confession in order to attribute a fundamental role to censorship, to taboos regarding speaking and thinking; one has to have an inverted image of power in order to believe that all these voices which have spoken to us so long in our civilization—repeating the formidable injunction to tell what one is and what one does, what one recollects and what one has forgotten, what one is thinking and what one thinks he is not thinking—are speaking to us of freedom. An immense labor to which the West has submitted generations in order to produce ... subjection (Foucault, 1978, pp. 59-60).

Though Foucault's understanding of psychoanalysis as a form of confession involves a serious misunderstanding of Freud and of the psychoanalytic process, he did nevertheless put his finger on a fundamental aspect of the transference and fantasies about psychotherapy. These fantasies, which we shall describe in more detail below, revolve around the simple narcissistic defense of idealization, in which primitive images of self-perfection are projected onto the object, who is imagined as omniscient, omnipotent, and potentially all-loving. This fantasy expresses itself as a compelling need to believe that the subject can be transformed and released from suffering, if only he or she can succeed in becoming "known" by the idealized object. From this point of view, Foucault was essentially correct in identifying a kind of manipulative twisting of the concept of repression in contemporary popular culture. While there is no reason to go along with him in assuming that confessionality, in the transferential sense, is exclusive to the West, Foucault's critical analysis of the repression hypothesis describes something very important about what happens when the therapeutic transference is amplified and hystericized in collective forms of behavior, such as media entertainment and popular "news." For purposes of this article, we have grouped such phenomena under the heading "therapeutic culture."

The central thesis of this chapter is that the rise of the therapeutic culture, with its emphasis on confessionality as a major theme, even genre, of modern popular culture, has played an important role in undermining the professional ethical precept of confidentiality, an essential prerequisite of psychoanalytic psychotherapy.

The therapeutic culture has tended to minimize and even to demonize the concept of privacy. Under the banners of "freedom of information" and "the personal is the political," privacy has come to be regarded even in sophisticated political circles as a form of resistance to social progress toward a less individualistic, more "transparent" society. Transparency has also become one of the bywords of bioethics. The term can sometimes be used to provide a disingenuous rationale for increasing bureaucratic powers of investigation and administrative control in government, private corporations, universities, and the "health care industry" itself (Levin, 2001). The emphasis on transparency has also encouraged a popular aesthetic of "outing" and lurid self-exposure that has turned into a kind of media equivalent of blood sport. Such trends are not entirely negative. They express, however crudely, an important theme in the dialectic of democratization: the demand for public accountability not only in representative government, but also in scientific research and in professional conduct. The experimental exhibitionism of much media culture can be interpreted as a side effect of real increases in individual and social self-awareness and responsibility brought about, in part, by the same media. Nevertheless, the therapeutic culture has also led to the relative devaluation of an important democratic principle, that of individual privacy. This has contributed to the erosion of the basic legal and cultural supports for the confidentiality of the psychotherapeutic relationship.

2. A Social Model of Confidentiality and its Intrapsychic Significance

Implied in the foregoing summary is the notion that neither privacy nor confidentiality is a universal concept with an independent status in logic or ethics. They are certainly rational concepts, but they are also products of intellectual and cultural history, part of the development of what we now, with some degree of confidence, describe as liberal democratic culture. Confidentiality is not simply a sub-category of privacy as a constitutional right, though it can be discussed meaningfully as such in judicial and professional discourse (L'Heureux-Dubé, 2003; Pyles, 2003). Nor can it be deduced or derived in the abstract from ethical precepts. It is a complex and heterogeneous notion with a long history, which is really the history of the emergence of different kinds of professional practice (Levin, 2001, 2003). In some cases, such as law or psychoanalysis, where it is a truly significant principle, confidentiality expresses the ethos of a particular kind of working relationship, and also the pragmatic underpinnings of that relationship. In both the common law and civil law traditions, the lawyer-client privilege and medical confidentiality, are forms of "relational privilege." Medical confidentiality also has cultural origins in the Hippocratic Oath, but both forms of privilege may be derived from the fact that the lawyer or the doctor is a kind of servant who, like the family slave, was protected under Roman law from testifying against his masters (Shuman, 1985). (Privilege = privus + lex = private law.) In civil law (France), this kind of protection has sometimes been raised to the level of a quasi "absolute" principle on deontological grounds. In the common law tradition (Britain, North America), speaking very generally, relational privileges have been justified on utilitarian grounds, namely that the greater public good, for example the institution of the law itself and the benefits provided by the legal profession, depend vitally on the protection of communication between the professional and the client. This kind of justification for a psychotherapy privilege finds its most important contemporary statement in the United States Supreme Court decision in *Jaffee v. Redmond* [1996].

The concept of confidentiality in psychoanalysis certainly shares historical roots with law, medicine, and other fields. One significant difference, however, lies in the fact that psychoanalysis does not just enjoin a relationship of *conscious* communication between the professional and the client. In fact, the analyst and analysand are generally striving to move beyond conventional social models of explicit communication in order to enable a much greater role than usual for unbidden and unconscious forms of mental activity and verbalization. The analyst is generally expected to "contain" his or her own subjective experience internally for working purposes, and to maintain a relatively "neutral" stance (the frame). In complementary fashion, the analysand is invited to give full reign to the verbal and emotional expression of whatever comes to mind (free association) (Furlong, this volume, pp. 13 ff.). In practice this means that the function of confidentiality in psychoanalysis is rather more complex than it is in many other fields. The point is only secondarily and superficially that confidentiality gives the analysand confidence or "trust" to reveal facts whose disclosure might otherwise bring harm or embarrassment (Forrester, 2003). It is true that psychoanalysis, like any other form of psychotherapy or counseling, would be impossible or very difficult if the analysand felt unable to reveal and discuss such facts. But far more important for the genuine practice of psychoanalysis is the possibility of creating an atmosphere conducive to the gradual emergence of complex unconscious patterns of meaning and motivation. Such patterns cannot simply be "disclosed," and their discovery does not in itself alleviate suffering or consolidate greater mental freedom; they have to be "worked through," and this can be a lengthy and painful process (Freud, 1912).

Contrary to Foucault's claim, the point of psychoanalysis is not confession or "self-disclosure" and the deeper function of confidentiality is certainly not to encourage such gestures in the name of healing. In fact, if that were the case, and confession were shown to have lasting psychological benefits, then the argument for confidentiality would be at serious risk of self-contradiction. Confidentiality would then seem merely to be another form of suffering in isolation, merely enlarging the sphere of pathological secrecy from one person to two and, therefore, a detrimental impediment to potentially much more dramatic and effective forms of healing based on *public* confession and self-disclosure.

In fact, the function of confidentiality in psychoanalysis has as much to do with the analysand's relationship with him or herself as with the analyst and the world. At the first level, the analyst's deep commitment to confidentiality, in the full sense of that term, is designed to protect the patient from the direct impingement of conventional social pressure and public morality, which may not only inhibit the free play of mind, but also reinforce harsh and self-destructive superego pathology or self-sabotaging self-representations of various kinds. In this way, a kind of "facilitating environment" (Winnicott, 1965) for the emergence and protection of unconscious communication can be established.

At the second level, which is somewhat more difficult to explicate, confidentiality protects the analysand from him- or herself and more importantly from the inadvertent countertransference impingements of the analyst and his or her forms of psychological pressure and morality. Of course, these factors can never be eliminated, they can only be minimized. The patient will certainly have internalized social pressures and prohibitions so that confidentiality at the first level of minimizing external impingement may not significantly reduce such inhibiting influences. Moreover, the analyst will be influenced in the same way by internalizations and identifications. In fact such "complexes" and fantasies are in significant measure internally driven in all of us; they develop in eccentric ways, and probably require only minimal social and environmental inputs in order to gain dynamic purchase on mental activity.

Whatever its faults, psychoanalytic training is expressly designed to help the analyst to recognize, contain, and learn from such external and internal influences, rather than to act them out in the countertransference unreflectively. When the analyst's practice is deeply informed by the ethos of confidentiality, he or she is much less likely to give in to the impulse to engage in a form of gossip with the patient *about* the patient. This has been referred to elsewhere as "blabbing about the patient *to* the patient" (Levin, 2003). It is easy to fall into, and at its worst, constitutes a perverse form of discourse, in which the analyst splits the patient into favored and denigrated aspects and in effect begins a process of telling on one side of the patient to the other. Analysands are easily seduced into this pattern of "analysis" or "therapy" in which the therapeutic alliance is distorted into a strategy of encouraging further internal splitting and suppression rather than internal recognition and integration. Sometimes, deliberately or inadvertently, the positive transference can be exploited to this end by the analyst, in effect establishing a regime of suggestion in which the negative transference is never successfully expressed by the analysand or engaged by the analyst. When this situation occurs, it can be said with justice that confidentiality in the deeper psychoanalytic sense has been violated, even though no public disclosure whatsoever has been made by the analyst. Many aspects of the therapeutic culture, media therapy, and related forms of entertainment to be discussed below are based on this distortion of psychotherapeutic interaction, taking it to a radical and, we believe, potentially damaging extreme.

The social model of confidentiality we have outlined strongly implies that the actual practice of confidentiality will be partially dependent upon and vulnerable to prevailing currents within the surrounding cultural and social environment, regardless of what the law of the land and professional codes of ethics may stipulate. Moreover, the intrapsychic significance of confidentiality suggests that this interdependence between culture and professional practice, and the vulnerability of the latter, is especially important in the case of psychoanalytic psychotherapy. These premises force on us a seeming paradox, which will be the subject of the remainder of this chapter, namely, that the therapeutic culture represents a serious challenge to the viability of psychoanalysis and most forms of psychoanalytically-oriented psychotherapy.

3. The Therapeutic Culture and Mass Entertainment

The idea that contemporary culture is becoming at least in part a culture of therapy has many sources and tendencies. It can be traced in part to Hannah Arendt's political critique of the erosion of the classical distinction between public and domestic life, involving a sort of dilution of the *polis* into a "gigantic, nation-wide administration of housekeeping" (Arendt, 1958, p. 28). The emphasis on the "therapeutic" as an important category of contemporary culture gained currency with Philip Rieff's portrait of "psychological man" in *The Triumph of the Therapeutic* (Rieff, 1968). Some aspects of these analyses and their numerous offshoots have turned out to be quite prophetic. There are now very obvious tendencies to reinterpret the purposes of the political process, public and private administration, and the law itself in therapeutic terms. The ever-rising demand for public safety at all costs and the generalization of the redressive logic of tort in political reasoning about social issues certainly suggest an unprecedented emphasis on therapeutic models and purposes across the social spectrum.

While these trends, and the debates about them, form the backdrop to the present discussion, the term "therapeutic culture" refers in this chapter to mass cultural permutations of the psychotherapeutic paradigm and their manifestation in popular electronic media. The *locus classicus* of this culture is surely *The Oprah Winfrey Show* (although there have been many significant precursors and competitors, including the now apparently nearly forgotten Phil Donahue). As almost every literate citizen of the English-speaking world must know, Oprah Winfrey is a whole industry unto herself, with a top-rated, unusually enduring syndicated television show, an eponymous magazine, *O: The Oprah Magazine*, an influential book reviewing operation, and endless publications based on her life story and her periodic efforts to lose weight and achieve emotional and physical well-being. The hallmark of these books is to share intimate and personal details with the reader, such as the fact that, during a memorable visit to Rome, it was painfully difficult for Oprah to go the distance jogging with her personal trainer the morning after she had some wine at dinner, as he had warned her.

One of the most successful *Oprah* spin-offs has been Phil McGraw, or "Dr. Phil," who appears weekly on the *Oprah* show and is the author of the best-selling self-help book *Life Strategies*. Winfrey originally met McGraw as a psychological consultant for her legal defense in a libel suit brought against her by the Texas cattle industry resulting from her derogatory comments about beef at the height of the mad cow disease news scandal. On the day of her acquittal, she presented McGraw on her show, stating: "It was Phil who gave myself back to me" (Peyser, 2002, p. 54). Eventually he became a regular guest on the show.

The McGraw style is not unlike that of the rough and ready radio therapist, Dr. Laura Schlessinger, though his style is considerably toned down for television consumption. Like Dr. Laura, he will rudely interrupt his guest client as he or she gropes for an answer to a pointed question; but he is not as sadistic as Dr. Laura in the way he elicits the client's confused feelings in order to set up his act. Dr. Laura will try to ambush the clients on the edge of maximum fragility in order to browbeat and humiliate them with grandiloquent denunciations of their stupidity and moral failure. In contrast, Dr. Phil's more congenial attitude toward the complexity of human experience is not so much to bury it alive as merely to make fun of it. His technique is basically to jolt the TV guest, to bring the guest up short, usually in tandem with Oprah as the disingenuously naive "straight man." The aim is to set up for some audience-pleasing mockery, followed by the famous "straight talk" in which the guest is dressed down by Dr. Phil for his or her failure to "get real."

A brief synopsis of a segment from the program *Sally* will conclude this introduction to day-time TV therapy programming. In this scenario, Sally struts before the studio audience, introducing a thirteen-year-old teenage run away who is working in a strip-tease joint and living with a pimp. Taped images of the girl curled around a show-dance pole in tight clothing and announcing her defiance of her mother accompany her entrance on the stage. As the mother is introduced to the audience amid gasps of sympathy and dismay, she is unaware that she is about to be reunited, if only temporarily, with her long lost daughter. The confrontation between the indignant mother and the superficially defiant but obviously embarrassed and shamed daughter unfolds pathetically until the moment when Sally chooses to intervene with a challenge to the daughter that she is showing no feeling, no remorse. This occurs just at the moment when the girl is visibly on the verge of tears, her fragile mask of defiant indifference clearly about to crumble before the cameras. The audience jeers and mocks as Sally berates the wayward child. Then, following a commercial break, framed by the now familiar video image of the girl wrapping herself around the strip tease pole, the resident *Sally* psychologist is ushered onto the stage. The psychologist paces back and forth aggressively behind the seated mother and daughter, occasionally swooping over the girl's shoulder as she speaks. She hectors the girl about her irresponsible and self-destructive behavior, climaxing with a loud and sarcastic "Hello-o-o! Excuse me, honey! What about AIDS?" to block the girl's spluttering attempt to answer her rhetorical questions. This dramatic moral triumph of the psychologist over the thirteen-year-old girl is met with audible approval and pleasure by the studio audience. Following another commercial break, the segment ends with a very stagy "off-stage" scene (even by comparison to the previous scenes) in which the psychologist speaks sympathetically to the girl and her mother, and the daughter tearfully apologizes to her mother and promises to reform. They embrace rather awkwardly before the next commercial intervenes.

4. Games People Play on TV

What clinicians call exhibitionism is a central feature of human culture and primate behavior; an important means of expressing social dominance, initiating sexual contact, and binding groups of affiliation through play and entertainment (Goodall, 1990). Exhibitionistic play, such as sport and spectacle, is a basic feature of known human cultures (Huizinga, 1955). These more or less spontaneous forms of self-display intercalate easily with other social agendas, such as social competition for power, the struggle for survival, and the organized discharge of aggression, for example, through scapegoating outsiders and preparing the group for war. A very common example of the latter is the cliché about the Imperial Roman technique of "bread and circuses," inciting and exploiting the blood lust of the Coliseum crowd as a means of dispelling through vicarious violence and scapegoating the latent hostility of the grumbling urban masses. The journalistic image of mass entertainment as a form of "blood sport" has been surfacing more and more frequently in recent years as popular television entertainment programming has evolved from the staged decorum of game shows like *Jeopardy* or *The Sixty-Four Thousand Dollar Question* to controversial but wildly popular scandal features, such as the *Jerry Springer Show*, which arrange emotionally violent confrontations in front of a live audience, sometimes leading to physical violence among the participants which may continue offstage, even to the point of murder (Wiltz & Farhi, 2000). (There are at least two cases of murder: an ex-wife on July 24, 2000 following the broadcasting of a pre-taped *Jerry Springer Show* confronting her with her former husband and his new wife; and a homosexual man after the taping of the *Jenny Jones Show*, on March 6, 1995, in which he confessed his love to a heterosexual male acquaintance.)

The original game show format can itself become quite lurid. In a Dutch game show reviewed on a Canadian Broadcasting Corporation (CBC) documentary, the studio audience was given the power to make life and death decisions about the contestants. In one series, the women contestants were actually dying of cancer and the competition was to have them persuade the audience, through pleas, arguments, and personal accounts of their illness, to award the prize money to herself rather than another in order to pay for a new experimental cancer treatment. The winner of this contest was then moved onto a final round, in which she squared off in a showdown with an Alzheimer's patient. Japanese television audiences also seem to be rather partial to these kinds of morbid and humiliating public invasions of privacy. The same CBC documentary showed clips of programs in which volunteer contestants are isolated in rooms with cameras broadcasting their performance of degrading tasks of endurance, or dropped into a Middle Eastern desert to fend for themselves. The sequences we saw were even equipped with a laugh track to mimic the *Schadenfreude* of the imagined TV audience (which is us). The bizarre recent Japanese film *Visitor Q.* satirizes this popular culture phenomenon with sometimes unbearably perverse imagery of violence, incest, drug addiction, and necrophilia in the family life of a television reporter who tries to use this personal material to improve his audience ratings. North American readers may be aware of United States network attempts to duplicate the success of this kind of programming, for example, by hiring the tabloid TV con-artist Giraldo to simulate the role of war correspondent during the recent invasion of Afghanistan; or by engaging the belligerent ex-tennis pro John McEnroe to moderate the serial televising of crudely degrading, revolting, or terrifying assaults on the sensibilities of apparently publicity-hungry volunteer contestants.

It was probably the phenomenon of "reality television" which consolidated the blood sport image of popular entertainment in media criticism. Reality TV shows have involved the near total isolation of groups of selected contestants in some form of heightened competitive situation, uninterrupted for weeks and months on end. The highest rated shows of this type in North America were *Survivor* and *Big Brother*, both objects of cult-like audience interest during the summer of 2000. Though denounced by media critics as decadent, and frequently compared to depraved gladiator sports, these shows were in fact tailored for "family entertainment" and were generally tamer than the European prototypes on which they were based. The Swedish precursor of *Survivor*, the first television show to isolate contestants on a desert island in order to film their game of progressive elimination over a period of months, led to the suicide of one of the "banished" and humiliated participants after he returned from the island to society.

The American *Big Brother* was copied from an original Dutch production that was also popular in Germany and Spain. The scenario was to select ten mostly young and unmarried adults of both sexes and to confine them in a sealed dwelling, the "Big Brother House," located somewhere in Los Angeles and rigged with twenty-eight cameras (permitting multiple camera angles and close ups in every room and from behind every mirror) and sixty highly sensitive microphones (making even the lowest whispered conversations between the contestants audible). In this Panopticon-like setting, it was impossible to go to sleep or to the bathroom without being observable. The object of the "game" was to eliminate the other contestants one by one through a procedure involving periodic, televised secret balloting. Much of the attraction for the television and Internet audience, as was also the case with *Survivor*, was to observe and discuss over a period of many weeks the evolution of a complex group dynamic, involving the interplay of personalities and the formation and dissolution of strategic alliances among the participants. Naturally, a great deal of sexual and aggressive tension emerged fairly quickly in these conditions of unrelenting group confinement. In the American version of *Big Brother*, the show's producers tended to diffuse this tension when it threatened to overflow into action, imposing restrictions when necessary. One strategy was to introduce a "surprise," a cute little puppy dog, during a difficult period in the house dynamic. Apparently the original European version let the sexual relationships develop and reach fruition on camera.

We taped and observed a majority of the weekly American *Big Brother* (BB) broadcasts, beginning in the middle of the first month of the show. These broadcasts consisted of a nightly half-hour digest of that day's interpersonal dramas and political maneuvering in "the house." The broadcasts were punctuated on Wednesday evenings by a full-hour studio audience special hosted by an attractive CBS celebrity interviewer. The competitive drama in BB was organized around the voting procedure for gradually winnowing the group down to a grand prize-winner ($500,000 U. S.) and two runners up. Each vote was a process that unfolded in a two-week cycle. During the first week, the house guests would calculate privately or in conspiratorial groups which two of their fellow guests they wanted to "nominate" for "banishment" in the eventual, televised secret ballot on Wednesday night. The two "nominees" were then announced live in the presence of the entire group and forced to live in suspense for another week while they waited for the TV/Internet audience poll to select which of them was to be removed on the following Wednesday's show. This cycle of choosing two victims and then waiting for the public to decide who would actually walk the plank was repeated fortnightly over a period of approximately twenty weeks until the process of elimination was complete. The full-hour Wednesday night extravaganza always included a review of the week's events, a studio encounter with the eliminated contestant in front of the live audience, plus interviews with the BB "health and relationships expert," Drew Pinsky, and the chipper America On Line (AOL) Internet analyst and polling consultant. All this was supplemented throughout the summer of 2000 by five continuous, twenty-four hour live Internet video feeds from the house on the CBS-AOL *Big Brother* Website, a small fragment of which we were able to observe.

Though trapped in this multimedia fish bowl, the ten contestants of the Big Brother house had no access themselves to any electronic or print media. There was little for them to do but be with one other for twenty weeks on end. They could congregate and disperse into different rooms or try to escape each other in the large walled-in patio at the rear of the house. The only alternative was to request a visit to the "Red Room" (reminiscent of the ominous "redrum" (murder spelled backwards in the Stephen King/Stanley Kubrick novel/film *The Shining*), a soundproof sanctuary where individual contestants could confide "privately" through the video connection with an invisible BB producer. Sometimes a contestant would be called into the Red Room to be interrogated or warned in *1984* fashion by the disembodied voice of a producer. Occasionally one of them would be rewarded with the privilege of making a telephone call in the Red Room, usually to a close relative. There was no other possibility of contact with the outside world apart from the sighting of partisan banners favoring or denigrating one of the contestants, which were flown over the house by privately hired aircraft.

The first contestant to be "banished from the house" was Will, a somewhat self-important Afro-American male with simply too many ideas and too many opinions for most of the others to bear. The consensus among the contestants to get rid of him was fairly swift and brutal. The main hold out on this strategy was an attractive and intelligent blonde ex-stripper, Jordan, who enjoyed Will's company and found the other contestants rather closed-minded and conventional in their thinking. She deeply annoyed the other women in the house, especially Karen, a sort of mother hen figure who curried favor by taking over the preparation of meals while secretly (and bitterly) plotting against her rival, Jordan. The engaging Jordan, initially popular with the audience, was indeed the next to go, but Karen followed her out the door two weeks later. The borderline features of Karen's personality structure had served her well during the crude early stages of paranoid maneuvering in the house, but her defensive manic friendliness barely concealed her miserable state of mind; consumed with guilt, her presence soon began to make the others feel uncomfortable, and she was executed in short order, ostensibly out of pity. (Karen knew she was doomed and provided the others with the excuse that she really wanted to be voted out so that she could return to her family.)

In the early going Karen had announced to the other "houseguests" (ergo, on national TV) that she had decided to divorce her husband as soon as she got out. This was news to her husband waiting patiently at home with his children in front of the TV and created one of the many BB soap opera sideshows on the Internet chat lines. Inevitably, he was interviewed by the BB host. He said he thought Karen would change her mind when she came out, and was present in the television studio to greet Karen after her banishment. By the following week, however, BB was broadcasting footage of Karen moving with her children in a van to Los Angeles, where she was planning to take up a new career. Another subplot involved her closest male ally and peer, George, an affable but ineffectual small town roofer and family man who had once accidentally shot and killed a friend in a hunting accident. The press managed to dig up this dirt on him, but no one in the house knew about it. All the other contestants were single, attractive, and poignant in their own way. The last woman to hang on in the final stages of the competition was an Afro-American United Nations employee, Cassandra, who stated in an interview that she had survived as long as she did by acting at all times as if her mother were watching her. This had made her behavior seem rather bland and inauthentic to the others, but also more difficult to single out for "elimination" than someone like Brittany, an obnoxious and devious infantile personality who dyed her hair a different lurid color every week, or Jamie, the attractive and ambitious would-be actress who chose to speak with a casting agent rather than her mother when given the chance to make one phone call by the producers. In the final two weeks, there were three eligible young bachelors left, a tough-talking, streetwise New Yorker who had lost one leg to cancer as a boy, a rather dreamy and feckless body-building orphan raised by an uncle, and a nerdy but tenacious Chinese-American yuppie. The man with only one leg won.

5. Surprised by Moralism: The Group Dynamics of Therapeutic Culture

There was some surprise and dismay when, at the end of the second cycle, the engaging and articulate Jordan was voted out by the public. There seemed to be a paradox in the audience decision, by overwhelming majority, to eliminate one who contributed so much to making the house dynamic interesting. However, Drew Pinsky, the BB health and relationship expert, commented that her elimination was an encouraging result. "I'm kind of relieved," he said. "I was concerned there was some sort of gladiator mentality out there and people would push a sort of draconian interest in drama and keep people in the house who are creating instability. Instead, they see people who are creating problems for other people in the house and they kind of vote them out. ... They're concerned about the *relationships* in the house." Not only the contestants but also the American public were more interested in stability and group cohesion than bloodthirsty competition; they had made an emotionally mature choice in favor of healthy and civil relationships, cooperative behavior, and traditional American family values. Pinsky made no reference to the fact that the BB houseguests were self-selected competitors who were in fact trying their best to eliminate each other; or that the attraction of a strategic "war of all against all" was the explicit marketing premise of the show and the conscious motive of the audience. In Pinsky's analysis, not only had "reality TV" become emotional reality, as opposed to a cynical simulation of it; this emotional reality was reassuring and benign, a mirror of essential human goodness.

Pinsky's ingenious rationalization reflected an important feature of the manifest discourse within the BB group itself. With the possible exception of the eventual winner, all the contestants tried to maintain that they were there to help and to support each other. To some extent, this version of their essential motive was plausible because the conditions of close confinement and relative sensory and intellectual deprivation must indeed have been difficult for them to bear. Alone in the Red Room, confiding in the BB producers and the TV audience, the contestants were just as concerned to appear unselfish. The tendency was to rationalize antipathy toward another member, or a sense of being threatened, with moral arguments. Whenever it was felt desirable for strategic or personal reasons to get rid of another houseguest, the explanation was usually grounded in judgments about the other's failings. As in "real" life, moralistic posturing of one kind or another was a dominant mode of interaction on the *Big Brother* show.

The obvious tendency was to vote out those who questioned the rationalizations of the group, those who created what Pinsky termed "instability in the House." The group clearly could not tolerate much emotionalism or aggression and so the first individuals to go were either too aggressive, too provocative, or too emotionally labile. As we find in human society generally, the pressure toward conformity and consensus was enormous in the House. The way to achieve this in BB was to eliminate where possible the apparent sources of conflict within the group and then to minimize the appearance of further conflict through the creation of a reassuring narrative about the individual and collective motives and meanings of behavior in the group.

BB seems to demonstrate that even when the stated purpose and overt rationale for a group's existence is conflict itself, the drive to simulate some kind of group solidarity based on moral consensus is overwhelming. We can take this hypothesis a step further: the deliberate staging of certain kinds of conflict serves as an effective context for the mobilization of value judgments whose overt expression reduces the sense of conflict within the group. From the audience point of view, BB actually represents a fairly elaborate form of this dynamic, one in which complex relationships between personalities and their ways of accounting for themselves evolve in real time. The gradual, at first quite brutal, then more measured negotiation of a *modus vivendi* and its justifying narrative is a fascinating process to observe. But the same drive to enforce solidarity can be observed even in the lurid antics of the *Jerry Springer Show* or the absurd therapeutics of *Sally* described above. What is striking about these shows is the intensity of the moralistic atmosphere, the harshness of the judgments expressed by the television personalities and therapists, cheered on by the studio audience's chorus of approval and disapproval. Consideration of the continuum from *Oprah* to *Springer* suggests that moralism itself has instinctual roots (Ury, 1997; 1998). The sensationalism gives TV critics the impression that boundaries of decency are being crossed, that something nasty and even wildly perverse is being introduced into the public consciousness. But the actual content of these shows is really nothing else but a very familiar kind of conventional, everyday excitement, otherwise known as indignation and outrage. The discharge of these emotions, or the feelings of pity and barely concealed hatred toward guests who are suffering or burdened with onerous difficulties, are a great source of disguised pleasure.

The governing logic of manufacturing one kind of conflict in order to create the discursive conditions for occluding another is everywhere in human culture. The seeming contradiction or paradox of this mechanism results from the fact that two very different kinds of conflict are involved. The staged conflict is always a pretext for the discharge of anxiety related to another, more deep-seated conflict. There is no end to the possible variations on this theme in human affairs, but the model we are using to elucidate the therapeutic culture is the following: the conflict being avoided is internal, idiosyncratic, and often unconscious; whereas the staged conflict is general and stereotypic, a shareable external object. There is a flight from internal reality into the archetypical constructions of the group. Our hypothesis is that the unconscious attraction of the modern therapeutic culture and its derivative forms of entertainment is to facilitate this flight from internal reality, to offer a secular image of salvation through solidarity, in a quasi-communal, mass media version of redemption through the simulation of divine intervention and moral absolution.

The central theme of therapeutic culture and its spectatorial, sensationalistic derivatives is a powerful confessional impulse, identified by Foucault, which lies at the heart of the basic transference orientation toward any idealized object. This confessional impulse represents the psychological flip-side of Foucault's (1979) better known Panopticon thesis regarding modern, non-directed, systemic forms of micro-social regulation. The traditional Christian confession ritual is only one variation on a fundamental moralistic drive informing many other institutions and activities, including contemporary popular entertainment. The difference between psychoanalysis and the various forms of therapeutic culture with which it competes lies in the way they handle this transferential construction of an idealized object. Psychoanalysis invites the full unfolding of the transference in the symbolic realm in order to explore its many forms and negative variants in the individual, with the aim of partially alleviating its tyranny over the internal life of the individual. In contrast, the therapeutic culture seeks to isolate and mobilize the idealizing transference in order to reinforce its hold on the individual by enacting it through the reassuring medium of a collective hallucination. The act of public confession, of revealing one's errors and sufferings to the media therapist or game show host, works psychologically in the same manner as an exorcism. The harnessing of the idealizing impulse is encouraged by massive splitting, in which the bad self and the bad object (the negative transference) are projected away from the group.

The transference wish is to establish contact and merge with an all-knowing, all-powerful, and benevolent infantile object (Ury, 1997). The need it expresses is very straightforward: I love you because in the good moments you are what comes to me in my hour of need and I would like my emotional universe to consist of just that, you and me, an ideal couple in which you are there for me when I need you.

But do you really love me? I love you, but I need you to love me in return in order to confirm my existence; I am prepared to do anything to secure your love, because without it I am forsaken. I know that you question me, that you suspect my paranoia, my disappointment, my rage, my *ressentiment*. Please believe me: these nasty feelings are only the result of my lack of faith, my inconstancy, my weakness. I can prove that my intentions are good. I will show you everything, disclose all of my faults, failings, and misdeeds as proof of my faith in your justice, goodness, and love. I will submit to you unreservedly. You are my Archaic Superego (Caper, 1995) and I will confess myself into blissful union with your divine understanding, I will join with the power of your recognition and acceptance, because in fact we are really the same; we are the perfect couple, separated only by the refractions of this false world that I am quite happy to forget and, in extreme cases, even to destroy.

The expectation, or illusion, that "finally, at last, after all this uncertainty and suffering, *I am recognized and understood*" is very important in human psychology. It promises an enormous, almost orgasmic prospect of emotional relief, unconscious though it may be in our daily lives. The sense of security thus engendered is not difficult to understand at the level of the individual sinner in relation to his Redeemer, which is characteristic of the positive transference in the early stages of the psychoanalytic relationship. The introduction of cameras and national television audiences ratchets this transference dynamic up to another, less intelligible level where the potential for understanding and working through the fantasy is replaced by the defensive enactment of the transference fantasy itself.

The individual in this situation is desperate to find security, the security established through the unconscious dyadic regime of like-mindedness, which seems to eradicate all ambivalence (Caper, 1995; 1997). Unwanted parts of the self are split off and projected, creating an unstable situation in the group. The negativity projected into the fantasy void floats dangerously in the group setting. It is at the level of the group that the possibility of an intrapsychic solution breaks down, and must be replaced by group action. Each individual has established a false self, the self that satisfies the archaic superego and group life is set as a pattern of interaction between the false selves. At some level, of course, there will always be a social game in which false selves jockey with each other, flirting with each other and skirting on the edges of near exposure, a frightening but also thrilling game of hide and seek (office politics and cocktail parties). The presence of the cameras in shows like *Big Brother* heightens this inherent drama. The aim of the group becomes the search to refind the equilibrium achieved in intrapsychic fantasy at the level of collective life. This promised state of collective security requires a sacrifice to the group of a token self-disclosure through the medium of the false self in order to pre-empt the threat of actual discoveries about one's own internal make-up, which are imagined in the form of humiliating self-exposure, irreconcilable conflict, and banishment. The psychologically overdetermined belief is that all of this can be achieved through the ritual enactment of a fantasy of reassuring identity. It is as if the problem of ambivalence can be solved at the level of social interaction. Hate, envy, and destructiveness are momentarily transcended through intersubjectively shared forms of splitting and projection, the best-known social enactment of which is scapegoating.

The flight from the internal world offered by the therapeutic culture also takes the form of promised wholeness. The psychology offered on day-time television programming usually simplifies and concretizes suffering and conflict by singling out particular kinds of symptoms and forms of abuse. The reality of these symptoms and abuses allows them to serve as metonymic external substitutes for the complexity of psychological life, fixing the sufferer in the role of innocent and passive victim. Everyone can identify with this imagined innocence and join together in condemnation of the abuse or the symptom. The salutary effect of such rituals on the ailing person can be very real in traditional communal contexts, but it is difficult to imagine the same emotional benefit deriving from an appearance on a media therapy show or from consenting to be interviewed on television about one's terrible experience of loss and grief following the death of a family member in a national tragedy. Nevertheless, through a kind of audience driven incitement to emote, such confessional acts do seem to recreate the dimly remembered sense of a community that has been lost. Unfortunately, when the victim agrees to participate in such televised rituals, there may also, in a deeper sense, be a pathologizing repetition of the real trauma. The sense of wholeness achieved through the ritual (re-)enacts the defensive identification with the damaged part of the self, singling out the traumatic moment as the defining moment of one's life. The repetition here is not of the literal trauma but of recoiling from the painful complexity of fragmentary, conflicting feelings and states of mind that have been intensified by the traumatic experience. By investing only in one part of oneself in order to establish the illusion of a unified identity through victimage, the victim is trapped in the search for illusory redemption through submissive identification with controlling and intrusive objects, such as cults, ideological groups, and the imagined audiences of public salvation.

6. Confidentiality and its Cultural Antithesis

Confidentiality in the psychotherapeutic sense depends implicitly upon a general acceptance within the dominant culture of certain social ideas and principles that have to do with the perceived value of individuality, autonomy, privacy, and freedom of thought. This is a culture in which it is deemed arduous but ultimately worthwhile to accord a very high degree of moral responsibility to the individual for the quality of his or her life. The interests of the individual may frequently and necessarily be subordinated, but the perspective of the individual is still felt to be irreducible to that of the social group and its coercive power. Under cover of this general liberal democratic system of values, with its legal protections and civil rights, psychoanalysis has been able to cultivate the distinction between external (or conventional) reality, and psychic (or internal) reality. This distinction is crucial for psychoanalysis and psychodynamic therapy. It is what gives confidentiality its special significance in the therapeutic context.

The basic psychological strategy of therapeutic culture is to reduce awareness of internal reality and to eradicate its significance. Emotional problems are acknowledged, but thinking about them is discouraged. There is a concrete notion that vigorous self-expression cures, which feeds the magical impulse to blurt out secrets, and also contributes to a growing social imperative to emote. Attention is directed toward simple ideas about what is right and wrong, the appropriate forms of behavior, practical reality, the sense of duty, and willpower. The emphasis on conventional morality makes inward reflection extremely difficult, especially because it snuffs out potential curiosity about what new thoughts and feelings might emerge spontaneously. The watchword is to monitor one's thoughts and to shape them in appropriate ways. Bad or illogical thoughts should be disregarded and replaced rather than explored for their meaning. Symptoms are seen as failures of adaptation and their causes are felt to be outside the mind, either biological or social (which they may be), but never personal or psychological in any profound sense. Apart from re-education and drug therapy, the essential technique is cathartic discharge in which the ailment, or alien element, is dramatically disclosed and dispelled.

The orientation of therapeutic culture makes confidentiality seem not only vaguely unnecessary, but also potentially harmful. The confidential relationship is felt to isolate the afflicted individual from the sympathy and succor of the group, or worse, to conceal antisocial tendencies that need to be exposed and dispelled. This implicit perspective of an overarching collective superego is especially apparent in the mass media expressions of therapeutic culture discussed above. There is a barely concealed hostility directed toward differences and eccentricities, which are seen as the origins of conflict and suffering. The emotional pressure to achieve a state of declared like-mindedness through externalization and projection discourages any serious focus on the complexity of one's own responses to what is going on and the puzzling differentness of others (Caper, 1995; 1997). Since it is extremely difficult under these conditions to maintain the privacy of one's own thought process, any preoccupation or knowledge which conflicts with the declared state of mind of the group tends to generate powerful feelings of guilt and shame pressing toward confessional discharge. The temptation here is not only to unburden oneself, but also to offer this part of oneself in sacrifice to the need of the group to identify a moral issue and to settle it through satisfying feelings of righteous action. Each individual's disturbing sense of internal nonconformity can by these means be split off and projected and thereby temporarily dispelled. The group will be grateful for the confession, though the need for sacrifice may make it difficult to reward the confessor openly when the group feels especially threatened.

This dynamic has a paradoxical effect within the group: there is an individual flight from the internal world, yet the influence of the latter predominates within the group. The more the internal world is disavowed, the more transferential the group's perception of external reality becomes. Whatever form the group dynamic takes, there is a strong likelihood that within the transference process there will be an element of projected omniscience and omnipotence. This element normally expresses itself in relation to the group's leader, or in the desire for a leader, but it can also be projected onto a perceived antagonist in a paranoid way. In fact, the relationship with authority within the group will tend to oscillate between idealizing and paranoid poles of feeling. The anxiety around this volatile aspect of the group dynamic is one of the reasons why the confessional mode of flight from internal reality is so tempting.

The role of the transference fantasy of a benignly omniscient object in promoting the confessional impulse is beautifully illustrated in a remarkable documentary about family violence entitled *The Trouble with Evan* (CBC 1994). With the laudable intention of exposing the terrible consequences of the verbal abuse of children, the highly regarded television news magazine series *The Fifth Estate* produced a program based on the videotaped home-life of an extremely troubled working class family. The family had been contacted by the CBC and seemed to come forward in the belief that the proposed public exposure of their problems would provide them with the curative relationship that had not been forthcoming from the public health and social service network. The parents agreed to terms in which they would have control over the functioning of the cameras, with power to review and destroy the tapes. In actual practice, they kept the cameras loaded and running constantly, handing over all the tapes without review (Docherty, 2000). The resulting footage was so harrowing that a minor scandal followed the eventual broadcast. The local children's aid society removed the 11 year old son, Evan, from his parents the following morning, and placed him with a foster family from which he had subsequently to be removed because the father turned out to have been a known child abuser (Docherty, 2000; Olsen, 2000). Evan was soon lost in the labyrinth of child correctional services. Meanwhile, the public response to the broadcast was more favorable and voluminous than any previous *Fifth Estate* program. *The Trouble with Evan* was entered into competition at the Cannes Film festival, but the local social services succeeded in persuading a judge to impose an injunction on the program. The tapes were retrieved from Cannes and the program is still banned from public airing (Docherty, 2000). *The Fifth Estate* did however produce another program featuring testimonials from individuals who had seen the first program and wanted to speak about their own childhood experiences as victims of verbal abuse.

This family's desperation to be found, at almost any cost, by someone influential enough to make a difference illustrates the power of the transference fantasy of cure through dramatic self-revelation. The parents were even willing to be filmed in counseling sessions discussing the problem of controlling their own horrible mistreatment of Evan. The intensity of this kind of emotional appeal for help naturally elicits a corresponding countertransference response, which is essentially an equally concrete fantasy of dramatic rescue through decisive action. In the absence of a learned capacity to distinguish between psychic reality and conventional reality, our normal reaction tends to be very literal, caught up in the sway of the transference demand, missing the opportunity to open up its meaning at the symbolic level. This is one of the reasons why the position of psychoanalysis within culture is often so precarious. By deconstructing the analyst's unconscious wish to become the ideal object, psychoanalysis may seem cruelly oblivious to the natural and normal, common sense response to human suffering.

The need to enter into a fusional relationship with an omniscient object is fed by the delicious prospect of release through a self-unburdening that will make us whole again. The attribution of this magical power to the object arises from the profound wish to be recognized and received in our true being. These fantasies make the impulse to objectify ourselves in the confessional mode difficult to resist. When the group is under pressure, the members are understandably inclined to be hostile, jealous, and suspicious toward the confidential relationship. The confidential couple may be perceived with envy as greedily hoarding salvation for itself, or to be plotting against the group, or to be withholding information vital for the survival of the group. Such fantasies quickly attach themselves to any pretext for questioning the wisdom of confidentiality. The most common among these are the notion that patients are or might be dangerous criminals and that information in the sole possession of the therapist might prevent a miscarriage of justice. Decontextualized speculations like these inevitably inflate the felt significance of the possible disadvantages of confidentiality, while clouding awareness of the much more serious consequences of undermining it. In this way, the political dramatization of public safety issues can directly influence legislative and judicial attitudes, so that confidentiality itself becomes the sacrificial victim in a public ritual of therapeutic exorcism (Bollas & Sundelson, 1995). Much more insidious, however, is the apparent erosion of respect for privacy in the culture generally. In the long term, this may represent a greater threat to confidentiality, and therefore psychoanalysis, than the vagaries of the law. As Freud pointed out, psychoanalysis is unlike confession in that the patient has somehow to say more than what he knows (Freud, 1926, p. 189). The conditions for enabling the emergence of this "more" are difficult to establish because they require both the analyst and the analysand to feel reasonably comfortable with nonconformity and unconventionality. It would be difficult to achieve this level of comfort in a culture that could not intuitively grasp the meaning and importance of confidentiality.

Acknowledgments

Earlier versions of this paper were presented to the conference "Confidentiality & Society" in Montreal, 14–16 October 2000; The Argyle Institute of Human Relations, April 2001, Montreal; and Toronto Psychoanalytic Society, Toronto, November 2001. We would like to thank Christiana Abraham, Neil Docherty, Victoria De Zwaan, John Fekete, and Edith Ury.

Works Cited

Arendt, Hannah. (1958) *The Human Condition.* Chicago: University of Chicago Press.

Bollas, Christopher, and David Sundelson. (1995) *The New Informants: The Betrayal of Confidentiality in Psychoanalysis and Psychotherapy.* Northvale, N. J.: Jason Aronson.

Caper, Robert. (1995) "On the Difficulty of Making a Mutative Interpretation," *International Journal of Psycho-Analysis*, 76: pp. 91–101.

———. (1997) "A Mind of One's Own," *International Journal of Psycho-Analysis,* 78: pp. 265–278.

Docherty, Neil. (2000). Personal Communication. Producer, "The Trouble with Evan," Canadian Broadcasting Corporation, *The Fifth Estate*.

Forrester, John. (2003). "Trust, Confidentiality and the Possibility of Psychoanalysis." In *Confidentiality: Psychoanalysis, Ethics and the Law*, ed. Charles Levin, Allannah Furlong, and M. K. O'Neil. Hillsdale, N. J.: Analytic Press (forthcoming).

Foucault, Michel. (1978) *The History of Sexuality*, transl. Robert Hurley. New York: Pantheon.

———. (1979). *Discipline and Punish: The Birth of the Prison.* Translated by Alan Sheridan. New York: Vintage Books.

Freud, Sigmund. (1914) "Remembering, Repeating, Working Through." *Standard Edition of the Complete Psychological Works of Sigmund Freud,* 12: pp. 147–156.

———. (1926) "The Question of Lay Analysis." *Standard Edition of the Complete Works of Sigmund Freud,* 20: pp.177–258.

Goodall, Jane. (1990) *Through a Window: My Thirty Years with the Chimpanzees of Gombe*. Boston: Houghton Mifflin.

Jaffee v. Redmond. [1996] 116 S. Ct. 1923.

Huizinga, Johan. (1955) *Homo Ludens: A Study of the Play Element in Culture*. Boston: Beacon Press.

Levin, Charles. (2001) "The Siege of Psychotherapeutic Space: Psychoanalysis in the Age of Transparency," *Canadian Journal of Psychoanalysis/Revue Canadienne de Psychanalyse,* 9(2): pp. 187–215.

———. (2003) "Civic Confidentiality and Psychoanalytic Confidentiality." In *Confidentiality: Psychoanalysis, Ethics and the Law*, eds. Charles Levin, Allannah Furlong, and M. K. O'Neil. Hillsdale, New Jersey: Analytic Press (forthcoming).

L'Heureux-Dubé, Claire. (2003) "The Right to Privacy: A Comment on the Production of Complainants' Personal Records in Sexual Assault Cases." In *Confidentiality: Psychoanalysis, Ethics and the Law*, eds. Charles Levin, Allannah Furlong, and M. K. O'Neil. Hillsdale, New Jersey: Analytic Press (forthcoming).

Olsen, Catherine. (2000). Personal communication. CBC Producer, *The Passionate Eye*.

Peyser, M. (2002) "Paging Dr. Phil," *Newsweek*, 2 September: pp. 50–56.

Pyles, Robert. (2003) "The American Psychoanalytic Association's Fight for Privacy." In *Confidentiality: Psychoanalysis, Ethics and the Law*, eds. Charles Levin, Allannah Furlong, and M. K. O'Neil. Hillsdale, New Jersey: Analytic Press (forthcoming).

Rieff, Philip. (1966) *The Triumph of the Therapeutic: Uses of Faith After Freud*. New York: Harper and Row.

Shuman, Daniel W. (1985) "The Origins of the Physician-Patient Privilege and Professional Secret," *Southwestern Law Journal*, 39: pp. 661–687.

Ury, Christine. (1997) "The Shadow of Object Love: Reconstructing Freud's Theory of Pre-Oedipal Guilt," *Psychoanalytic Quarterly*, 66: pp. 34–61.

———. (1998) "The Nietzschean Monster: Considering Guilt in Developmental Theory," *Canadian Journal of Psychoanalysis/Revue Canadienne de Psychanalyse*, 6(1): pp. 51–74.

Wiltz, Teresa, and Paul Farhi. (2000) "TV Confrontation the Final Humiliation," *The Montreal Gazette*, 29 July: p. D–2.

Winnicott, D. W. (1965) *Maturational Processes and the Facilitating Environment: Studies in the Theory of Emotional Development*. New York: International Universities Press.

Part Three

ETHICS

Six

THE MORAL FRAMEWORK OF CONFIDENTIALITY AND THE ELECTRONIC PANOPTICON

Michael Yeo and Andrew Brook

1. Introduction

Patients' faith that what is said in the consulting room stays in the consulting room is utterly necessary for effective psychotherapy. Unless a patient has complete confidence in the confidentiality of the process, he or she will not be candid about matters that are embarrassing or shameful and certainly not about matters that may involve moral turpitude or illegality. Although few would disagree about the importance of confidentiality in psychotherapy, there is considerable controversy about its limits, that is to say, about the circumstances under which it may justifiably be breached. So far, this debate is mainly structured around two lines of argument. One line, the main reference point of which is the *Tarasoff v. Regents* [1976] case, debates the limits of confidentiality vis-à-vis the so-called "duty to warn," the duty to prevent harm. The second line, exemplified by *Jaffee v. Redmond* [1996] and in Canada by *R. v. Mills* [1999], debates the limits of confidentiality vis-à-vis the need for probative evidence in the administration of justice.

However, a new context in which limits of confidentiality are asserted is emerging. We believe that it deserves a *lot* more attention than it is receiving. It is related to monumental changes in the health system generally. Two related trends are particularly relevant to confidentiality in psychotherapy.

The first is the trend to computerization. In digital form, information can be more readily and inexpensively searched, reproduced, indexed, collated, aggregated, and shared. This considerably enhances its usefulness or value for a variety of purposes, including financial and social policy purposes. Second, as information becomes easier to use, new policy contexts are creating bottomless demands for ever more health information. The new watchwords are "accountability," "audit," "quality assurance," "research," "efficiency," "evidence-based" and "cost effectiveness." All these objectives are information hungry.

These trends have resulted in arguments that breaches of confidentiality are justified that have nothing to do with the old considerations of prevention of harm and the administration of justice. The old context focused on prevention of individual harms. The new context focuses on broad social objectives and the benefits that informed social policy can confer. Indeed, the very concept of confidentiality may be shifting. This new context, in our view, has not received the attention it deserves.

Throughout the western world, psychotherapy has been less integrated into the general changes that health systems are undergoing than most other areas of health care practice. Experience in places where that is beginning to change, for example in the United States with the introduction of managed care, suggests that where psychotherapy does become more integrated, it immediately begins to feel the same confidentiality-threatening pressures (see, for example, Kremer and Gesten, 1998; Tuckfelt, Fink, and Warren, 1997). In this new context, not only payers and insurers but also auditors, researchers, licensing bodies, governments, and other members of the health care "team" seek access to information for reasons and under circumstances that have little or nothing to do with traditional claims about "third party harm" or "administration of justice." Psychotherapy everywhere is bound to be drawn increasingly into this new context.

In this paper, we want to map the territory of this change, elucidating certain foundational issues and delineating the dimensions of the shift. We begin by laying out a framework of ethical concepts for thinking about confidentiality and justifications for breaching it. Then, using this framework, we show what the traditional way of thinking about confidentiality was like and just how different the concepts that animate the new context are. These differences matter because policy issues concerning health information appear very different depending on which conceptualization one adopts and one will be inclined to very different resolutions of issues concerning confidentiality. Next we sketch some aspects of the digital revolution in health information management that have led to the development of these new concepts and lay out some of the financial and policy developments behind the ever-increasing demands for health information. First we examine the digital revolution as it is affecting health care generally, then we turn to the threats and promises of information technology for psychotherapy specifically.

Matters of great importance are at stake as "the information age" becomes a major factor in health care. The final judgment about whether changes underway today will prove to be for good or ill will turn on choices that we will soon have to make, indeed in some cases are already making. The values we affirm or negate in making, or even in not making, these choices are not just about technology but about what counts as ethical treatment of people, therapeutic relationships, and what the rights and responsibilities of everyone involved are. Ultimately, they are about the kind of society we are and wish to become. As we said, surprisingly little attention has been paid so far to the ethical, legal, and social issues to which the increasing use of information technology in health care give rise.

2. Two Moral Foundations for Confidentiality

There is clearly a tension between the demands of confidentiality in psychotherapy and a variety of worthwhile social objectives concerning the health system: research, disease tracking, better health care, more efficient health care, control of irresponsible or abusive health care professionals, and so on. Where one comes down on the spectrum of possible resolutions of these tensions will be profoundly affected by how one understands confidentiality and what gives it its value.

Confidentiality is closely related to privacy and the value of confidentiality is linked to the value of privacy. Here is how we understand the two.

Privacy concerns the subject of information and his or her rights or interests with respect to whether others come into possession of that information and if so, who and under what circumstances.

Confidentiality concerns anyone who has come into possession of such information and his or her duties in connection with respect to sharing or not sharing that information with third parties.

To say that information is private is to say something primarily in relation to the subject of the information; to say that information is confidential is to say something primarily in relation to someone other than the subject to whom the information has been revealed.

Of these two issues, the important one for psychotherapy has always been confidentiality but let us say just a word or two about privacy. Privacy is a notoriously elusive concept, and different definitions highlight different aspects of the phenomenon. Commentators typically begin with Chief Justices Warren and Brandeis' (1890) famous "right of the individual to be let alone." Confidentiality would then be the right to expect that those to whom one discloses information will not allow it to be used so as to interfere with one's right to be let alone. In psychotherapy, confidentiality protects the patient's right to be let alone to explore personally important issues with another person without anyone else knowing about it. Privacy and confidentiality here are as much about freedom to reveal as freedom to conceal. The key thing is to be able to prevent or control access by third parties.

Confidentiality and privacy are closely linked. Confidentiality is important because privacy, being able to do or say certain things without others coming to know about them, is important. Nonetheless, confidentiality is the central issue with respect to psychotherapy and it is the one on which we will concentrate from now on.

A. Two Bases for the Value of Confidentiality in Psychotherapy

When may confidentiality justifiably be breached? This is where the two contexts that we sketched earlier enter. Let us call them the *traditional view* and the *emerging view*.

i. Traditional View

On the traditional view, confidentiality is vital to the therapeutic process. It has a close connection to the right to keep information about oneself private if one so chooses. On this way of thinking, information about a patient can be disclosed only under very special conditions (usually including rigorous protection of identity) and/or only for very powerful countervailing reasons, to prevent serious harm or a serious miscarriage of justice, the reasons introduced at the beginning of the paper. The question of who has the right to release or consent to release information is fundamental. In traditional liberal theory, consent on the part of the person whom information is about is at least a necessary condition for justified disclosure in contexts like the current one. Since, as we will see, consent is itself a vexed notion in psychotherapy where transference, primitive regressions, and so on may be taking place, in practice the therapist takes the patient's place and makes the decision as to when, if ever, circumstances are sufficiently severe to warrant a breach of confidentiality. (Note that in practice, the circumstances that leave therapists feeling justified in disclosing information about their patients in the traditional context are broader than harm to others and miscarriage of justice. So long as identities are disguised and anonymity is preserved, most therapists feel justified in disclosing information about their patients, in the form of clinical vignettes and case studies, in seminars, when supervising training therapists, in publications in professional journals, and so on. It is another question, of course, whether these breaches *are* justified, certainly in individual cases or even at all. We return to this issue briefly below.) This role is not unlike schools acting *in loco parentis.*

ii. Emerging View

On the view that is emerging in the context of the new technologies and new demands for health information, confidentiality is viewed as a matter of protecting or prompting patients' *interests*, not a matter of rights of the patient or duties of the therapist. On this new view, the question of under what conditions a patient's interests are protected (by deleting identity, aggregation, and so on) is not necessarily a matter for the patient or even the therapist to decide. This question can legitimately be decided by third parties; for example, insurance companies, policy planners, legislators, or the courts.

Clearly, the traditional view is the view of most psychotherapists and the emerging view is advanced by policy planners, insurance companies, legislatures, and the courts and on the basis of general social benefits that may result, not (or not just) the rights and duties of the individuals involved in the therapeutic relationship.

B. The Foundations of the Traditional View

The traditional view, as we will see, has two main foundations. One is rooted in the dignity and autonomy of the individual. The other is rooted in the value of psychotherapy and therefore the value of the conditions for doing it successfully. The traditional view is not without its stresses and strains. Liberalism with its emphasis on the value of liberty and the human individual is the underlying political philosophy of the democratic world. It might be thought that the traditional view of the values and limits of confidentiality flow out of liberalism in a fairly direct way. Interestingly, that is at most only partly true. Let us start with what a strict foundation in liberal theory for the value and justifiable limits of confidentiality might be like, then look at how the foundation in liberal theory gets modified or supplemented in actual debates about confidentiality within the traditional view.

i. Pure Liberal Basis for Protecting Confidentiality

On a pure liberal justification for the traditional view, individuals have a right to privacy and confidentiality, a right that flows from the value of autonomy and dignity. To be autonomous, to have dignity, with respect to something it is at least necessary that you control it; that what happens with respect to that thing is solely up to you. Either your decision or your consent is required for anything to happen justifiably with respect to that thing. Put differently, with regard to a domain over which one has a right to autonomy, one has a right to exclude others.

On this account, confidentiality protects autonomy and dignity. Usually the best way to ensure protection of autonomy is to guarantee that those affected have control over matters of concern to them. When these are matters of information, to have such control entails that information can be released only with the consent, in fact the informed consent, of the person concerned. Informed consent is therefore central. Defending confidentiality (and privacy) on the basis of preservation of autonomy and dignity goes with arguing for tight limits on the right of the state or other third parties to intervene in the lives of individuals.

That is a strict liberal defense of what the right to confidentiality might look like. The key point is that confidentiality is viewed as necessary for protection of autonomy. In practice, psychotherapy has always modified pure liberalism in two significant ways, even prior to the new context sketched earlier. The first flows from the problem about informed consent that we have already introduced.

ii. Consent and the Psychotherapeutic Dyad

Because of transference (the rekindling of ancient, powerful feelings in a patient, now directed at the therapist), regression, and so on, consent in psychotherapy, as we said, is more complicated than pure liberalism would suggest, in at least two ways. First, patients are often highly dependent on the therapist emotionally for a period of time, to such an extent that even their capacity to judge situations in the therapy accurately may be affected. Second, some therapists tend to believe that they know what is in the best interests of their patients, sometimes even better than the patient him- or herself. For both these reasons, in psychotherapy, therapists tend to act as their patient's agent in the matter of deciding what information gets released, to whom, and in what form (usually without the patient consenting to the therapist assuming this role). That is, the therapist makes decisions for the whole patient/therapist dyad.

When this happens, it is clearly paternalistic and contrary to liberal principles, as many therapists realize, but they believe that they are better able to exercise the function of giving or withholding consent on behalf of both parties than the patient is. From a liberal standpoint, this practice could certainly be questioned, consent being what determines whether information can be disclosed or not for liberals. One of the few places where there is anything close to a consensus that patient consent is not definitive in therapeutic relationships is with respect to sexual relationships with therapists. Even if a patient consents to a sexual relationship, that consent, it is now generally accepted, does not absolve the therapist from blame for entering the relationship. However, this situation is different from the situation with respect to release of information. In the sexual relationship situation, consent is not sufficient but lack of consent would make the violation even more egregious. In the situation with respect to information, consent is not even necessary—whatever the patient's view, it is the therapist who makes the decision about release or non-release of information.

As we said, therapists assuming the right to make decisions on behalf of patients with respect to disclosure or nondisclosure of information could be questioned from a liberal point of view. Nonetheless, it is a standard feature of much psychotherapeutic practice.

iii. The Harm Principle in Psychotherapy

The second place where at least some psychotherapists depart from pure liberalism concerns what is often called the *harm principle*. Indeed, people holding the traditional view often experience some real conflict over the harm principle.

Most liberal theorists subscribe to the view that the autonomy rights of one person can be infringed or restricted when it is necessary to do so to prevent harm: certainly harm to another, perhaps even harm to self. A well-known example of this harm principle is Mill's example of shouting "Fire" in a crowded theater: if acting as you wish here will create significant risks for, or cause significant harm to, others, your right to act as you wish can justifiably be abridged.

In psychotherapy, the harm principle gets invoked in at least four contexts:

(1) where the patient reveals that he or she intends to or is harming another or others,
(2) where the patient reveals that he or she has harmed others, and,
(3) where the patient reveals that he or she intends harm to self.
(4) where the information is needed in order for the courts to treat someone else justly.

The first is the land of *Tarasoff*—the patient in this case revealed that he intended to harm his estranged girlfriend. The second is the realm of boundary violations and abuse to children and the reporting laws that go with these things in many jurisdictions: if you reveal to your therapist that you have abused a patient or a child, she is legally obliged to report you. Notice that the exception in this case is quite different from the case of shouting "fire!" in a theater. In this case but not in the standard case in liberal theory, the issue is not risk of causing harm, it is harm already caused. The third is the domain of suicidal patients: if you reveal that you intend to harm or kill yourself, that is sufficient in many jurisdictions to allow your confidentiality to be breached in any way necessary to have you committed to an inpatient psychiatric care facility involuntarily. The fourth consideration comes up most frequently where someone has been accused of sexual or other abuse and either the accuser or the complainant, being in therapy, may have said something to his or her therapist relevant to determining the truthfulness of the accusation.

The trouble is this. Whereas within liberal theory, the harm principle is widely accepted, in psychotherapy it is controversial. There is simply no agreement among psychotherapists about when, or even if, a patient's right to confidentiality can legitimately be abridged in any of (1) to (4). As *Tarasoff v. Regents* shows, there is no agreement over whether a patient's right to confidentiality or the therapist's duty of confidentiality can legitimately be overridden and third parties informed *even when* the patient has expressed a clear and credible intention to harm or kill someone else. There is a similar controversy over whether a breach of confidentiality can be justified even when the patient has expressed (clear and plausible) plans to commit suicide, or has confessed to abusing a child or a patient. In our judgment, there is not likely to be any general agreement here. Two values fundamental even within liberal theory, namely, preserving the confidentiality of the patient and protecting others or punishing a perpetrator are at war and there is no easy way within an autonomy-based approach to confidentiality to reconcile them.

On the issue of consent and the issue of harm, then, many psychotherapists part company with a traditional liberal analysis of the value to confidentiality and the conditions under which it can be abridged. However, psychotherapists within the traditional approach do not just modify liberalism when they set out to justify confidentiality. Many of them add an entirely different kind of justification, one based on *social good.*

iv. A Social Good Basis for Protecting Confidentiality

When psychotherapists and others switch to an argument based on social good for confidentiality, the social good to which they usually point is the social good of psychotherapy itself. Effective psychotherapy, the argument runs, is a good thing to have available in a society and if therapists are allowed, even worse if they are required, to breach confidentiality at certain points, for those patients in those circumstances, psychotherapy will be impossible. And we see this already. In jurisdictions with reporting requirements, there is no longer any effective psychotherapy available for abusers of children and patients. The position is well stated in *Jaffee v. Redmond:*

> Effective psychotherapy . . . depends upon an atmosphere of confidence and trust in which the patient is willing to make a frank and complete disclosure of facts, emotions, memories, and fears. Because of the sensitive nature of the problems for which individuals consult psychotherapists, disclosure of confidential communications made during counseling sessions may cause embarrassment. . . . For this reason, the mere possibility of disclosure may impede development of the confidential relationship necessary for successful treatment. . . . The psychotherapist privilege serves the public interest by facilitating the provision of appropriate treatment for individuals suffering the effects of a mental or emotional problem (*Jaffee v. Redmond* [1996], III).

The point is also well made by the Surgeon General of the United States (United States Department of Health and Social Services, 1999), who further argues for the importance of therapeutic relationships to the goal of promoting the mental health of the population.

Whatever we may think of this kind of argument, notice that the ground has shifted dramatically. Whereas on the liberal view, the starting point was protecting the autonomy and dignity of the patient, from the social good view one starts from the *social* value of psychotherapy and the need for uninhibited speech if one is to do psychotherapy. The basis for protecting confidentiality has shifted from the autonomy rights of the patients to the social good of psychotherapy. Both views require that breaches of confidentiality be few and far between, but they do so on entirely different bases. On the social good account, confidentiality is merely an instrumental good, a means to an end. If good psychotherapy could be achieved without confidentially, confidentiality would no longer have a special value. That would never be the case on the autonomy account.

So far we have focused on the differences between the individual rights-based and the social good justifications for protecting confidentiality. Note that there are also some important similarities, similarities that mark them both off from the emerging view. First, both flow from liberalism. Second, they both focus entirely on the patient and the therapeutic setting. Third, although they assign importance to the protection of information in the therapeutic relationship for different reasons, they agree that protection of this information is of fundamental importance and any exceptions need a deep-running justification. The new, emerging context for thinking about confidentiality does not focus on the individual and argues that massive breaches of confidentiality are justified, so long as they are done in the right way.

C. The Foundation of the Emerging View

The new way of thinking about confidentiality, one becoming increasingly prevalent in debates about health information, frames the right to confidentiality in terms of interests: patients' interests, therapists' interests, and society's interests, that is to say (more aptly), the achievement of social goods. The traditional view is based on rights and duties, especially the duty to preserve confidentiality. The emerging view is based on achievement of social objectives and the interests of various parties.

Concerning confidentiality, the key question for the emerging view is: What interest does a patient or therapist have in keeping something confidential? It is those interests that we should be protecting, not autonomy or the ability to choose as such. The interests on which theorists of the emerging view tend to focus are harms to patients and they look to protective measures such as de-identification of data, strict security rules, confidentiality contracts, prohibitions on using information to discriminate against people, and assurances that information will not be used for administrative decisions against a person. Whether the individual has consented to use of the information is not important. On this view, when there is an important social objective and access to the information in question would not adversely affect the person the information is about, no confidentiality right is infringed, whether or not the patient or therapist has given consent.

As we just argued, those who argue for this conception of confidentiality tend to be concerned about the subject of the information only to the extent of protecting that individual from harm, where harm is fairly narrowly construed. Thus, they seldom pay much attention to more abstract and subtle things such as autonomy and dignity and the harm that can be done to them. Their main interest is in facilitating the movement of information for purposes unrelated to individual treatment aims (purposes such as financial control, accountability, and health policy). For further reflections on the emerging view, see Etzioni (1999).

D. Comparing the Two Views

The two views of confidentiality that we have been considering run partly in parallel with a deep-running distinction in ethics generally, the distinction between deontological and utilitarian justifications of ethical propositions. On the deontological view, what we are justified in doing flows from the rights and duties of the parties concerned. On the utilitarian view, it flows from what will maximize social goods, including the good of protecting the interests of those involved. To be sure, the parallel is not complete. As we saw, even within the traditional view, there is often a resort to a “social good” argument, namely, the social value of psychotherapy, to defend confidentiality. Nonetheless, even this “utilitarian” move by the traditional view yields a rights-based conclusion: the social value of psychotherapy argues for granting patients a right to, and therapists a duty to defend, confidentiality; a right or duty that can be abridged, except when harm is at issue, only with the concurrence of the therapist, the patient, or both. Thus the parallel is broad and important. Let us from now on call the traditional view that reaches deontological conclusions the *autonomy* view. And let us call the emerging view based entirely on utilitarianism arguments the *social objectives* view.

Both the autonomy and the social objectives views accept sharp limits on the disclosure of information to third parties. The grounds for limiting disclosure are quite different, however. Because of the supreme value of individual autonomy and dignity on the first view, one must have the concurrence of the therapist, the patient, or both, or demonstrate that the information is necessary in order to prevent or correct or punish a serious and imminent harm. (Even these limited grounds, as we saw, are controversial with many psychotherapists.) On the second account, access or disclosure is justified so long as the interests of the subject of the information are protected.

An example may help. Suppose that you are in a therapy session and unbeknownst either to you or your therapist, you are being observed, let us say by a researcher. Suppose further that this person does not know or recognize you, does not care about who you are, and that protections are in place that will ensure that nothing you say or do could possibly rebound on you.

On the viewpoint of protection of autonomy, your rights have nonetheless been violated. Someone has come to know things about you that you would not want them to know and the person had no remotely adequate reason (that is a reason having to do with preventing or correcting or punishing a serious harm) to gain access to this information. Whether or not you have been harmed, you have been wronged. However, your interests have not been adversely affected so, on the kind of rights that the interest-based account focuses on, your rights have not been violated.

This example may seem fanciful but in the digital age, closely analogous situations could arise on a regular basis. Information about a person, once digitalized, may be accessible to any number of third parties without the person's knowledge and against the person's wishes. Those who argue for confidentiality on the basis of autonomy deny that third parties should have access to information about us without our consent or the proxy consent of our therapist (except for the harm-based exceptions we have considered and we saw that even they are controversial). Those who argue for only as much confidentiality as is needed to protect the interests of patients tend to focus on how to ensure that third parties are constrained so as to protect these interests. Once such interests are protected, disclosure to the third parties is no longer an issue.

The circumstances under which it is permissible for information to be disclosed without the concurrence of the patient and/or the therapist is the heart of the matter. This question is the crux of current debates about health information and legislation governing health information. Generally speaking, governments and various third parties who seek access to health information disclosed in the therapeutic relationship tend to favor broad exceptions enabling, or even mandating, the disclosure of information whatever the patient and/or therapist may think about it. Requiring concurrence or consent on the part of either party is viewed as a significant impediment to the achievement of important social goals. Indeed, in the absent of any requirement of concurrence or consent, the threshold of the test for whether information should be disclosed is often sufficiently low as to actually *favor* disclosure.

The confrontation between the two approaches is going on even as we write. As Timothy Caulfield has put it,

> in the past few years . . . governments have enacted or initiated the development of new health information legislation [that] has the potential to dramatically impact the legal framework within which health information is collected, stored and shared. . . . The emerging conflicts between existing common law [which is based on the liberal conception of autonomy rights] . . . and new health information legislation illustrates the profound policy

dilemmas created by the rapid advances that are occurring in the biomedical field (Caulfield, in progress).

An example. A huge debate is currently taking place in the United States about whether the requirement that patients sign consent forms before information can be disclosed should be done away with, to be replaced by supposedly failsafe controls on how information is collected, aggregated, and used. Here is Donna Shalala of the United States Department of Health:

> We recommend that the traditional control on use and disclosure of information, the patient's written authorization, be replaced by comprehensive statutory controls on all who get health information for health care and payment purposes. The reality of the present authorization process is that the patient has little actual control of information. The approach we recommend would replace the often ritualistic authorization with direct statutory controls and a realistic and effective opportunity for patient intervention in instances where the patient finds it truly necessary (United States Secretary of Health and Human Services (Shalala), 1997).

This statement applies to all health care. As we argued earlier, psychotherapy is special because consent is itself a vexed issue. However, statutes mandating disclosure with or without consent would undercut the mechanisms at work to protect information in psychotherapy too, including therapists' strong sense of obligation to protect the confidentiality of their patients and their conviction that, in addition to or even sometimes instead of the patient, only the therapist has the knowledge and sensitivity to determine what disclosures (if any!) are compatible with protecting the autonomy and dignity of the patient. Professional and patient groups argue for extremely sharp restrictions on disclosure without the agreement of the therapist and/or the patient. As we saw, therapists often resist even the standard liberal reasons for disclosure without consent; namely, risk or fact of harm to self or other. Many patient groups agree with them on this. Such convictions would be completely negated by legislation such as Shalala proposes.

The tension between the traditional and the emerging views is reflected in a current controversy about codes of ethics and the law. The codes of ethics of many health care professions require that members obey the law. Such a provision is in the spirit of the emerging view because, as everyone involved knows, the laws in question include disclosure laws such as laws requiring the reporting of misconduct, laws requiring the disclosure of information to the courts, and laws requiring the disclosure of information for financial or health policy reasons. Since these laws usually require disclosure whether or not the therapist and/or patient has given consent, any requirement that members obey them is sharply contrary to the traditional view. For this and other reasons, the requirement that members obey the law has become controversial in many professional associations and a number of associations have removed such provisions from their codes of ethics. Once such provisions are removed, if a member decides to break the law in order to protect patient confidentiality, even if he or she goes to jail rather than breach confidentiality, that becomes merely a matter between the therapist and the state. It would no longer count as professional misconduct and would not affect the therapist's standing in his or her profession.

3. Factors Obscuring the Shift

Our claim, then, is that a major shift is taking place from an individual, largely rights-based view of the value of confidentiality to a view in which confidentiality becomes just one social good among others, free to be sacrificed so long as no one's interests are harmed. So far, we have focussed on psychotherapy but the same shift has been happening in health care generally. If such a major shift is taking place, why is there not more discussion of it? We see at least three reasons.

First, obfuscation and ambiguity concerning key terms is getting in the way of seeing the size of the shift. From the traditional perspective, things are very clear. Disclosures without patient and/or therapist concurrence are breaches of confidentiality. They may be justified by some other consideration but they are breaches. Indeed, some proponents of the traditional view hold that even disclosure *with* concurrence breaches *confidentiality,* whatever other values may be at stake and however well protected the identity of the patient. On this strict reading, even presentation of case materials for purposes of advancing science, supervision, and teaching are violations of confidentiality. The emerging view obscures the issues here. Is an *authorized* or *legally mandated* disclosure a breach? If it is authorized and thereby not reprehensible, how can it be a *breach* of anything? If a government can legislate away a patient's right to confidentiality and a therapist's duty to protect confidentiality, then what duty of confidentiality remains? The new conceptualization of confidentiality at the heart of the emerging view starts with broad social goods and tries to tease some anemic notion of rights out of this starting point. Nothing but obfuscation can result from talking about a right to *confidentiality* in this new context. For present purposes, however, the important point is that when social and financial agents continue to do so, this talk obscures the magnitude of the shift taking place at the moment.

The second thing obscuring the magnitude of the shift is closely related. Policy-makers have also continued to use rights talk when they speak of confidentiality. Sometimes this talk is appropriate, for example, in the recognition of strong privilege in *Jaffee v. Redmond.* This case and the subsequent incorporation of that privilege in federal law in the United States are clearly in the liberal tradition of rights-based moral analysis and are significant steps forward. In other contexts, however, a lot of rights talk is confused. Although people on all sides of these issues speak of confidentiality as a right, when one probes the rhetoric the underlying defense of confidentiality is very frequently not based on rights at all. It is based on interests of the parties and broad social objectives. The use of the term "rights" is therefore simply misleading here. Whatever the rhetoric, broad social goods are the center of focus, not the rights of individuals. Policy development, development of statutory law, and the demands of insurers and funding agencies are now often moving in directions quite opposite to those embedded in the liberal tradition of individual rights.

The third reason obscuring the magnitude of the shift is that many of those most concerned have often not seen it happening yet. In the psychotherapy literature, debate concerning confidentiality is still centered on the harm principle: is it justified to disclose information without consent to prevent or punish harm (physical or emotional harm or the harm of wrongful conviction). These issues are extremely important, of course. But the bar is moving and the therapeutic community has yet responded. More and more, the issue concerning statutory disclosure of information is the desirability of achieving broad social objectives, not harm or anything else having to with individuals in a therapeutic relationship. The managed care controversy in the United States has sensitized psychotherapists to certain dimensions of the issue but the emerging threats to confidentiality extend far beyond managed care. To be sure, achieving social objectives is a worthy pursuit and any adequate policy or legislation will probably take into account social objectives, not just individual autonomy rights. However, a shift to ever-greater attention to social objectives is occurring and the magnitude of the shift is not receiving the attention it deserves.

This completes our sketch of a framework for thinking about confidentiality. We have attempted to lay out how both autonomy rights and social good figure in traditional thought about confidentiality in psychotherapy and how this traditional view is being supplanted or at least supplemented by a new way of thinking about confidentiality based entirely on social objectives and the interests (rather than the rights) of those concerned. Let us turn to some recent developments in information technology (IT). IT is playing a rapidly growing role in health care. The information demands generated by this technology are creating some unique threats to patient confidentiality, threats that theorists have hardly begun to address. We will first consider the threats to confidentiality in health care as a whole, then turn to the specific threats the new IT poses for confidentiality in psychotherapy.

4. The Expanding Role of Information Technology in Health Care

As we said at the beginning of the paper, new technology is making it ever easier to process vast amounts of information, and new policy initiatives are developing to take advantage of this information-processing capacity. First the new technology.

A. The Technological Context: Proliferation of Information Technology

Although the health care sector has been less quick to capitalize on the potential of computerized health information than other sectors of the economy, it has been crucial to some of the most dramatic changes in the health system in recent years. Examples include:

(1) plans in most countries for (as it is called in Canada) a "Health Information Highway";
(2) the development of health information systems and networks with the capacity to link information from a variety of institutions and systems;
(3) the growth of the Internet and its use for the transmission of personal health information for consumers and providers alike seeking health information;
(4) the emergence of a robust e-health industry delivering various products and services over the Internet;
(5) initiatives concerning the development of the electronic health record;
(6) the use of telehealth for a variety of applications, including remote consultation, diagnostics, and patient care;
(7) the proliferation of databases and registries;
(8) the deployment of IT in comprehensive health and disease surveillance systems.

Market trends and a commitment by governments to investment in health infrastructure make it extremely likely that technological developments along these lines will accelerate.

Computerization can enhance the value and usefulness of health information. For example, once patient information has been entered into a computer, subsequent retrieval and processing of that information for various purposes becomes much easier than when the information is recorded in paper form. Enhanced capabilities include:

(1) the ability to produce electronic copies of all or parts of the information relatively quickly effortlessly, and economically;

(2) the automated ability to search, process, aggregate, and reformat the information into new files or databases and to gather information from different records under select headings, whether for the same patient or for different patients;
(3) the ability to link information from a variety of sources in a common database that may be instantly accessible by any number of users;
(4) the ability to automate a variety of administrative tasks.

B. Health Policy and Ideological Context

Now the policy context. As computerization puts patient information in a form that is much more readily accessible to a variety of users than ever before, changes in health policy and health policy ideology are intensifying or even creating "needs" or any rate demands for health information for a variety of purposes and by a variety of users. Here are some of the activities and policy objectives calling on ever-increasing amounts of information and ever-increasing power and sophistication of IT.

Efficiency and Cost Containment: For some decades, the health care system was perceived to be growing constantly as a percentage of GNP (gross national product). There is some debate about the actual factors but the perception was enough by itself to give rise to intense scrutiny of the health system from the point of view of cost containment and even reduction. The computerization of health information has the potential to facilitate this. For example, the centralization of patient information and the possibility of linking databases from diverse sources could promote the detection of fraud or inappropriate use of the health system, could identify less expensive ways of trying to deliver a given kind of health care (one of the main motives behind Health Management Organizations in the US), and could assist system planners in deciding how best to allocate resources to achieve the greatest value per unit of money spent.

Accountability: Cost consciousness has prompted increased scrutiny of the accountability by various players in the health system, trying to determine if the results they achieve warrant the resources they use. This has led to the development of devices very alien to the context of health care such as outcome measures, performance indicators, and report cards. Whatever one may think of such initiatives, it is clear that they could not work without intensive use of information and sophisticated IT. Since many forms of psychotherapy are time- and therefore resource-intensive and since these new measures make extensive information demands and therefore threaten confidentiality, they are of particular concern to many parts of the psychotherapy community.

Evidence-Based Decision-Making: The imperative to base medical decision-making on evidence requires extensive therapeutic information.

Quality Assurance: Activities such as utilization review and audit may be expedited and enhanced by greater access to, and use of, patient information. While commendable on the face of it, the move to evidence-based decision-making and quality-assurance measures are often invoked in the name of increased accountability.

Health Surveillance: Information systems make possible health and disease tracking, and also tracking of such problems as practitioner abuse of or irresponsibility toward patients, parental abuse of children, and so on, to a much greater degree than any previously-existing technology. However, health and disease tracking requires mandatory reporting, which gives rise to all sorts of questions about the autonomy rights of patients and the need for confidentiality, especially where illegal or unethical conduct may be at issue.

Patient Participation: Many patients are assuming a more active role in their own health care. The growth of the Internet has made health information much more accessible to patients and has spawned an industry providing health information to consumers.

Health Research: In many jurisdictions, the amount of public and private money being devoted to health research is ramping up very fast. Plans regarding IT and such things as the development of registries and databases are part of this expansion, as are new demands for accountability and hopes for improving efficiency.

Health System Reform: Many of the trends currently driving health care reform, trends for example toward integrated health care systems and managed care, mandate increased and more ready access to patient information.

Population Health: The goal of improving and safeguarding population health by addressing the broader determinants of health is aided by patient information, especially aggregated in cumputerized form. Moreover, because the population health framework extends to other sectors besides health care, including social services, there is a demand that databases and information linkages extend well beyond the health system into virtually all other areas of social and economic service and policy.

The Commodification of Health Information: Health information, in a variety of forms, has become increasingly valuable as a commodity. The growth of markets in health information, and private sector involvement as buyer, trader, or seller, increases as health information becomes increasingly valuable.

Private/Public Partnerships: The involvement of the private sector in health care is increasing, especially in the area of health information. The mixture of public good purposes and the for-profit incentive in partnerships being formed for information infrastructure development, research, and other initiatives, gives rise to a variety of ethical tensions and issues concerning such matters as conflict of interest.

These trends are "information hungry." In particular, many of them are generating huge increases in the demand for patient information. In many cases, the purposes for which the information is being demanded are not the purpose for which health information used to be collected: for the immediate benefit of the patient from, or about, whom the information is being collected. The purposes now often have to do more with broad social objectives.

5. Some of the New Issues to which Computerized Health Information Has Given Rise

The issue of primary concern raised by the ever-expanding role of IT in the health care system and the new policy initiatives that have been developed to exploit this new capacity is the threat to confidentiality. We will first sketch this issue and related issues as they arise for health care in all its forms, then in Section 7 turn to confidentiality and related issues in the specific context of psychotherapy. Note how the conflict between the traditional and the emerging view of confidentiality arises in issue after issue. Some of the issues overlap.

Ownership and Sale of Health Information: Health information is becoming increasingly commercially valuable, particularly as amassed in large databases. Who owns health information? Where health information includes a significant component contributed by the clinician, does this make the information in question the clinician's intellectual property? What rights do patients have concerning revenues that might be generated from health information? Is it appropriate for health care providers or data custodians to sell health information, with or without patient consent?

Genetic Information: Advances in genetics are occurring in step, and converging with, health information initiatives, as recent events concerning the Icelandic database demonstrate. Iceland has had a stable population for a long time, so its genetic record is particularly valuable. When the Icelandic government began to market it, questions arose almost immediately. What standards should apply to genetic information? Who owns the information? What provisions should be in place to protect patients from powerful commercial interests? What protocols for consent are appropriate when information collected from one person also reveals something private about the genetic make-up of another? What protections should be in place to ensure adequate protection from inappropriate discrimination based on genetic information?

Provider Information: Health information includes information about health professionals as well as about patients. The demand for health provider information is growing in the name of such things as cost containment and accountability. What rules should govern the collection, use, and disclosure of information about providers? What rights do providers have in their information? Under what circumstances should it be collected, used, or disclosed without their consent?

Registries and Databases: Registries and databases are proliferating in health care. The focus on the potential benefits to be accrued often occurs at the expense of due attention to privacy and other ethical concerns. What rules should govern registries and databases? Should inclusion be premised on consent? Should there be limits on what data can be matched with other data? Should there be common privacy and security standards for databases?

Telehealth: Telehealth involves the translation of information (text, images, sound, what is felt, and so on) into digital form and the transmission of this information between locations that are typically quite distant. Are the general standards that obtain in health care adequate for telehealth or does telehealth introduce complexities requiring additional standards? Should the standards applied be those pertaining to the patient or the provider? What constitutes appropriate consent in the telehealth context?

E-health: The Internet is spawning a variety of health-related initiatives, including web-based electronic records. Most of these are in the private sector and sustained on a commercial, for-profit basis. Several codes and ethics statements have been advanced to address the many issues that arise concerning privacy and confidentiality, advertising, accuracy of information, conflict of interest, sale of information, and so forth, but such codes are themselves contentious. How should e-health be regulated? What standards should govern e-health initiatives? Who should set the standards? How might e-health impact on patient rights and on quality of care, and how might it enhance or disrupt the patient-physician relationship?

Electronic Health Record: The electronic health record is becoming a subject of increased debate. Who should have control of the record? Who should fund it? What rights of access do patients have to their own record? Who should be able to provide input into it? What information should it contain, and what linkages should it facilitate? Under what circumstances, if any, would it be appropriate for access to occur without patient knowledge or consent? Should patients be able to opt out of having their information in an e-record or an electronic database? What security protocols are appropriate?

Data Flows: The data flows in the health system are becoming increasingly complex. Whose responsibility is it to describe and track information flows? What controls should there be on these flows? What do patients and the public need to know about information flows in order for their confidentiality to be protected and their participation in the health system to be autonomous?

Private, For-profit Enterprises: Insurers and other private-enterprise bodies require information for a variety of purposes, including to rate risk, determine eligibility, and verify claims. How much information are they entitled to require? Should they be limited in their ability to require information when doing so might impede patients from seeking tests for fear the information generated might disadvantage them or create legal, social, or personal risks for them? How should patients and health professionals respond in the face of broad "consent" forms for insurance purposes? Should there be standards to govern such forms and limit the information they can require?

Impact Assessments with Respect to Privacy and Confidentiality: The idea of conducting privacy and confidentiality impact assessments prior to the introduction of new information systems is attracting a lot of attention.

What kind of considerations should be looked at in such an assessment? Should standards be developed? What role should such assessments play in system planning?

Transparency and Accountability: There is very little public information about current health information policies and practices and little public knowledge about how extensive and interrelated existing databases are. How can these practices and policies be made more transparent and subject to public scrutiny? What obligations do data custodians have to inform data subjects and the public about their practices?

The Role of the Public: The issues that need to be resolved as rules for collecting, managing, and using health information are developed touch upon fundamental values and have far-reaching implications for society. They are not technical or expert issues but rather public issues, and the public should be involved in debating and resolving them. How should the public be educated about the issues? What methods and processes best facilitate meaningful democratic public involvement in debating and resolving issues? What role should public opinion play in forming the rules of the game?

The issues we have just outlined indicate how broad the range of issues posed by the computerization of health information is and sketch some of the potential benefits and risks. The issues are becoming increasingly complicated and legislative and policy initiatives concerning health information and IT are not only generating a lot of contention; they are falling ever farther behind the state of the art in the technology. It is unlikely that things will become more settled or more adequate in most information-intensive countries any time soon.

6. Potential Benefits of Computerized Health Information

The situation with respect to the new information technology and health care is not unremittingly troubled and gloomy. Indeed, IT in health care holds the promise of much benefit, not just to society (we sketched some of those benefits) but also to individuals.

By facilitating ready access to personal information when it is needed for purposes of care, computerization has the potential to enhance patient care by providing treating professionals with tremendous stores of information about their patients and about treatment. Indeed, with appropriate controls on access, IT could even do a lot to address concerns about confidentiality across the health care professions. It could improve patients' ability to control their health information, enable health professionals to guarantee virtually unbreachable confidentiality, and increase trust in the therapeutic relationship.

IT also has the potential to empower patients to become more involved in managing health and disease by facilitating ready access to generic health information. The Internet in particular is a very powerful tool for patients to do research and become better informed about health matters of concern to them. However, the Internet is evolving with a very strong marketplace orientation and countervailing factors can undermine the potential for patient empowerment. In particular, the problem of unreliable or just plain false "information" on the Internet is becoming very serious. The interests of information compilers and providers in generating revenue do not perfectly coincide with patients' interest in accurate, unbiased, and trustworthy information. Whether empowerment is achieved will depend on how the Internet evolves to mitigate against misinformation, manipulation, and exploitation and on the existence of a robust primary care system with trusted health professionals available to help patients interpret information they have obtained from other sources.

The potentials described above are from the perspective of patients interested in enhancing the direct care they receive, becoming better informed about their health and possible diseases, and in limiting third parties access to information they provide for the purpose of receiving care. These objectives are in some tension, of course, with the objectives of third parties seeking access to patient information for purposes such as system planning, research, fraud detection, accountability, and quality assurance. To be sure, the use of information for purposes other than direct patient care can also enhance patient care (although this is not something to be taken on faith). The research of today can produce better treatments for tomorrow; reduced costs can help to free up money for patient care; and quality assurance can lead to improvements in the quality of care available. Whether, or to what extent, the benefits will be achieved and the risks avoided will depend in part on how well we anticipate and manage the issues that we have identified.

Except possibly for the devices to protect confidentiality, these benefits do not accrue to psychotherapy patients in the same way as they accrue to patients of other kinds. Neither the treating professional having access to information about the patient nor the patient having access to information about his or her condition connects to the treatment situation in such a way that direct benefits to the treatment clearly ensue. There are also costs and risks special to psychotherapy. For example, the way that threats to confidentiality from IT relate to psychotherapy is different from the way they relate to other kinds of health care.

7. Confidentiality and the Specific Situation of Psychotherapy

Many of the initiatives designed to promote broad social objectives that use electronic health care information systems threaten confidentiality (and therefore trust in the therapeutic relationship) wherever they are found in the health care system.

> Impact on Confidentiality: The usual way to protect confidentiality in situations where information-gathering threatens it is to require patient consent. (Thus, any proposed information collection activities that do not require consent are suspect for that reason alone.) Even where consent is required, hard questions arise. Under what circumstances, if any, is it acceptable to use or disclose information without consent? In cases where consent is required, what form should the consent take? How much does a patient need to know for consent to be sufficiently informed? Are blanket consents ever appropriate? Under what circumstances, if any, can consent be implied? Are "opt out" regimes acceptable in some cases? Is consent ever an adequate gatekeeper for confidentiality and privacy? Are there some things to which people should not be permitted to consent? Should they be able to selectively block parts of their health information? Would it be justified to require people in countries with universal health coverage to forego the right to consent as a condition of enjoying the benefits of a publicly funded health system? In psychotherapy, however, other considerations arise, because, as we saw earlier, in psychotherapy consent is not the gold standard for protection of confidentiality.

In addition to the problem of how to think about protection of confidentiality in psychotherapy, the expanding role of IT in health care gives rise to some other issues peculiar to psychotherapy.

> Impact on the Therapeutic Relationship: In psychotherapy, mandatory reporting requirements affect the therapist/patient relationship directly by distorting the development of affect, fantasy, and transference in the patient. An obvious example has to do with requirements that psychotherapists report boundary-violating and other transgressive patients. Such a requirement makes psychotherapy with such people essentially impossible. If potential patients know or even fear that something they say about themselves could end up in a database cross referenced to databases used by the police or potential employers, they simply will not be candid in therapy. How should these potential consequences be weighed in the development of rules for health information?

> Impact on Clinical Practice: Closely related to the issue of impact on the therapeutic relationship is the potential of IT to change clinical practice. Should information practices of psychotherapists be standardized with respect to information about their own techniques and practices, so as to enhance communication with other practitioners and potential or actual patients? Should the needs of various secondary users of health information influence what information psychotherapists provide about themselves?

So protecting confidentiality, the therapeutic relationship, and clinical practice gives rise to special issues in psychotherapy. Consent is not a safe protection because, as we saw earlier, in the context of transferences, primitive regressions, and so on, the notion of informed consent is itself inherently vexed. Yet breaches of confidentiality can have much more profound effects in psychotherapy than in other areas of medicine. My oncologist revealing to someone that I have cancer might infuriate me and undermine my confidence in her, but it is not likely to have much effect on how well the chemotherapy she has prescribed works. By contrast, if my psychotherapist reveals to someone that I am in psychotherapy, that could destroy the therapy. Likewise, because of the enormous individuality of clinical practice in psychotherapy, measures requiring standardization of clinical practice are likely to have far more profound effects on psychotherapy than on, for example, oncology. So how should we think of the threats to confidentiality in psychotherapy posed by the new demands for information?

What is special to psychotherapy is that disclosure of information to third parties is a violation of a patient's legitimate expectations and therefore autonomy and threatens the treatment *whether or not the patient consents.* Psychotherapy requires that certain kinds of information be kept private to the patient and therapist. (The teaching and research practices of psychotherapists pose a threat of their own to this requirement and we will come back to it.) If consent is not an adequate protection of confidentiality in psychotherapy, what would be?

We might look to the very technology that caused the problem. There are promising developments in the field of privacy- and confidentiality-enhancing technology, including such things as anonymization software. Can these technologies protect confidentiality in psychotherapy? Should, for example, anonymization provisions be mandated in all health care information systems? We might also look to securing databases where information about psychotherapeutic treatments is housed. Security includes both human and technological measures to protect information against unauthorized access, use, or disclosure. Here we would have to decide what level of security is appropriate for such information. Perhaps some of the developing security provisions such as secure

Internet sites could be used to begin to protect confidentiality. If information is going to be collected about psychotherapy, with or without patient consent, even if collected anonymously, everything that can be done should be done to enhance privacy and confidentiality, of course. We doubt, however, that provisions such as these are likely to ensure the level of confidentiality needed for effective psychotherapy any time soon, for the following reasons.

First, in psychotherapy the standard of confidentiality that must be met is very high. Patients of means have been known to insist that they pay the whole treatment themselves and that the treating professional not take notes. Here is how Herbert Sacks, a psychiatrist and former president of the American Psychiatric Association, describes the situation in that country:

> [A] grave concern . . . has to do with . . . the demands of managed care organizations for full medical records. They claim they need them for accountability. That is not true. . . . [Plus,] there are leaks all over the place. In my private practice dealing with . . . patients who work in corporations, banks, and the media, perhaps half of them who have coverage will not use it. They pay out of pocket because of their concern about these breaches, because of what they observe in their own workplaces (Sacks, 1996).

Such a concern can have many motives: clinical paranoia; holding down a highly sensitive job; risk that professional effectiveness would be diminished if it were known that the person had been in psychotherapy; or prior illegality or immorality or fear that earlier actions might have been illegal or immoral. *For purposes of psychotherapy*, these are *all* legitimate reasons for absolute confidentiality. Paranoia, for example, may or may not be justified but it is an entirely appropriate reason for seeking psychotherapy and the therapy will not work unless the patient can trust that nothing will violate the confidentiality of his or her information.

With the confidentiality bar set this high, not just the demands of health policy initiatives but also the standard liberal exceptions to do with harm to self or other begin to look like they should be resisted. Both because of the rights-grounding autonomy and dignity of the individual and because psychotherapy is a highly valuable social good, psychotherapy needs a near-unbreachable standard of confidentiality. For this reason, we doubt that the confidentiality needs of psychotherapy, on the one hand, and the legitimate demands of courts and child protection agencies and the agencies charged with developing health policy are reconcilable. In our own view, in all cases or nearly all cases of conflict, the value of effective psychotherapy to a society is greater than almost any value that could be achieved by violating confidentiality.

What is sauce for the goose, however, is sauce for the gander. Treating confidentiality as nearly unbreachable would cut against some common practices of psychotherapists too: clinical case studies, for example, and use of cases, vignettes, quotations from sessions, and so on in teaching, supervision, and research. Probably private clinical conversations between therapists would not constitute a breach of confidentiality even under the stringent regime we are proposing, but a lot of communications with groups of clinicians might turn out to be violations of confidentiality. Indeed, can information about individual patients, transcripts of what patients say, and the like be so much as *generated* without distorting the therapeutic process? And once the information has been generated, can it be used without threatening confidentiality? The standard protection is to remove identifying material. But (1) can one remove identifying material without distorting the rest of the material, and (2) can one ever disguise material so as to make it unrecognizable even to the patient concerned? (Patients read journals, too.) In general, is there any way to use information from psychotherapeutic sessions that is accurate enough to be scientifically useful and yet poses no threat to confidentiality?

8. Conclusion

The goal of this chapter has been to contrast the traditional and the emerging frameworks for thinking about confidentiality and to lay out some of the risks to confidentiality in the information revolution currently going on in health care. The prospects for avoiding these risks are not good if we as a society continue to demand more and more information about highly sensitive, emotionally-wrought activities such as psychotherapy. We think that it is past time for the community to shift from its near-exclusive focus on the individual treatment context and how therapists should respond to the harm principle and to begin to think about the implications for psychotherapy of the new risks to confidentiality deriving from every-increasing demands for information to help us achieve broad and for the most part admirable social objectives.

There should be much more debate in the therapeutic community, patient community, and the general public than there is. In the absence of debate, the agenda of users of health information with large resources and political clout are apt to prevail. Their point of view has been the dominant one in the design and regulation of health information systems so far. Serious things are at stake, such as the very possibility of effective psychotherapy. It is imperative that the providers and beneficiaries of health care identify the issues clearly and face them squarely. By delineating the very different value foundations at work in current thinking about confidentiality, we have tried to take a first step in this direction.

The choice with respect to confidentiality is to think about it on the basis of autonomy, modified perhaps by a qualification about harm to self or other, or to think about it in the context of social objectives or the needs of financial or other institutions. The first approach is built on respect for patients' autonomy but comes at some cost to third parties and the good of society generally. The second approach may achieve some important social objectives but at the cost of seriously damaging psychotherapy, itself a major social good, and, often, treating both patients and health care professionals paternalistically.

Acknowledgments

We would like to thank the editors: Christine Koggel, for reviewing the reviewing the paper a number of times and making innumerable important suggestions; Allannah Furlong for an additional set of very helpful suggestions; and Charles Levin especially for saving us from seriously distorting how confidentiality is actually handled in psychotherapy.

Works Cited

Caulfield, T. (In progress) *Tissue Banking, Patient Rights, and Confidentiality: Tensions in Law and Policy.*

Etzioni, Amitai. (1999) *The Limits of Privacy.* New York: Basic Books.

Jaffee v. Redmond. [1996] 64 LW 4490 (Sup Ct, 11 June 1996).

Kremer, Thomas G, and Ellis L. Gesten. (1998) "Confidentiality Limits of Managed Care and Clients' Willingness to Self-Disclose.," *Professional Psychology: Research and Practice*, 29 (6): pp. 553–558.

R. v. Mills. [1999]3 S. C. R. 668.

Sacks, Herbert S. (1996) "Connecticut Section," *The New York Times*, 27 October.

Tarasoff v. Regents of University of California. [1976]17 Cal. 3d 425, 551 P.2d 334, 131 Cal. Rpt. 14 (Cal. 1976).

Tuckfelt, Sondra, Jeri Fink, and Muriel Prince Warren. (1997) *The Psychotherapists' Guide to Managed Care in the 21st Century: Surviving Big Brother and Providing Quality Mental Health Services.* Northvale, N. J.: Jason Aronson Inc.

United States Department of Health and Social Services. (1999) "Confidentiality of Mental Health Information: Ethical, Legal and Policy Issues." In *Mental Health: A Report of the Surgeon General*, Chapter 7.

United States Secretary of Health and Human Services (Donna Shalala). (1997) *Confidentiality of Individually-Identifiable Health Information: Recommendations of the Secretary of Health and Human Services, Pursuant to Section 264 of the Health Insurance Portability and Accountability Act of 1996* (September 1997 Report to Congress).

von Tigerstrom, Barbara, Patrick Nugent, and Vanessa Cosco. (2000) "Alberta's Health Information Act and the *Charter*: A Discussion Paper." *Health Law Review,* 9(2): 3–21.

Warren, Samuel D., and Louis D. Brandeis. (1890) "The Right to Privacy." *Harvard Law Review* 4 (5): 193-220.

Seven

CONFIDENTIALITY IN THE LIBERAL TRADITION: A RELATIONAL CRITIQUE

Christine M. Koggel

1. Introduction

Privacy has tended not to be articulated in Western liberal constitutions as a right in itself. However, what gives privacy its value fits with the value given to other individual liberty rights central to liberal democratic societies. In the broad sense, privacy captures the idea that individuals ought to have the freedom to shape their own interests, projects, and goals without interference from other individuals or the state. What is done in the privacy of the home or in personal relationships, for example, is understood as expressing individual freedom. The other sense of privacy concerns personal information conveyed to another. Confidentiality asks that information about oneself and the relationships in which that information is disclosed be kept private. Confidentiality is the practical outcome of valuing freedom and autonomy in a liberal democratic society. In our society, the law recognizes and protects confidentiality in specific sorts of relationships such as that between a husband and a wife and a lawyer and a client. A wife cannot be forced to testify against her husband and what a client reveals to his or her lawyer is privileged information. The protection of confidentiality in relationships between doctors and patients, however, has not had the same privileged status in the law as the other two relationships have had. In fact, the increased monitoring of health care costs by insurance companies and governments; the proliferation of data banks for purposes of medical research; and demands that medical records be disclosed to the courts are examples of greater erosions of confidentiality between doctors and patients now than in the past.

While all these encroachments on confidentiality between doctors and patients present interesting moral dilemmas in their own right, in this chapter I concentrate on the particular relationship between psychotherapists and their patients to critically evaluate the importance and value of confidentiality in this context. More specifically, I am interested in examining justifications given by the state for breaching confidentiality in those cases where what a patient tells a therapist is taken to be relevant to determining the innocence or guilt of a third party. While my argument for protecting confidentiality in these cases may have implications for other situations such as breaching confidentiality when a patient reports having committed a crime or threatens to commit one, I will not be exploring these here. I focus instead on the argument that confidentiality is justifiably breached in service of the state interest in protecting an individual's right to full answer and defense. This argument is being challenged because these cases raise important equality considerations for feminists committed to eliminating oppression for women and members of other disadvantaged groups.

I shall proceed in the following way. First, I outline the way in which the debate on confidentiality in liberal democratic societies has been framed in terms of two competing values: an individual's right to privacy, with the corresponding need to protect confidentiality in relationships between psychotherapists and patients, and society's interest in providing full answer and defense for the accused, leading courts to require production of information disclosed by the complainant to her therapist. I do not question the importance of these values or the idea that they need to be balanced one against the other. Rather, I question restricting the debate on confidentiality in liberal democracies to these two primary values. I shall argue that attending to the social relations and political context that form the backdrop against which individuals enter into relationships with psychotherapists moves us beyond the well-accepted and familiar defense of confidentiality as merely an individual's right to privacy or of breaches of confidentiality as simply fulfilling an individual's right to full answer and defense. The gist of my argument is that the broader social context in which members of traditionally disadvantaged groups exist in and are shaped by unequal relations makes it necessary to reconceive the right to privacy in the therapeutic relationship as an individual *and* a social right. While feminists have drawn attention to these background issues of inequalities and their relevance to questions of policy and legislation, they have tended to be ignored in the mainstream debate on confidentiality. Eliminating discrimination and achieving equality are goals that both psychotherapists and lawyers/judges ought to take into consideration not only in their respective professions, but also in formulating policies regarding confidentiality.

2. The Political Context: Relevant Background Issues

The approach I defend in this chapter is feminist: our social and political context of continuing and entrenched inequalities of women and other disadvantaged groups is relevant to an understanding of privacy and to an adequate account of policies with respect to confidentiality. A discussion of these background features has been virtually absent in a debate about confidentiality that is generally framed in terms of competing individual rights. In the traditional debate, on one side is the individual and the need to protect that individual's freedom to enter into these relationships and keep them private. In the specific context of psychotherapy, it is generally agreed that this relationship works best if information shared in it is kept confidential. On this side of the debate are therapists who defend confidentiality as a quality of care issue: confidentiality is an essential part of what it means to care for a patient and for the treatment to be successful. On the other side are said to be the interests of the collective and its need to protect social goods such as public safety and the right to a fair trial. Revealing the names of people who are a threat to public safety or upholding the right to full answer and defense are taken to be justifiable restrictions on the interests of therapists and patients in preserving the confidentiality of psychotherapeutic and other personal files. On this side are lawyers and judges with a legitimate interest in having all the information before them, including what is disclosed in therapeutic relationships, in order to uncover the facts of a case and determine innocence or guilt. The framework within which the debate has traditionally been structured has been depicted as a "clash of cultures" between psychotherapists/analysts and lawyers/judges (as it was by numerous speakers at the "Confidentiality & Society" Conference in Montreal in October 2000).

Yet, while the competing values are thought to be those of the individual right to privacy on the one hand and the societal objective of full answer and defense on the other, what actually takes place in court is a conflict between particular individuals, one with the right to privacy and the other with the right to full answer and defense. Reframing the conflict as one between individuals is useful for highlighting the emphasis in liberal theory on the individual, the negative rights to freedom that are given priority, and the contours of legitimate restrictions on individual freedom. In liberal theory, negative rights are primary in the sense that what is important is not what the state can *do* to provide for its citizens but what the state must *refrain from doing* to maximize individual freedom. Moreover, negative rights tend to be thought of in the abstract as attaching to isolated individuals viewed as similarly situated and virtually interchangeable. The details about the lives of individuals are taken to be irrelevant to questions of breaching confidentiality as are the social practices and political contexts in which these individuals can exercise their rights without interference from the state or others. Underlying this understanding of individuals and the emphasis on negative rights is a particular understanding of equality as resting on the basic idea that people are essentially the same; similarly situated and deserving equal treatment under the law. From this perspective, the moral and legal question of the protection of confidentiality is answered in terms of whether one individual's right to privacy can be overridden by another individual's right to full answer and defense.

In *Perspectives on Equality*, I sketch a relational theory that takes an analysis of the kinds of relationships people are in to be essential to an account of whether equality obtains (Koggel, 1998). The traditional liberal focus on individuals, each having basic needs and capacities that make them equal and worthy of respect, is not jettisoned in the kind of relational account that I and other feminists such as Susan Sherwin, Sue Campbell, Jennifer Nedelsky, and Lorraine Code defend. A relational conception provides a picture of individuals as born into and necessarily shaped by relationships throughout their lives: some chosen, some not; some maintained, some ended; some damaging to self-concepts; and some aids to self-development. Relational theory begins with an understanding of people as beings that cannot survive let alone flourish on their own and of relationships as places where interactions can help or hinder a person's ability to develop the capacities of rationality, autonomy, and self-development so valued in liberal democratic societies. If we take seriously this account of how individual lives are embedded in and shaped by relationships, the basic liberal notion that each individual ought to have the freedom to pursue his or her interests, projects, and goals without interference from other individuals or the state needs to be understood differently. A person's interests, projects, and goals are shaped by the relationships in the particular social and political context in which he or she is situated; including the relationships between psychotherapists and patients as they have developed in our own liberal democratic context. I argue that we need to understand how these kinds of private relationships function not only in the lives of individuals but also in the broader network of relationships in the public realm.

A relational account moves us away from assumptions that all individuals are similarly situated and have the same levels of freedom and the same opportunities to develop talents, projects, and goals and to be full participating members of a community. It takes the details of lives shaped by specific relationships that exist in particular social practices and political contexts to be relevant to an understanding of inequalities and of how to remove them. It explains that we do not pay sufficient attention to what is needed to achieve genuine equality unless we learn how perceptions and stereotypes of individuals who are members of traditionally disadvantaged groups continue to limit opportunities and shape identities and self-perceptions. Acknowledging the impact of relationships on people's lives and on levels of freedom and self-respect reveals inequalities that tend to be ignored in moral, legal, and political theory in traditional liberal theory.

To give substance to this account of the relevance of relationships, let us imagine a context different from our own and work out the implications of this for a discussion of confidentiality on the issue of psychotherapeutic relationships dynamically different from our own. The goal is to highlight the deficiencies in any liberal conception of an individual right to privacy that fails to take into account the significance of relationships, social practices, and political contexts to an analysis of policies regarding confidentiality. In "Confidentiality in the Formerly Communist World: A Case Study in Mental Health Reform," Richard Bonnie provides a picture of a context different from our own: a totalitarian regime in the former Soviet Union that violated privacy rights and abused confidentiality in psychotherapeutic relationships for purposes of state control. Here the therapeutic relationship was not a place for individuals to pursue moral and intellectual development, but rather a tool for the state to thwart individual protest and unrest (Bonnie, 2000). Few would defend these sorts of violations of privacy and individual freedom. But now imagine a society different from both our own and the former Soviet Union. This society is committed to promoting freedom for each and every individual, but it does this by ensuring that the basic needs of all of its citizens are met through strong social welfare programs. In this society, positive rights to food, shelter, health, and work, for example, are understood as fundamental to individuals being able to exercise negative liberty rights such as privacy, speech, and association. Citizens of this hypothetical society would consider it meaningless to think that a person in a social and economic context that tolerates homelessness has the same right to work or to speak freely or to own property as the person with even a moderate level of wealth. While in our liberal democratic society we tend to believe that freedom is achieved through non-interference, here state interference in the lives of citizens through positive measures such as provisions of food, shelter, health, and work is thought to enhance rather than undermine individual freedom.

Imagining the beliefs and values of people in societies other than our own makes it clear that people in these contexts legitimately may not give individual negative liberty rights the kind of primacy they have in liberal societies. At the very least, they may believe that positive social and economic rights enhance the negative liberty rights we take for granted. We can extend the exercise to imagine the kinds of relationships that might emerge. It is not implausible to think that a society concerned about promoting equal relationships through strong welfare measures may generate a different kind of therapeutic relationship than those occurring in our own social and political context. We need not idealize this society as one without inequalities, abuses of power, or unequal relationships to conceive of a potentially different role for relationships between therapists and patients. For example, our hypothetical society might ensure that there is funding for psychotherapy for those living in and damaged by unequal or oppressive relationships; that all its citizens have genuine freedom to make use of these health care resources; and that the special function of these relationships in this context would be supported by the enactment of strong policies protecting confidentiality. Because the therapeutic relationship would be viewed as a vehicle for addressing inequalities in the private lives of its citizens, state protection of privacy would be understood as promoting equality; just as positive rights to food, shelter, work, and health, for example, are taken to eliminate inequalities in public relationships.

Imagining a context different from our own provides us with a different picture of what might be needed to treat human beings with respect, promote social relations in which all human beings can flourish, and establish social harmony and stability. The lesson is not that negative liberty rights are unimportant. Rather it is that values taken for granted in our liberal democratic context cannot be understood in the abstract. They need to be examined as specific to and deriving their meaning from particular social and political contexts. Thus far, I have defended the idea that a relational approach provides a needed analysis of private and public relationships existing in specific political contexts and sustained by particular social practices. In the section that follows, I apply relational insights to an analysis of the seemingly quintessential individual right of freedom of speech so central to liberal democratic societies. This critical analysis of a liberal conception of free speech will turn out to be highly relevant to the question of protecting confidentiality in relationships between psychotherapists and particular sorts of patients; those who are members of traditionally disadvantaged groups.

3. Freedom of Speech and Privacy

At first glance, the right to freedom of speech might be thought to be in conflict with the right to privacy. While one promotes the value of being able to speak freely in public, the other asks that a person's thoughts, beliefs, and relationships be kept private and out of the public realm. In "Do You Mind if I Speak Freely? Reconceptualizing Freedom of Speech," Lisa Heldke evaluates two liberal arguments for freedom of speech. The first, inherited from John Stuart Mill, is the argument that society needs to allow individuals to speak freely because having an open marketplace of ideas serves the useful purpose of weeding out bad ideas and allowing a society to arrive at truth. The second is the argument that individuals need to be able to speak freely to achieve intellectual and moral self-development. Applying relational insights to each of these arguments for free speech and then concentrating on a critical evaluation of the second will illustrate that the two arguments are more connected than may at first appear. A relational reading of both shows how the autonomy aspect of the first argument combines with the communal aspect of the second to make better sense of both. Reconceiving speech as relational provides an account of the role of speech in the process of self-development and of how relationships and whole communities can hinder or help this development.

The first argument for freedom of speech continues to be important to the liberal defense of free speech. Mill argued that only in a context that allows all ideas to be expressed, even those that are odious, obscene, immoral, or false, is it possible to arrive at truth. Put immoral and false ideas into the marketplace and ultimately they will be revealed for what they are. Censor ideas in advance and the result is an impoverishment of ideas and a threat to the valuable process of having a whole range of ideas that can be explored, tested, accepted, or rejected on the road to acquiring truth. In Mill's philosophy, the state is only justified in restricting speech if it causes direct harm to another. The frequently cited example of yelling "fire!" in a crowded theater is taken to be a clear case of speech that causes direct harm. For most liberals, the harm has to be imminent and direct.

This account of freedom of speech and the very narrow range of circumstances acceptable as justifiable restrictions of speech are notorious in debates about pornography in liberal democratic societies. A person does not have to like or approve of what pornographers produce or of what consumers read or view, but should tolerate an individual's right to produce and to consume as fundamental to having the community examine a full range of views as a legitimate way of exploring and answering moral questions about human sexuality. Unlike the second argument for free speech, Mill's argument acknowledges that exploring, testing, and improving ideas and arguments is fundamentally a communal activity and project. The underlying assumption is that all individuals are equal participants in the activities of uttering speech and exploring its validity and truth. Inequalities in wealth, power, position, and status are rarely if ever recognized by liberal theorists as relevant to an evaluation of whether there is a genuinely free marketplace of ideas. The absence of recognition of factors of power and status is particularly evident in the second traditional liberal argument for freedom of speech.

The second argument is based on the idea that allowing individuals to speak, to say what is on their minds, is fundamental to people's intellectual and moral development. If there are limitations to my utterances, then there is a sense in which the monitoring of my speech, either from the outside or the inside, prevents me from being the person I am or want to be. My freedom is restricted in the fundamental sense of my being unable to express and explore the beliefs, desires, values, and projects that constitute who I am. Whereas Mill's argument for the utility of testing ideas in an open marketplace acknowledges that human intellectual and moral development is a communal enterprise, the second argument for speech as an individual right implies, at the very least, that intellectual and moral development is a solitary project and that expressing ideas is a way of asserting independence and developing autonomy on one's own. I am not claiming that there are liberals who actually argue that speech is solitary in this way. Rather, in defending a relational conception of the self I am interested in highlighting what is missing in the liberal conception of speech as allowing individuals to develop morally and intellectually.

In my estimation, we undermine the very notion of the importance of free speech to self-development unless we take into account the significance of the interactions and relationships in which utterances are made. A fundamental feature of what it is to shape and develop one's own beliefs, desires, values, and projects is that this is done in relationships in which those beliefs, desires, values, and projects are examined, questioned, endorsed, accepted, or rejected with and by others. These reactions to our utterances in turn shape future utterances, which in turn shape and reshape our beliefs, desires, values, and projects. All of this is fundamental to self-development in that this context of relationships and interactive speech is vital to the promotion of individual autonomy and independence so valued in liberal theory. Very little sense can be made of the notion of self-development unless we assume listeners, reactions, interactions, and relationships. The liberal conception assumes that speech can be discussed in the abstract and apart from contexts in which speaking and listening takes place. When we focus on the kinds of relationships particular individuals are in and who does the listening, we make room for understanding the ways in which speech always has the potential to do harm or good for people living in the context of unequal opportunities, status, and levels of power.

Heldke develops the idea that speaking is an inherently relational act that involves a speaker *and* a listener. One aspect of conceiving speech as relational picks up on the argument in the previous section about how individuals are "constituted as persons in part through our connection with others" (Heldke, 1991, p. 680). Here the emphasis is on the importance of listeners to the development of autonomy and independence and to the promotion of moral and intellectual growth. Conceiving speech as relational has obvious implications for and applications to the relationship between a psychotherapist and patient. This relationship is one in which the person speaking needs and often has selected a listener with the express purpose of disclosing information in the process of assessing and reconstituting the self. The success of this process depends on the patient trusting that the disclosure and self-evaluation be kept private, particularly from those close to the patient. After all, much of the information that is disclosed and assessed will be about the people and relationships central to this person's life. Free speech in this context requires privacy. But there is more to the analysis of speech as relational than the importance of this kind of listener to this kind of speaker.

Another aspect of conceiving speech as relational involves thinking about the effects of one's speech on the listener: "Unless you always talk only to yourself, whenever you speak you are entering into a relation with someone who stands to be affected by what you say" (Heldke, 1991, p. 680). Heldke elucidates the ways in which listeners are made invisible in the liberal conception of free speech and argues that this invisibility actually facilitates or enables a silencing. Sexist speech in a classroom, for example, harms by having the effect of silencing and thus restricting the speech of those who are the targets of such speech. Contrary to the liberal conception that focuses on the right of the speaker to make utterances, Heldke argues that "it is not only the current speaker whose freedom may be curtailed; listeners/potential speakers may also suffer limitations on their freedom. ... Speaking in a particular situation is not free if my talking silences (or in other ways harms) another person through threat, intimidation, or oppressive generalization" (Heldke, 1991, p. 681).

These insights about the role of and effect on the listener can be applied to the psychotherapeutic relationship in two ways. First, given the nature of this private relationship and the purpose of speech within it, the responsibility of the therapist to listen well and respond appropriately is heightened. Second, placing this private relationship into a network of relationships in a public realm, and understanding the role of therapeutic relationships in our social and political context, highlights the way in which threats and intimidation by courts to obtain records further silences those who are already silenced in other private and public relationships. The point is that the "speech" of the courts that permits access to the personal records of patients who are members of traditionally disadvantaged groups entrenches rather than alleviates inequalities.

Heldke writes: "[w]hen I conceive of myself as a being in-relations-with-others, and of speech as an activity that places me in relations with particular others, I must also regard my speech as a thing that may build or disrupt those relations. In other words, I cannot consider my freedom-to-speak outside of the context in which I am speaking" (Heldke, 1991, p. 681). We need to understand the importance of the value of confidentiality in our own social and political context in which women who seek therapy come into this relationship of differential power as members of a disadvantaged group. An account of the inequalities that women and other disadvantaged group members continue to suffer is essential to understanding and evaluating not only the value of the social good of achieving equality for all but also the concept of confidentiality itself. As just illustrated, a central aspect of a relational approach is that it allows an examination not only of the role and responsibilities of both the speaker and the listener in a particular therapeutic relationship, but also how this sort of speaking-and-listening relationship functions in the broader societal context. It thereby also highlights a society's responsibility to prevent the harm of silencing those who are most vulnerable. Recognizing that psychotherapeutic relationships are vital to self-development and the shaping of autonomy and independence of certain classes of disadvantaged citizens means conceiving of confidentiality as a way of alleviating and eliminating particular kinds of entrenched inequalities. The protection of confidentiality is one vehicle for creating relationships that enable free speech and promote self-development. In this context, the right to free speech is enhanced and made meaningful when confidentiality is strengthened through legal protection.

Heldke defends the idea that "a transformation in the ways we think about free speaking" (Heldke, 1991, p. 683) can have the effect of teaching us about the potential harms of our speech on listeners, thereby inducing some self-monitoring of what we say. Heldke's focus is on transforming the speaker who utters harmful speech so that thought is given to the effects on others of what is uttered. My focus is on the speaker who is silenced by listeners such as the state when they provide too easy access to psychotherapeutic records. Power determines who gets to speak freely and who is silenced. Relational theory transforms the liberal understanding that rights to speech and to privacy are held by and are of value to individuals as separate and isolated entities into a conception of these rights as hindered and damaged by relationships of power and inequality. In line with the position Heldke defends, we should not be pessimistic about the possibility of transforming our thinking about the role and function of therapeutic relationships in the lives of those who are marginalized and disadvantaged. But I would argue that more than a transformation of thinking is required concerning the issue of confidentiality. Here is one place where policy matters. Feminists have shown that challenges to and the curtailment of the legal protection of confidentiality have the effect of increasing instances in which the courts demand disclosure of the therapeutic records of members of disadvantaged groups.

4. Feminist Concerns about the Courts and Confidentiality

The first step in applying relational insights to questions of policy regarding confidentiality is to acknowledge the relevance of the broader context in which women and members of other disadvantaged groups continue to suffer inequalities in status, position, and opportunities. These are inequalities that are shaped by perceptions of women's proper roles and the relationships of unequal power and authority within which they are confined. These factors in turn shape the perceptions women have of their own experiences and the stories they tell about themselves. In other words, they not only shape women's effective levels of freedom to speak, but also what listeners hear them say. Margaret Denike argues that in a context in which men's experiences and perspectives structure the justice system, women are not taken to be credible reporters of their own experiences, particularly of their experiences of sexuality and of sexual encounters. Denike takes "knowing and seeing the gender inequality at the heart of evaluating, interpreting, deciphering and declaring what counts as truth, what counts as credible speech" to be central to understanding how the law treats victims of sexual assault and complainants in sexual assault proceedings (Denike, 2000, p. 6). Unequal treatment under the law is apparent in the fact that the overwhelming number of requests for records disclosure are in response to cases in which women come forward to report instances of sexual assault.

Denike cites a 1997 study by Karen Busby that reveals that "120 out of the 140 cases involving defense counsel requests for access to third-party records were cases where the accused was charged with a sexual assault offense" (Denike, 2000, p. 14). The assumption is that these records are relevant to determining whether the assault took place and to judging the credibility, character, and motive of the complainant. The background context within which personal records are requested and disclosed is thus relevant to the moral and legal question of whether there should be full disclosure of personal records in therapeutic relationships.

Katherine Kelly points out that "the social context of sexual assault involves discourses about sexual assault, gender and, with the use of personal records, about women and mental illness" (Kelly, 1997, p. 181). We cannot ignore the perceptions of women that form the backdrop against which the values of equality before the law and a fair trial get their meaning. "The dominant discourses that apply to our understanding of the speaker and these types of events are critical to any assessment. They provide us with informational filters, for example, that certain individuals are more likely to lie or to be mentally unstable or to have perceptional problems" (Kelly, 1997, p. 190). Women's speech about their experiences of sexual assault are interpreted from the perspective not only of the perpetrator, but of lawyers and judges who share beliefs about women's lack of credibility. Those who speak about sexual assault have tended to be silenced not only by these interpretations of them as lacking credibility, but by legislation that explicitly takes factors such as past sexual experiences or a relationship to the accused to be relevant to the determination of consent. Perceptions of women's inferior status and the law's treatment of women as less than credible agents in turn shape women's self-concepts in ways that result in lower levels of self-esteem and self-respect and higher levels of self-blame. In the language of a relational conception of speech, making it possible for the courts to have easy access to therapeutic records has the effect of further silencing those who are the victims of sexual assault.

A number of feminists have highlighted the consequences of the Canadian Supreme Court decision in *O'Connor*, which in endorsing defendants' access to complainants' personal records, opened the floodgates, as Karen Busby's 1997 research has shown, to defendants seeking "access not only to counseling, therapy and psychiatric records but also records from abortion and birth control clinics, child welfare agencies, adoption agencies, residential and public schools, drug and alcohol abuse recovery centers, other doctors, employers, the military, psychiatric hospitals, the Crown on unrelated charges against the complainant, and personal diaries, reporters' notes, and criminal and Young Offender records" (Busby, 1997, p.149). In its neutral and abstract determination of individuals and their liberty rights, the majority decision in *O'Connor* did not raise the issue of women's inequality as relevant to the specification of criteria for disclosing personal records. This might be thought to be remarkable given that the complainants in the *O'Connor* case were four aboriginal women charging a bishop, and former principal of the native residential school where they were students, with sexual offenses. In reviewing the release ordered by earlier courts of all the medical, psychiatric, and counseling records of these women, the Supreme Court set up a two-stage procedure for determining when such records could be disclosed. While the decision was meant to regulate what at that time was an increased demand for personal records as a result of constitutional challenges to legislation that restricted access, the clarification of guidelines had the untoward effect of opening access to these records, an effect that the Supreme Court attempted to then rectify in their subsequent decision in *R. v. Mills* [1999].

In "Dependence in Client-Therapist Relationships: A Relational Reading of *O'Connor* and *Mills*," Sue Campbell borrows from my own work on a relational account of equality to argue that a contextual analysis of women's inequality is relevant to the determination of criteria for records disclosure. She argues that in upholding restrictions on records disclosure, the Supreme Court decision in *Mills* has provided the sort of contextual and substantive interpretation of equality missing in *O'Connor*. She finds in *Mills* a move away from an individualist notion of privacy to an "approach that stresses the role of privacy in creating certain relational possibilities" (Campbell, 2002, p. 28). When interpreted in this way, the Supreme Court decision in *Mills* can be viewed as defending therapeutic relationships as playing a vital role in the lives of those who need these resources to develop and make possible other relationships of trust and equality in both the private and public spheres. I take the goal of creating relationships of trust and equality to be an argument strengthening the case for protecting confidentiality in the context of therapeutic relationships and will develop this further later.

O'Connor and *Mills* demonstrate that feminists have had some success in the Canadian context in making equality arguments heard and articulated in the formulation of legislation and in Supreme Court decisions. Denike warns, however, that the successes have been hard won and are often followed by reversals: "every one of the legislative reforms introduced since the 1970s to inflect jurisprudence with considerations of women's equality and human dignity have been continually subjected to constitutional challenges. And in each instance they've been made on the same grounds: the compromise they make to the rights of the accused" (Denike, 2000, p. 10). There is no doubt that the right to a fair trial and to full answer and defense are extremely important. I have not set out to undermine their importance, but rather to provide a relational reading of the right to privacy that expands our understanding of it and thereby strengthens arguments for confidentiality. But there are objections that can be raised to my reasoning thus far and they need to be addressed; even if only briefly here.

My argument about the relevance of political contexts to an analysis of rights could suggest that the right to full answer and defense is even more important in political contexts where the death penalty is allowed. This is an interesting consideration that should affect the way the right to privacy is discussed and defended in the United States, for example. One could argue that the need to have access to personal records to prove a person's innocence is more pressing when the possible consequence is being sentenced to death. The right to full answer and defense in this context might be thought to take precedence over the right to privacy, but I want to question this and will do so after outlining the second and related objection. One could also object that my approach calls for the application of relational insights to the right to full answer and defense in the way that I have applied it to the right to privacy. There are cases in which members of disadvantaged groups are falsely accused of crimes, for example, and where the therapeutic records of the complainant might be thought to be relevant to the determination of innocence. Admittedly, I have not examined the right to full answer and defense fully here or given it the kind of relational reading I have provided for the right to privacy. That would seem to be a different and similarly complex project. But I want to say two things in answer to these sorts of objections.

First, I am not defending the idea that psychotherapeutic relationships should have *absolute* privileged status with respect to confidentiality. In Canada, for example and at this time, current legislation and policy favors the protection of confidentiality while providing criteria for determining when it can be justifiably breached in particular cases. This sort of case-by-case analysis fits with the contextual and relational approach I have been advocating. However, the brief discussion of the Supreme Court *O'Connor* and *Mills* decisions shows that there is more to the analysis than a defense of confidentiality on a case-by-case basis. I have argued that the criteria for determining justifiable breaches need to be informed by a relational understanding of inequalities. Individuals are not similarly situated with equal amounts of power and influence either in their private or public relationships. These factors should be treated as relevant to the determination of criteria for records disclosure. In examining these factors we have discovered that we need to pay attention to the right to privacy, and arguments defending it, when not doing so has had and continues to have a detrimental impact and burden on members of disadvantaged groups. But there is another argument on the side of assigning greater weight to protecting confidentiality over the right to full answer and defense: access to psychotherapeutic records will not satisfy the right to full answer and defense in any case. A relational approach can help to illustrate this.

A relational approach provides the kind of careful, detailed, and contextual analysis of what happens in both the psychotherapeutic relationship and the courts that can explain why it is far from clear that the information disclosed in these relationships can be conceived as revealing the kind of facts the courts are looking for. This point has been made by psychotherapists and analysts, who argue that the therapeutic process presents an entire spectrum of thought and emotion often conflicted and conflicting over time (for support of the idea of a fundamental conflict between the function of the psychotherapeutic relationship and the function of the courts, see Allannah Furlong and Paul Mosher in this volume). What is recorded by psychotherapists is inherently subject to misinterpretation and is unlikely to have the probative value that aids the fact-finding mission of the law. In fact, Canadian Supreme Court Justice Claire L'Heureux-Dubé acknowledged this argument about the inherent lack of probative value in therapeutic records in her dissent in *O'Connor* (*R. v. O'Connor* [1995], paras. 109 and 144).

A relational approach adds complexity to this analysis by pointing out how particular relationships, both at the personal and public levels, shape the thought and emotion of those who are disadvantaged in ways that undermine their trust and confidence in their own beliefs and assertions. For such clients, therapeutic records that document conflicts of this sort are likely to be interpreted as confirming judgments about their lack of credibility, integrity, and stability. Stereotypical perceptions of those who are disadvantaged infect not only the recording of what is said by patients in therapeutic relationships, but also how the courts interpret that speech. An illustration will demonstrate the force of the argument that these records not only lack probative value, they are also inherently prejudicial.

To treat statements recorded in a therapeutic relationship as disclosing facts is extremely problematic when we think about cases in which a woman tells her therapist that she has pangs of guilt because she wonders whether her behavior constituted consent to the sexual assault she has reported. In a context in which women are told that they need to be careful about what they wear, how late they go out at night, and where they go with acquaintances, feelings of guilt and doubt about one's sexual choices are perfectly reasonable. This context of social expectations that women should restrict their activities and choices also explains why this woman's expression of guilt when taken out of context may be used to justify the plaintiff's claim that he had reason to believe that the complainant consented. We then need to add to this complex network of relationships the difficulties involved in recording and interpreting how the same feelings and beliefs explored over the space of time in treatment can be rejected, embraced, evaluated, scrutinized, or revised. Busby examines a real life case of this sort in *Osolin*, where after undergoing a grueling cross-examination in court about her behavior on the day the rape took place, the complainant was also expected to comment on a report in the psychotherapist's records to the effect that she "is concerned that her attitude and behavior may have influenced the man to some extent and is having second thoughts about the entire case" (Busby, 1997, pp. 159–160; Busby in this volume).

5. The Psychotherapeutic Relationship as a Space for Promoting Equality

A relational account asks us to examine the very relationships that get scrutinized when personal records are accessible to the courts. All of the relationships examined above, including those between psychotherapists and patients, are ones of authority and power. Issues of power were magnified in the case of the aboriginal women in the native residential school, who in dealing with and speaking to priests, doctors, and therapists already had reason to distrust these relationships. Elements of power and authority are magnified when patients are members of traditionally disadvantaged groups. In our social context, relationships between those in power and those who are members of traditionally disadvantaged groups are effected and shaped on both sides by the stereotypes about and self-perceptions of what it means to be a woman, or disabled, or a person of color in a context in which these factors continue to result in inequalities of various sorts. These relationships, already characterized by differences in levels of power, are susceptible to high levels of mistrust on the part of the patient and of misunderstanding on the part of the therapist and others in power. Both of these factors are further enhanced in milieus of considerable differences in the life experiences of patient and therapist. These factors not only call for responsibility and accountability on the part of professionals in these kinds of asymmetrical relationships; they also call for an understanding of the importance of these relationships as social mechanisms for creating a context of trust, enhancing self-understanding, fostering self-respect, and promoting equality.

We think of relationships in which people seek counsel or get help with a life crisis as ones that allow individuals the privacy they need to improve their lives, enhance self-development, and increase opportunities and levels of self-respect. However, once we place the therapeutic relationship into the broader context of a network of institutional, public, professional, and political relationships, the fragility of the trust so necessary to sharing feelings and personal information emerges starkly in relationships between psychotherapists and members of disadvantaged groups. As Campbell points out, "we may have a general idea of autonomy as the ability to direct one's life, or of privacy as limited accessibility, but we need to understand how to give content and support to these ideals in the specific contexts within which they may be applicable. For this, we require information about people's identities, self-concepts, and circumstances" (Campbell, 2002, p. 6). Thus the harms of breaching confidentiality need to be understood in the context of the particular lives effected by that breach and of the sorts of relationships a society ought to promote.

Distrust, fear, lack of confidence and self-respect, and self-blame are likely to be background features in the life of the disadvantaged person who seeks out and then works within a therapeutic relationship. For many, this relationship may be virtually the only place where a person shattered by relationships of abuse and powerlessness feels safe and develops a sense of self-worth. These features of particular persons and their identities, self-concepts, and circumstances should be weighed by the state in determining when records of what has taken place in a therapeutic relationship should be disclosed to the courts.

Disclosing the records of the therapeutic relationships of members of oppressed groups results in breaches of trust at many levels. When it is possible for judges and lawyers to obtain these records, members of disadvantaged groups may be more hesitant to seek help through these avenues. As argued earlier, state "speech" that defends broad policies of disclosure has the effect of silencing citizen listeners who are particularly vulnerable to feelings of distrust. These patients may have even less reason to trust that psychotherapists will protect them or resist court orders of disclosure. Trust in the probable success of the therapeutic relationship may be undermined when psychotherapists are forced to be careful about what they record and patients are forced to be careful about what they say. When the institutional message is that members of disadvantaged groups cannot be believed or trusted to tell the truth about their experiences, it is reasonable to think that they may not trust that psychotherapists will believe them either. Members of disadvantaged groups, particularly those who have been abused, often enter into therapeutic relationships reluctantly; believing that they asked for or deserve the abuse. They may conclude that they cannot work through these thoughts and feelings openly with psychotherapists precisely because these sorts of statements can be and have been used to "prove" their guilt in court. Moreover, when courts make statements shared in confidence the grounds for doubting the person who accuses another of abuse, this feeds back into beliefs that members of oppressed groups cannot be trusted to tell their stories accurately. Trust can be undermined in all these ways when breaches of confidentiality are legitimized and mandated by the courts in the very relationships that are potential spaces for building this trust. In short, breaches of trust are more harmful for members of oppressed groups than for those with power and privilege. If we think of the therapeutic relationship as containing possibilities for promoting self-development, we also think of it as a place to eliminate rather than maintain damaging and unequal relationships.

Making reference to my work on a relational account of equality, Campbell writes: "feminist theorists have argued that, within the context of substantive inequalities, we must pay particular attention to relationships that undermine persons, their self-concepts, abilities, and opportunities; that shape values and structure continued interactions in ways that entrench rather than ameliorate inequalities" (Campbell, 2002, p. 7). We promote the goal of equality for individuals who are members of disadvantaged groups when the psychotherapeutic relationships they are in are protected from intrusion and examination by the courts. Trusting that accounts of our feelings and life experiences will be listened to and respected is but one way of undoing the damage to autonomy and self-respect perpetuated by unequal personal and public relationships.

6. Conclusion

I have argued that reconceiving the right to privacy in our context of continuing inequalities and unequal relationships expands the debate so as to make equality considerations central to questions of policy regarding confidentiality. Confidentiality can then be understood as promoting equality. However, I need to clarify that I have not argued that protection of confidentiality is absolute and trumps all other values, particularly that of an individual's right to full answer and defense. Nor have I argued that the law needs to accord special protection of confidentiality for members of disadvantaged groups only; though my argument favors an understanding of confidentiality as an affirmative action type measure (broadly conceived) that can help to alleviate inequalities for members of disadvantaged groups. I, thus, embrace rather than reject Bruce Archibald's concern that "equality analysis pushed to the limit could raise personal or relational privilege to the level of an instrument of affirmative action for certain classes of persons suffering from discrimination" (Archibald, 1999, p. 43). This said, the main purpose of the chapter has been the more modest goal of expanding the debate beyond the narrow purview of competing individual rights and showing that equality arguments are relevant to policies and legislation with respect to confidentiality.

We need to extend the terms of the debate on confidentiality and to transform liberal notions of individuals, rights, and equality. A relational approach to confidentiality and the corresponding defense of the protection of it reconceives the individual rights valued and taken for granted in liberal democratic societies and, more particularly, the individual right to privacy. The right to privacy is indeed respect for an individual's freedom to pursue therapeutic relationships as a way to shape and reshape his or her life, identity, and values, but it cannot be understood in the abstract apart from social conditions and practices that further undermine that right for some individuals. The goal of this chapter has been to strengthen arguments for confidentiality by showing that it needs to be conceived relationally as both an individual right and a social good in our political context of entrenched and continuing inequalities. Reconceiving the right to privacy and the value of confidentiality relationally explains why psychotherapeutic relationships deserve special protection. A relational approach defends confidentiality as one way of increasing equality for those who are members of disadvantaged groups. The debate on confidentiality needs to take these factors into account in its evaluation and formulation of appropriate psychotherapeutic practices, of social policy, and of legislation regarding confidentiality.

Acknowledgments

This paper was first presented at the "Confidentiality & Society" Conference in Montreal in October 2000. The reaction I got from psychotherapists there, which was that broader issues of inequality and discrimination of members of traditionally disadvantaged groups is not taken by them to be relevant to an account of confidentiality, motivated me to articulate the relevance of equality considerations to policies regarding confidentiality. I am also grateful for the feedback I got when I presented the paper at Queen's University, in particular that from Alistair Macleod. I also want to thank Sue Campbell, Jay Drydyk, Michael Yeo, Andrew Brook, Allannah Furlong, and Charles Levin for the comments and suggestions they provided in the process of revisions.

Works Cited

Archibald, Bruce P. (1999) "The Uncertain 'Revolution' in the Canadian Law of Evidentiary Privilege: What Principles Take Us Where?" Presented at the Second World Conference on New Trends in Criminal Investigation and Evidence, Amsterdam, The Netherlands.

Bonnie, Richard. (2000) "Confidentiality in the Formerly Communist World: A Case Study in Mental Health Reform," Presented at "Confidentiality & Society: Therapy, Ethics and the Law, Social, Philosophical and Psychoanalytic Perspectives" in Montreal, 14 October.

Busby, Karen. (1997) "Discriminatory Uses of Personal Records in Sexual Violence Cases," *Canadian Journal of Women and the Law,* 9: pp. 148–177.

Campbell, Sue. (2002) "Dependence in Client-Therapist Relationships: A Relational Reading of *O'Connor* and *Mills.*" In Law Commission of Canada, ed. *Personal Relationships of Dependence and Interdependence in Law.* Vancouver: University of British Columbia Press, pp. 3–37.

Code, Lorraine. (1991) *What Can She Know? Feminist Theory and the Construction of Knowledge*. Ithaca, NY: Cornell University Press.

Denike, Margaret. (2000) "Credibility and Feminist Legal Strategy," Presented at the Conference on the Feminine Principle, University of Texas at Arlington.

Heldke, Lisa. (1991) "Do You Mind if I Speak Freely? Reconceptualizing Freedom of Speech." *Social Theory and Practice,* 17(3): pp. 349–368. Reprinted in *Moral Issues in Global Perspective*, ed. Christine Koggel. Peterborough: Broadview, 1999, pp. 676–686.

Kelly, Katherine D. (1997) "'You Must be Crazy if You Think You Were Raped': Reflections on the Use of Complainants' Personal and Therapy Records in Sexual Assault Trials." *Canadian Journal of Women and the Law,* 9: pp. 179–195.

Koggel, Christine. (1998) *Perspectives on Equality: Constructing a Relational Theory.* Lanham, MD: Rowman & Littlefield.

———, ed. (1999) *Moral Issues in Global Perspective.* Peterborough, Ontario: Broadview Press.

Nedelsky, Jennifer. (1989) "Reconceiving Autonomy: Sources, Thoughts, and Possibilities." *Yale Journal of Law and Feminism,* 1(7): pp. 7–36. Reprinted in *Moral Issues in Global Perspective,* ed. Christine Koggel. Peterborough, Ontario: Broadview Press, pp. 510–522.

R. v. *Mills.* [1999] 3 Supreme Court Reports 668.

R. v. *O'Connor.* [1995] 4 Supreme Court Reports 411.

Schoeman, Ferdinand D., ed. (1984) *Philosophical Dimensions of Privacy: An Anthology.* Cambridge: Cambridge University Press.

Sherwin, Susan. (1998) "A Relational Approach to Autonomy in Health Care." In *The Politics of Women's Health: Exploring Agency and Autonomy.* The Feminist Health Care Ethics Research Network (Susan Sherwin, coordinator). Philadelphia: Temple University Press, pp. 19–47.

Eight

SEXUAL INEQUALITY AND THE CRISIS OF CONFIDENTIALITY: THE MYTH AND THE LAW ON PERSONAL RECORDS

Margaret Denike

1. Introduction

Psychiatrists, psychotherapists, counselors, and crisis workers have expressed grave concern about the recent "invasion of privacy" and the "crisis of confidentiality" concerning their relations and recorded communication with their clients. Personal records, widely viewed as private, confidential, and/or privileged, have become accessible to the public, and particularly to the courts, to be used as evidence in civil and criminal trials. Over the past decade, rape complainants and/or their counselors or psychotherapists have been increasingly compelled by the courts to produce and disclose personal information to assist in determining the "truth" of the allegations brought against the accused. The justification for this relatively new feature of Canadian sexual assault trials typically invokes the fundamental rights of the accused: it is necessary to ensure that the accused be granted a "fair trial" and, to this end, the information on or about the complainants and plaintiffs, such as their medical or psychiatric records, is for use to assist in his defense. The judiciary has not only tolerated such requests; together with a responsive legislature, it has implemented, refined, and codified procedures for securing their access, assessing their relevance, and producing them to the court (*R. v. O'Connor* [1995]). While the disclosure of personal, medical, and psychiatric records for such public proceedings was relatively unheard of until about a decade ago, once the courts ruled that such records may shed evidentiary light on a complainant's credibility or her ability to testify, it quickly became a "standard practice" used by defense counsel, typically in sexual assault trials (Busby, 2001, 1995; F. Kelly, 1997). Within the next five years, it became known to feminists as the leading defense strategy for intimidating and humiliating complainants and for deterring them from pursuing criminal charges or civil remedies.

This chapter offers a feminist analysis of the "crisis of confidentiality," with a view to the socio-semiotic, political, and legal context in which records requests are made and continue to prosper. I begin by addressing the fact that applications and orders to produce such records do not occur in just any and every criminal proceeding, but quite specifically and overwhelmingly in sexual assault trials. In this respect, to make sense of what the "invasions" of privacy are all about, we need to look at what has been going on in sexual assault law and the kinds of rights and interests that are presumed to be at stake in it. For the purpose of this chapter, this includes an analysis of the myths and representations around which our systems of meaning and value are organized and that structure social relations and the laws that govern them.

In the first part of this chapter, I elucidate the roles played by certain time-honored representations and prescriptions about women's character, behavior, and status, including those that foster the sexual guilt and shame of their ascetic and religious heritage: namely, those that have tended to characterize women as deceptive and vindictive seductresses; or those who imagine, following the leading interpretations of the creation myth in *Genesis*, that men may be at risk from the allure and the trickery of female sexual voracity, as she plots to bring about his fall from grace. Such myths define and represent woman's thoughts and actions from the point of view of men in a way that ensures male access to and control over her sexuality, by making it far less likely that she would be believed if she speaks of resisting or refusing his sexual advances, that is to say, if and when her account (of rape) differs from his (of consensual seduction). The objective of my analysis is to make evident the need for social policy and law reform initiatives to come to terms with such myths and their critical role in perpetuating sexual inequality; that is, in shaping the laws and logos of legal reasoning governing social relations. To develop effective responses to the crisis of confidentiality, we need to address such myths because they have precipitated the practice and procedure of records' disclosure and reduced legal proceedings for sexual violence to a matter of assessing the credibility of its survivors. More generally, and in other contexts, they have given form to various common law principles pertaining to the rights of the accused and to the treatment of and obligations imposed on sexual assault complainants. They have skewed the very perception and meaning of "rights"—such as the right to a "fair trial" or to "full answer and defense"—and the very perception and meaning of relationships shaped by these rights (including social and sexual relations of power, respect, trust, care, responsibility, and accountability).

For an operative definition of equality employed in the context of Canadian social policy, I have in mind the Supreme Court of Canada's definition, which is set out in the *Law* decision, in its summary of the objectives of the Section 15 equality guarantees of the *Canadian Charter of Rights and Freedoms*, "to prevent the violation of essential human dignity and freedom through the imposition of disadvantage, stereotyping, or political or social prejudice, and to promote a society in which all persons enjoy equal recognition at law as human beings or as members of Canadian society, equally capable and equally deserving of concern, respect and consideration" (*Law v. Canada* [1999], para. 51: for another account of equality under the *Charter*, see *Law Society of British Columbia et al. v. Andrews et al.* [1989]). With the aim of bringing a substantive equality analysis to the topic of confidentiality, rethinking the rights presumed to be at stake, and seeking direction for responsive laws and social policies, I draw on the legal theory of Jennifer Nedelsky, and particularly her analysis and critique of liberal and individualist conceptions of rights, such as privacy and autonomy. Her examination of the metaphoric import of rights discourses, and the nature of the relationships they reflect and reinforce helps to identify some of the limitations we would face in demanding the right to privacy or making the claim to privilege as a response to this crisis. Insisting that we recognize the extent to which individuals are social creatures immersed in networks and hierarchies of relations, Nedelsky urges us to look closely at the myths and metaphors used to give meaning and texture to rights, and to inquire as to the relationships they support or foster. If we do so in the context of sexual assault law, we come up against an individualizing conception of rights that dwells almost exclusively on the singular relation between the accused and the state, and that construes and defines power and oppression as a matter of the male subject's vulnerability to the malicious and vindictive actions of the state (or, for different reasons, of women, for that matter). We also confront the extent to which rights are reified as things that the accused "has" as a limit to the state's negative and abusive treatment of him. Informed by misogynist myths and stereotypes, and buttressed by a liberal tradition of anti-statism, these rights reinforce relations of power along such lines as gender, class, race, among others. Nedelsky convincingly demonstrates the importance of "rethinking rights," not as possessions (be they property, speech, belief, a fair trial), nor as "limits" or "trumps" to state action or intervention. We need to think of them instead as *capacities* to form or to foster certain relationships around values such as care, respect, and trust. In "rethinking rights as relationships," we are also pressed to reconfigure our strategies of social and legal reform by reconceptualizing the role that the state could play, not in "staying out" of the private domain or ceasing to interfere with confidential relations, but in fulfilling its positive obligation to actively guarantee "essential human dignity and freedom from stereotyping and social and political prejudice" (*Law v. Canada* [1999], para. 51), that is, to *promote* equality and to foster the relationships that enable equality to flourish. Although the rhetoric of individualism that has pervaded rights discourse works to conceal the fact, these rights and/or values always speak of social and political interrelations, in this instance between social groups that have been historically at risk of the exploitation and the disadvantage born of stereotyping or prejudice.

2. The Problem with Myth

As many feminist writers have noted, a definitive feature of western patriarchy is its deep ambivalence toward femininity and female sexuality. Enduring patterns of myths and metaphors that speak of a deep-seated fear of, and desire for, women are evident across the centuries of representations constitutive of Western Judeo-Christian cultures. Among the dominant themes of patriarchal monotheism's mythic universe, is the association or equation between woman/seduction and sex/sin (Kristeva, 1982; Brown, 1988; Brundage, 1987). A quick glance at Christian theological literature and doctrine makes apparent the extent to which this equation is repeatedly constituted and reinforced through the deployment of certain creation myths, such as that of Eve's inaugural temptation and seduction. It is to Eve that the sexual ascetics and founders of early Christianity first looked to account for the introduction of sin into what they saw as an otherwise edenic world, and for bringing about the expulsion and fall of "man" (Kvam, Schearing & Ziegler, 1999). The subjection of woman was inseparable from this. Countless other stories that have been told by men about women and woman's desire, including the widely influential Pauline doctrine that dominates the New Testament, which rationalizes concerns about the "weaker sex" to justify her silence and obedience to men. Such practices have been extensively documented, for example, with James Brundage's major work, *Law, Sex and Christian Society.* Brundage provides ample evidence of the ways that the negative attitudes about the "indecency" and "impurity" of sex, which are commonplace in the ethos of western Judeo-Christianity, are related to the misogyny entrenched in many Christian beliefs and practices and the restrictive roles imposed on women. Such literature provides a vast and diverse archive of how the theological view of woman as "the embodiment of sexual allure and temptation" was largely the basis for stripping women of credibility and "systematically excluding women from primary roles of power and authority in the Christian establishment" (Brundage, 1987, p. 609). They have also served the political objective of holding women accountable for sexual transgression, while effectively facilitating male access to, and control of, women's sexuality.

Archaic, misogynist stereotypes about how women "lure" men into sexual sin would be hardly worth mentioning were they mere relics of the distant past. Their historical tenacity and predominance in contemporary laws have been an obstacle to the achievement of social equality and to our ability to foster the kinds of social relations that will grant dignity and freedom to all individuals. Consider, for example, the longevity of ascetic doctrine of early Church Fathers like Tertullian (circa 160–circa 225, Common Era), whose deep distrust of women's malign, seductive wiles pervades almost two millennia of Canon and secular law related to sexual practices. In his treatise, "On the Apparel of Women" (Tertullian, 1997, circa 202, Common Era), Tertullian rebukes women for her provocative dress, speech, gait, manner, and demeanor, and he looks to such features to account for how she tempts otherwise honorable men into the evil of fornication, as she did in causing the fall of man from grace (Tertullian,

1997, pp. 25–52). Woman's chastity, which *is* her value in the political economy of patriarchy, is not in her control. It is not a matter of how she actually acts or conducts herself, but of how men respond to her sexually, *despite* what she does or wears: "it's not good enough to be known by God to be chaste … one must *seem* to be chaste" as well (Tertullian, 1997, p. 49).

However absurd or inappropriate they may seem, it is not uncommon to find articulated as law many such views about female chastity and about the relation between her appearance, reputation, and her culpability for sexual transgression. Take, for example, the reasoning of Alberta Court of Appeal judge, John McClung, in the 1998 sexual assault case of Mr. Ewanchuk. For McClung, although the complainant explicitly refused Ewanchuk's persistent sexual groping during a job interview, he reasoned that her consent to his sexual advances was "implied" by the fact that she was not a virgin, that she had lived with her boyfriend, and by how she was dressed at the time. "It must be pointed out that the complainant did not present herself to Ewanchuk or enter his trailer in a bonnet and crinolines. … She was the mother of a six month-old baby and ... along with her boyfriend, she shared an apartment with another couple" (*R. v. Ewanchuk* [1998], para. 4). It was on this basis that Ewanchuk was acquitted.

It would be nice to think that most law makers and triers of fact would agree with the Supreme Court's decision in this case (written by Claire L'Heureux-Dubé and Charles Gonthier) that such "archaic beliefs" should have no place in Canadian law. The problem, as Madame Justice Claire L'Heureux-Dubé puts it, is that we are up against a rather long history of entrenched myths permeating judicial discretion, which has left the law in this area "saturated" with stereotypes. Historically, such misogynist sexual morality has animated common law rules and procedures for rape, such as the need for a complainant to show evidence of penetration, the requirement that her testimony be corroborated, the requirement that she report the incident immediately after it has occurred, the requirement that juries be warned about convicting an accused on the basis of the complainant's testimony alone, and the judicial toleration of using complainant's sexual history to impugn her credibility (Sheehy, 1999). This sexual morality has given "meaning and texture" to the rights we presume to be at stake in these trials. It has made sexual assault trials unique among criminal proceedings for their aggressive treatment of complainants through the latitude granted to defense counsel to shift the question of culpability to her from the accused, just as had been done under Tertullian's dictum on chastity. These prejudicial representations are critical to understanding the latest manifestation of such tactics: the proliferation of applications by defense counsel and the judicial orders for the disclosure of the personal records of rape complainants and/or their counselors, psychotherapists, and so on, as disputed evidence to establish the facts on trial.

To the extent that the court grants currency to the unfounded notion that sexual assault complainants are more likely to lie or to maliciously launch false allegations than complainants in other criminal trials, special and exceptional rules are considered necessary to protect an accused. They have rendered rape law a matter of man's freedom (from false accusation), and in doing so, they detract consideration from the systemic inequalities and social tragedy that the sexual politics of rape is all about and from how sexual violence is institutionally sanctioned across lines of sex, race, age, ability, and other grounds. Furthermore, they pre-empt the positive obligations of the government to find effective means, remedies, and language to curb, much less to eradicate, sexual violence and to support and enhance relations of social and sexual equality.

3. The Context and Significance of *O'Connor*

It is well documented that the overwhelming majority of requests for third party records occurs in criminal cases where the accused is charged with a sexual offense. Among the case law studies and comparative analyses of requests made for these records, conducted in the wake of the "crisis in confidentiality" following the *O'Connor* (1995) Supreme Court decision, Oleskiw and Tellier's showed that sexual offences made up eighty five percent (120 of 140 cases accessible on Quicklaw) (Oleskiw and Tellier, 1997, pp. 5–8; also Busby, 1995). This pattern has also been acknowledged by Parliament and by the Supreme Court of Canada (*R. v. Mills* [1999]).

In December 1992, Bishop O'Connor first stood trial for several counts of sexual assault and indecent exposure committed in the 1960's against students at a Native residential school where he had served as principal. Without issuing any notice to the complainants prior to the trial, O'Connor sought and obtained an order for the defendants' personal records. In addition to ordering Crown to produce names and contact information of any therapist, counselor, psychologist, or psychiatrist who had treated the complainants and all educational and employment records kept while the complainants attended the school, the court issued an order that authorized "all therapists, counselors, psychologists, and psychiatrists who have treated any of them with respect to allegations of sexual assault or sexual abuse, to produce to the Crown copies of their complete file contents and any other related material including all documents, notes, records, reports, tape recordings, and videotapes, and the Crown to provide copies of all this material to counsel for the accused forthwith" (*R. v. O'Connor* Case on Appeal, Volume 3, Order, pp. 422–423; see Van Dieen, 1997). On appeal by the Crown, the British Columbia Court of Appeal established what it saw as a "fair" scheme for "balancing" the rights of complainants with the fair trial rights of the accused. It devised a two-step procedure for obtaining and producing personal records of sexual assault complainants, which was subsequently adopted and slightly modified by the Supreme Court of Canada. At the first stage, before records are disclosed to anyone, the accused applies to the judge to determine in camera whether the records in question are "likely relevant" to the issues at trial or to the competence of the complainant to testify. If the records are determined to be "likely relevant," they are turned over to the judge. At this second stage, the task is for the judge to "balance" the competing rights and interests at stake before deciding if they are to be further disclosed to the court and to the accused. For an analysis of the disclosure procedures, see Feldthusen (1996), Busby (1997), Frances Kelly (1997), and Sampson (1998).

The sheer breadth and scope of the original order should give rise to concern about the racial and sexual politics that were at play. Would such a sweeping order have been issued if the accused had not been of such stature within the church or if the complainants had not been native women? To what extent does such an order reflect the judicial presumption that these women lacked the kind of credibility that would have been unquestioningly granted to him and that they were likely to have launched malicious and false accusations about such an authority? What is it that could possibly make "all" available and recorded information about the complainants relevant evidence in this trial? What could justify the constitionalizing of the right for their accused rapist to be granted unlimited access to their personal records?

It is significant that the crisis of confidentiality has occurred just when those who are among the most historically colonized, disenfranchised, and silenced, such as aboriginal women and children of residential schools, have refused to be silenced about sexual abuse and have demanded accountability, redress, and compensation from their governments, their institutions, the authorities who ran them, and their abusers. When O'Connor was sentenced to two years for the sexual assault of former students, the big story for the media was that he was the "highest church official" yet to be sentenced for such a crime. As we know, this does not mean that he was the first among his rank to be accused, nor the first to concoct new tactics to silence his accusers. It does mean that those who are being accused have a tougher time counting on the secrecy and privilege that kept them above and beyond the law. Consider, for example, the thousands of cases involving church and other institutional officials currently under investigation or in mediation, the public inquiries and hearings into institutional abuse recently engaged by the Law Commission of Canada, and the pilot projects and other restorative justice and redress programs launched by provincial, federal, and territorial governments over the past decade. In retrospect, it appears that O'Connor's trial was but the tip of an enormous iceberg, only a small part of which will ever come into view, and some of which has been made to disappear, discretely, from public scrutiny. But the fact that the most disenfranchised and colonized individuals and groups can be, and have been, heard at all on the matter of sexual transgression (at least to the point of seeing charges laid against such authorities) in such public forums as the courts and national commissions, is rather remarkable in its own right. It amounts to an insurrection against traditional, hierarchical relations of power and privilege (with all the implications for credibility, responsibility, and accountability)—a crisis of confidence, so to speak.

These direct challenges to the historical sanctioning of sexual abuse, and this scrutiny of the integrity of institutional authority has not been without persistent resistance and backlash. As various feminists have noted, now that "rape" shield reforms, and particularly those implemented through Bill C–49 in 1992, have imposed restrictions on the defense ploy of using a complainant's sexual history to impugn her credibility, defense counsel have simply resorted to another ploy, namely, that of using her personal records. The latter is generally recognized as the leading tactic for shifting the culpability from the accused back to the complainant and effectively reasserting the masculinist standpoint about whether and how her consent was implied. The tactic exploits the myths that women "cry rape," falsely remember or reconstruct sexual scenes, or maliciously fabricate accusations (Busby, 2001; Sheehy, 1999; K. Kelly, 1997; Mack, 1993). The tactic also shifts the discourse of the rights and/or relations that are at stake in sexual assault trials from that of responsibility and accountability to eradicate systemic violence against vulnerable groups to the accused's individual vulnerability to women's vindictive lies. This shift entrenches and reinforces relations of illegitimate power and the correlative discriminatory myths that constitutional litigation should instead erode.

Consider, for example, the language used by the majority of Supreme Court judges in *O'Connor* to frame the disclosure procedures. As Bruce Feldthusen has pointed out, the fact that they emphasize the need to balance the accused's "fundamental right" to full answer and defense against the complainant's "interests" in privacy reflects that the scales of justice are tipped in the accused's favor from the outset. As was also evident in the post-*O'Connor* rulings involving records requests (Busby, 2001), the complainant's privacy and equality rights matter very little, if at all. "If the judge finds that there is a reasonable possibility the information in the records is relevant to the accused's right to make full answer and defense, no abstract privacy concerns will ever tip the scales against production" (Feldthusen, 1996, p. 555). For all of the talk about "balancing" competing rights, and all the nuances to the tests and procedures, "the production of private therapeutic records in a sexual assault trial will turn on one thing only: whether the judge determines they are relevant to the accused's right of full answer and defence" (Feldthusen, 1996, p. 558). The *O'Connor* guidelines offer the appearance of objective assessment of relevance, all the while concealing the reality of the subjective ideas about women's credibility and sexuality central to assessing the need for such extraordinary evidence as personal records. The fact that the test exists at all betrays the underlying assumption that rape complainants, and especially those who have sought any form of counseling, are either less trustworthy or less capable of truthfully testifying about sex and that the records would be evidence of this. The myths alone translate into a presumption of the relevance of her records. While there is no evidence to suggest that rape complainants are more prone to lie than complainants and witnesses for any other crime, the presumption remains, and it is left to judicial discretion to determine if and when personal records are needed to establish the truth. As long as there is currency to the stereotypes and myths about rape complainants, the privacy of "all" personal records can only be tenuous. The gates have simply been opened to regulate and facilitate access. This has been born out in practice (Busby, 2001).

Parliament was quick to respond to *O'Connor*, and to draft legislation (Bill C–46, May 1997; now sections 278.1 to 278.91 of the Criminal Code) to codify a modified and restrictive version of the *O'Connor* guidelines. This progressive legislation essentially attempted to do damage control for the *O'Connor* decision, and to bring to the *O'Connor* guidelines the equality considerations and analysis that were lacking in that decision. The preamble to this legislation stressed concern about the prevalence of sexual violence, Parliament's desire to encourage the reporting of incidents of sexual violence, and Parliament's recognition that the compelled production of records would deter the reporting of offenses or the seeking of counseling or advice by complainants. Under the new statute, section 278.5 details the factors that must be taken into account by the judge before he or she can order records to be produced. They include consideration of whether the request is based on discriminatory belief and the effect of the disclosure on the personal dignity and privacy rights of the accused. They also added to the *O'Connor* guidelines the further requirement that the production be "necessary in the interests of justice." A key point is the protection of the integrity of the trial process (now section 278.5[2][g]) and the effort to eliminate the myths and stereotypes that thrive in judicial discretion.

The fact that the new statute forced judges to make these additional considerations of the complainants was immediately contentious. Although the use of complainant's personal records was a recent development in criminal proceedings, many critics reacted as if any limits to the full disclosure of the sort ordered by the trial judge in *O'Connor* was a "flagrant violation" of the accused's fundamental rights. From the moment the legislation was passed in May 1997, civil libertarians and defense lawyers cried to the media and to the courts that Bill C–46 "went too far" in favoring the complainant, and this despite the fact that the spirit of the Bill was to bring the treatment of sexual assault complainants in line with those of witnesses and victims of other crimes. Writing for the *Alberta Report*, Davis Sheremata described it as a "legal travesty" as egregious as leaving men falsely accused of rape by vindictive women languishing in prison. Bill C–46, he says, "will make it harder for people falsely accused of rape to mount a full and complete defence by making counseling records of rape complainants virtually off limits" (Sheremata, 1997, p. 28). The unsubstantiated suggestion, of course, is that unlike allegations made of any other crime, those made about rape may well be false, and that the "rights" of the accused to full answer and defense should include having free reign to try to show this. Similarly, the headline in *BC Report* lamented that under the new legislation, those who are accused of sexual assault are effectively "[g]uilty until proven innocent: a new law will deny rape counseling records to defendants" (Verbug, 1996, p. 35). As journalist Peter Verbug describes it, the legislation "places the complainant's right to privacy in sexual assault cases ahead of the defendant's right to a fair trial" (Verbug, 1996, p. 35). Such media coverage worked to perpetuate the view that the primary rights at stake in such trials were a matter of men's vulnerability to deceitful women, all the while preempting the possibility that freedom from male sexual violence might be a consideration.

Various members of the judiciary reflected and reiterated such views: the lower courts were quick to accept constitutional challenges to the C–46 legislative reforms on the basis that the additional equality-minded considerations violated the accused's right to a fair trial. Of particular note are the decisions in the *Mills* and *Lee* cases, which both declared Bill C–46 unconstitutional within weeks of it having become law (*R. v. Lee* [1997]; *R. v. Mills* [1997]). It is no wonder that those who are prone to sympathize with accused rapists, and who begin with the presumption that accusations against them are false, would be bothered by this legislation: its whole point is to control the currency of the very discriminatory presumptions they are specifically vested in. It was designed to bring a measure of equality to relations of power and to curb the practices that violate women's human dignity and freedom through stereotypes and social prejudice.

Considering such facets of the social, legal, and political context of this "crisis of confidentiality," we might ask, what kind of response is appropriate or effective, and what shape and tenor should there be to the rights that we would collectively and democratically hope to advance? What is the nature of the relationships targeted by the courts' interpretations of rights claims? How do they compare to the relations we want to foster, if they are not ones that we know to be discriminatory or ones that reify relations of power, control, and sexual access or deter victims of violence from seeking counseling, support, or redress? And what approaches should we take, or call upon our governments to take, to help us get there? I pose these questions with a view to problematizing what appears to be the simple solution: demanding recognition of interests in and rights to privacy.

4. Reacting To the Crisis: Is Privacy the Solution?

In the therapeutic community, the confidentiality of client-therapist communications and records is widely understood to be a necessary condition of relations of trust and essential to the integrity of this relationship. Evident at forums such as the Montreal Conference on "Confidentiality & Society" (October 2000), there is a clear sense within this community that the courts simply do not understand that the confidentiality of communications between counselors, analysts, therapists and their clients is a necessary condition for the provision of effective treatment. In the same year that the *O'Connor* guidelines were affirmed by the Supreme Court, psychoanalysts Bollas and Sundelson described what they saw as a state-sanctioned "invasion" and "incursion" into a private and privileged domain, in response to which they call for collective defiance and resistance, an "organized political protection of psychoanalysis by its own practitioners" (Bollas and Sundelson, 1995, p. 166). They recommend that psychoanalytic societies and organizations adopt a clear statement or code asserting the absolute privilege of the analyst/client relation and their communications, much like that enjoyed by lawyers and priests (Bollas and Sundelson, 1995, p.166). They specifically suggest adopting the following code: "The contents of a psychoanalysis are strictly confidential and any and all disclosures by the psychoanalyst—such as discussing a patient with colleagues, arranging for a hospitalization, acting in the interests of a child patient—must be given in the understanding that confidentiality is maintained and that in all circumstances privilege is retained by the psychoanalyst" (Bollas and Sundelson, 1995, p. 156). Furthermore, they speak of defying court orders to disclose records, of resisting laws that "they know to be incorrect" (Bollas and Sundelson, 1995, p.172), and of maintaining, at the risk of arrest, a zero tolerance of any "incursions" on patient-psychoanalyst confidentiality (Bollas and Sundelson, 1995, p.175). Even abusive individuals, such as a patient who discloses that he is molesting his child, they argue, can be "managed" within the psychotherapeutic community by providing referrals to a clinic or to counseling (Bollas and Sundelson, 1995, p. 175). The clinic, and not the courts, they argue, could function "as a responsible partner for the remediation of the problem" (Bollas and Sundelson, 1995, p. 175). They use as an example a British case, which involves what they describe as an otherwise "decent man, hardworking, loyal, supportive," who was also "childlike and impulsive" enough to have been "sexually molesting two pre-adolescent daughters for several years" (Bollas and Sundelson, 1995, p. 174). The case, they say, was successfully resolved without using criminal intervention. The problem was kept "in the family," so to speak, as each family member was referred to a clinic, and the "father's problem, which had been deeply disturbing and confusing to his children and also to his wife, became an object of the whole family's right to redress" (Bollas and Sundelson, 1995, p. 175). Their insistence on advocating the "privilege" of the psychotherapeutic relationship in this way appears primarily to rationalize the autonomy and authority of their own institution (which is largely inaccessible to most victims of sexual violence, as they tend to be among the poor, marginalized and socially disadvantaged). Their recommendations directly undermine the possibility that our legal system could and should take a proactive role in ending such sexual exploitation.

Bollas and Sundelson's response to the "crisis" treats the state as the primary threat to values such as autonomy, privacy, and security and not as an entity that could be called upon for positive, remedial action to the practices that undermine them, or that could cultivate and foster the relations we value, and the values we cherish. They idealize a vision of liberal individualism, of being "left alone" by the state, which looms as menacing, invasive, and abusive, be it at the level of the judiciary or of law enforcement. The tropes of insulating, barricading, and protecting the "private"/"privileged" psychoanalytic and clinical setting are the very sort of "boundary metaphors," as Canadian legal scholar Jennifer Nedelsky calls them, that thrive in the discourse of liberal constitutionalism. In this tradition, individual values of freedom, autonomy, privacy, and security are very often depicted in terms of "bounded spheres," which, she contends, reflect "the original and lasting focus on property" (Nedelsky, 1991, p. 163) of constitutional law and the (propertied) few that the drafters designed these rights to protect. In this political and symbolic context, rights are typically conceived of as "trumps," as "limits to the legitimate scope of the state" (Nedelsky, 1991, p.162) or on how far state officials can go, for example, to pursue an investigation, to search for evidence, or to ensure an arrest or conviction.

Consider Nedelsky's example of the lasting image of "a man's home is his castle." This representation may well capture how man's security is tied to a sense of property that is "off limits," outside the reach of the state. However, such imagery says a very different thing about woman's security, especially considering that the greatest threat to her autonomy and freedom, and the greatest likelihood of being victimized by violence, as an abundance of social-scientific evidence clearly shows, occurs within such "bounded spheres" of man, namely the private sphere of his home/castle. Or consider, in the wider historical context, how it has been only quite recently that entitlement to property was even an option for women, much less for racially identifiable groups, who were basically counted as the property of man.

Such representations of autonomy and security, Nedelsky posits, construe rights in a way that reifies relations of power along racial, class, and gender lines and that sees citizens not in terms of their relationships with others, but as individuals in isolation, in a way that negates these relations and that excludes others. The "boundary metaphor," she concludes, "provides the wrong focus for exploring the best possibilities of human autonomy," in part because it sets such values in opposition to social relations of responsibility and accountability. In conjuring visions of individuation and isolation, the idea of "respecting boundaries," she notes, draws our minds away from relationships, and in effect, prevents us from giving "the relationships or the legal concepts that mask them the critical scrutiny they deserve" (Nedelsky, 1991, p. 178). We need a better way to articulate the relationships we want to foster. "We need a language of law whose metaphoric structure highlights rather than hides the patterns of relationship its constructs foster and reflect." She encourages us to develop "new mythic structures, new visions and metaphors" (Nedelsky, 1991, p. 163), and particularly ones that do not subordinate social and political rights to civil rights.

Through Canadian common law, the courts have tended to take a "trump"-like, boundary-setting approach to rights in general and to privacy rights in particular. Since *Hunter v. Southam* [1984], the Supreme Court has recognized that the right to privacy falls under section 8 of the *Charter*, which specifically provides "the right to be secure against unreasonable search and seizure." Privacy is thus tied to the same "legal rights" drafted by 18th to 19th century liberal philosophers with a view to the dark designs of a powerful state: fears of state intrusions on the private domain, of unannounced or unwarranted searches and seizures for damning evidence, of unjustified arrests and detentions, or of the denial to an accused of the ability to provide full answer and defense to the charges against him. As such, these rights have been interpreted to be primarily procedural in focus (that is, they have been applied primarily to defining what is fair and proper procedure for criminal investigations, trials, and imprisonment) and they are framed by what is presumed to be an adversarial relation between an aggressive, invasive, and oppressive state and a vulnerable rights-bearing citizen. Such a view has been expressed in several cases by the justices of the Supreme Court of Canada: in Justice LaForest's words, "privacy is at the heart of liberty in a modern state" (*R. v. Edwards* [1996], para. 427). In Justice Cory's words, privacy includes "the right to be free from intrusion or interference" (*R. v. Dyment* [1998], para. 50).

We see the same metaphors in the international human rights arena, particularly when nation states, led almost exclusively by men, demarcate the private, "cultural," or "religious" beliefs and practices of female genital mutilation, dowry killings, and the criminalization of divorce and abortion as being exempt from scrutiny and accountability to "public" international laws and standards of equality. Feminists have consistently argued that international human rights law rests on and reinforces a distinction between the public domain of state regulations and accountability and the "the inner sanctum of the private realm, where the pervasive human rights abuses against women prevail (Charlesworth, 1994, pp. 68–69), such that the latter is "cordoned off" from state accountability. The public/private distinction has political implications that are not unlike those of domestic sexual assault law, as discussed above: it concerns itself almost exclusively with men's rights to be protected against abusive government regimes and relegates women's "issues" or "interests" (including state-sanctioned sexual abuse, the lack of reproductive rights, pervasive practices of violence and femicide, and the traffic in women) to the "private" domain

(Gaer, 1998, p. 13).

As Catharine MacKinnon has argued, "the legal concept of privacy can and has shielded the place of battery, marital rape, and women's exploited labor; has preserved the central institutions whereby women are deprived of identity, autonomy, control and self-definition; and has protected the primary activity through which male supremacy is expressed and enforced" (MacKinnon, 1987, p. 101; also Romany, 1994; Cornell, 1998; Nussbaum, 2000). The refrain of privacy doctrine to the effect that the state should "stay out" of the home, the bedroom, the family, or marriage—or even out of the sanctity and privilege of the Church's jurisdiction—is basically code for "staying out" of sexuality, such that the "private" practices of inequality can stay intact,

> [B]y staying out of marriage and the family, prominently meaning sexuality... the law of privacy proposes to guarantee individual bodily integrity, personal exercise of moral intelligence, and freedom of intimacy. But if one asks whether women's rights to these values have been guaranteed, it appears that the law of privacy works to translate traditional social values into the rhetoric of individual rights as a means of subordinating those rights to specific social imperatives (MacKinnon, 1987, pp. 96–97).

This is not to say that there is something inherently problematic about advancing privacy rights for women, especially considering how, historically, women have not really had any. Rather, it is a matter of making the way we understand, interpret, and apply them more consistent with values such as social equality, more attentive to the fact that we are social creatures living in and through our relations with others (whatever form they take), and more vested in optimizing values of respect, care, trust, and responsibility in those relationships (Nedelsky, 1991, p. 169).

In the recent sexual assault appeal of Brian Joseph Mills, while the majority of the Supreme Court of Canada (per L'Heureux-Dubé, Gonthier, McLachlin, Iacobucci, Major, Bastarache, and Binnie JJ) affirmed the traditional interpretations of "privacy" (a matter of state intrusion/invasion), they also gestured in the direction of such contextual and relational analyses, acknowledging that to many commentators, "privacy is also necessarily related to many fundamental human relations" (*R. v. Mills* [1999], para. 81). Mr. Mills challenged the constitutionality of the new legislation (Bill C–46) that restricted his access to and use of the complainant's personal records. The Supreme Court rejected the challenge, citing among other things, the importance of privacy in "fostering the underlying values of dignity, integrity and autonomy" and privacy's "essential" role in maintaining relationships of trust, as was stressed in "the eloquent submissions of many interveners about counseling records" (*R. v. Mills* [1999], para. 82). As

McLachlin and Iacobucci wrote, "The therapeutic relationship is one that is characterized by trust, an element of which is confidentiality. The protection of the complainant's reasonable expectation of privacy in her therapeutic records protects the therapeutic relationship and the mental integrity of complainants and witnesses" (*R. v. Mills* [1999], para. 82). Furthermore, they ruled that the interpretation of both the privacy rights of the complainant and the fair trial rights of the accused were to "be informed by the equality rights at play" and that a contextual approach to the interpretation of these rights was important to understanding how this balancing should occur.

While we might applaud the Court's concern that the rights and interests to be balanced in records requests be mindful of equality, the fact remains that the very existence of these procedures, to the extent that they rely on and reinforce misogynist myths and representations of women's sexuality and credibility, masks a deeper and more systemic inequality pervading private and public relations. It masks what a quick glance at the social and political context of the short history of records production reveals: the extent to which the law is built on the basis of discriminatory myths and assumptions about rape complainants, and so much so that the very meaning of the rights to a "fair trial" or to "full answer" for an accused can be made to include forcing survivors to hand their personal records over to their rapist or subjecting them to aggressive intimidation tactics and fishing expeditions aimed at deterring them from proceeding with charges. Their existence masks their own implication in the social tragedy of sexual violence and the hierarchical and destructive relations of power reflected and reinforced by it.

Typical responses to the high court's decision in *Mills* by the defense make apparent how deeply invested some are in the stereotypes that infuse the individualist rhetoric of accused rapists' rights, and how much work is yet to be done to re-think and reconfigure rights in a way that frees them from time-honored misogynist myths. For example, when the decision was released, Alan Gold, the president of the Criminal Lawyers Association, was quoted in the Globe and Mail for his damning criticism of the way Bill C–46 "stacked the deck" against the accused, and the way that the court lacked "a sense of the terrible predicament of an accused person, or that there can be wrongful convictions" (Makin, 1999). As Gold sees, it, the ruling "elevates the sensitive feelings of complainants above the appearance of justice" (Makin, 1999). Focussing so exclusively on the reified rights of man, and trading on the presumption of women's lack of credibility and propensity to lie, Gold's understanding of how and where the deck is stacked, and how we might want to re-shuffle it even, fails to include consideration of contextual factors such as the prevalence of sexual violence and the way in which it constricts the lives of women. Gold's "appearance of justice" also does not include a consideration of the relationships that we foster in and through the way we speak and think and advocate for rights. To take such things into account or to account for the way the courts have tended to favor men's perspectives about women's sexuality or the way the law structures social relations in such inequitable ways is not to disregard the rights of the accused. As Nedelsky notes, "It is to recognize the consequences of those rights as traditionally understood, and to see the incompatibility of those consequences with equality" (Nedelsky, 1993a, p. 1294).

Following Nedelsky's line of inquiry, we need to ask ourselves what kinds of relationships we want to foster. Such an inquiry entails continuing the work of developing conceptions of our basic values for achieving and affirming social equality (for example, as the Supreme Court has in defining the objectives of the equality guarantees with respect to concepts such as "human dignity" (*Law v. Canada* [1999]), or more recently, "mental integrity" (*R. v. Mills* [1999]), and asking about the kinds of relationships that are entailed in or required by those values, and, more fundamentally, about what formulations of rights could foster those relationships (Nedelsky, 1993a, p. 1290). In posing such questions we are drawn away from the singular focus on the one relationship, between the state and the accused, that dominates judicial thinking and practices, and toward a consideration of the many possible roles the state and state officials could play, not in "staying out" of relationships, but in positively cultivating, supporting, and enabling them.

Works Cited

Bollas, Christopher, and David Sundelson. (1995) *The New Informants: The Betrayal of Confidentiality in Psychoanalysis and Psychotherapy.* Northvale, New Jersey: Jason Aronson.

Brown, Peter. (1988) *The Body and Society: Men, Women and Sexual Renunciation in Early Christianity.* New York: Columbia University Press.

Brundage, James A. (1987) *Law, Sex, and Christian Society in Medieval Europe.* Chicago: University of Chicago Press.

Busby, Karen. (1997) "Discriminatory Uses of Personal Records in Sexual Violence Cases: Notes for Sexual Assault Counselors on the Supreme Court Decisions in *R. v. O'Connor* and *L .L. A. v. A. B.*," *Canadian Journal of Women and the Law*, 9: pp.148–177.

———. (2001) "Third Party Records Cases Since *R. v. O'Connor*," *Manitoba Law Journal,* 27: pp. 335–373.

Charlesworth, Hilary. (1994) "What are 'Women's International Human Rights'?," in *Human Rights of Women: National and International Perspectives*, ed. Rebecca Cook. Philadelphia: University of Pennsylvania Press, pp. 58–84.

Cornell, Drucilla. (1998) *At the Heart of Freedom: Feminism, Sex, and Equality.* Princeton: Princeton University Press.

Feldman, David. (1997) "Privacy-related Rights: Their Social Value," in *Privacy and Loyalty,* ed. Peter Birks. Oxford: Clarendon Press.

Feldthusen, Bruce. (1996) "Access to the Private Therapeutic Records of Sexual Assault Complainants," *The Canadian Bar Review,* 75(4): pp. 536–563.

Forrester, John. (1994) *The Seductions of Psychoanalysis.* New York: Cambridge University Press.

Gaer, Felice. (1999) "The Struggle to Establish Women's Rights as Human Rights," in *The International Human Rights of Women: Instruments of Change*, eds. Carol E. Lockwood, Daniel Magraw, Margaret Spring and S. I. Strong. New York: American Bar Association, Section of International Law and Practice. Reprinted in *Sourcebook for the Advocates Roundtable on Linking National and International Women's Human Rights.* Toronto: York University Centre for Feminist Research, pp. 1–78.

Hunter v. Southam Inc. [1984] 2 S.C.R.

Kelly, Frances. (1997) "No Disclosure Workshop: Background Legal Information," in *Proceedings of the No Disclosure Workshop.* Vancouver: Feminist Research Education Development Action Centre, pp. 1–16.

Kelly, Katharine D. (1997) "'You Must be Crazy if You Think You Were Raped': Reflections on the Use of Complainants' Personal and Therapy Records in Sexual Assault Trials," *Canadian Journal of Women and the Law*, 9(1): pp. 178–195.

Kristeva, Julia. (1982) *The Powers of Horror: An Essay on Abjection*, trans. Leon S. Roudiez. New York: Colombia University Press.

Kvam, Kristen E., Linda S. Schearing, and Valerie H. Ziegler. (1999) *Eve and Adam: Jewish, Christian, and Muslim Readings on Genesis and Gender.* Bloomington: Indiana University Press.

Law Commission of Canada. (2000) *Restoring Dignity: Responding to Child Abuse in Canadian Institutions.* Ottawa: Minister of Public Works and Government Service. Available online at URL = http://www.lcc.gc.ca.

Law Society of British Columbia et al. v. Andrews et al. [1989] 1 S.C.R. 143.

Law v. Canada [1999] S.C.J. No. 12.

Mack, Kathy. (1993) "Continuing Barriers to Women's Credibility: A Feminist Perspective on the Proof of Process," *Criminal Law Forum,* 4(2): pp. 327–353.

MacKinnon, Catharine. (1987) "Privacy v. Equality," in *Feminism Unmodified: Discourses on Life and Law.* Cambridge: Harvard University Press, pp. 93–102.

———. (1982) "Feminism, Marxism, Method and the State: An Agenda for Theory," *Signs*, 7: pp. 515–544.

Makin, Kirk. (1999) "Top Court Bows to Will of Parliament," *Globe and Mail*, 26 November.

Nedelsky, Jennifer. (1991). "Law, Boundaries, and the Bounded Self," in *Law and the Order of Culture*, ed. Robert Post. Berkeley: University of California Press, pp. 162–189.

———. (1993a) "The Practical Possibilities of Feminist Theory," *Northwestern University Law Review* 87: pp. 1286–1301.

———. (1993b) "Reconceiving Rights as Relationship," *Review of Constitutional Studies,* 1(1): pp. 1–26.

Nedelsky, Jennifer, and Craig Scott. (1992). "Constitutional Dialogue," in *Social Justice and the Constitution*, eds. Joel Bakan and David Schneiderman. Ottawa: Carleton University Press, pp. 59–83.

Nussbaum, Martha. (2000) "Is Privacy Bad For Women?" *Boston Review* (April/May): pp. 1–9. Available online at:
URL = http://bostonreview.mit.edu/BR25.2/naussbaum.html.

O'Donovan, Katherine. (1992) "Sexual Divisions in Law," in *The Hidden Gender of the Law*, eds. Regina Graycar and Jenny Morgan. Annandale, New South Wales: The Federation Press.

Oleskiw, Diane, and Nicole Tellier. (1997) *Submissions to the Standing Committee on Bill C–46, An Act to Amend the Criminal Code in Respect of Production of Records in Sexual Offence Proceedings*. Ottawa: National Association of Women and the Law.

R. v. Dyment. [1998] 2 S.C.R.

R. v. Edwards. [1996] 1. S.C.R.

R. v. Ewanchuk. [1998] A.J. 150 [QL].

R. v. Lee. [1997] (O.J. 3796 [QL]) Ont. C.A. Gen. Div. (23 September 1997).

R. v. Mills. [1997]12 C.R. (5th) 138 and 163 (Alta. Q.B.).

R. v. Mills. [1999] 3 S.C.R.

R. v. O'Connor. [1995] 4 S.C.R. 411; affirming [1994], 29 C.R. (4th) 40, 89 C.C.C. (3d) 109 (B.C.C.A.); revising [1993]18 C.R. (4th) 98 (B.C.S.C.).

Roberts, Alexander, and Donaldson, James, eds. (1997) *The Ante-Nicene Fathers: The Writings of the Church Fathers down to 325 AD.* Reprint of the Edinburgh edition. Albany, Oregon: Ages Software.

Romany, Celina. (1994) "State Responsibility Goes Private: A Feminist Critique of the Public/Private Distinction in International Human Rights Law," in *Human Rights of Women: National and International Perspectives,* ed. Rebecca Cook. Philadelphia: Univ. of Pennsylvania Press, pp. 85–115.

Sampson, Fiona. (1998) "The Production and Disclosure of Complainant's Personal Records in Sexual Assault Trials," *METRAC Conference Proceedings: Can Confidentiality Survive?* Toronto: METRAC, pp. 3–6.

Sheehy, Elizabeth. (1999) "Legal Responses to Violence against Women," *Canadian Woman Studies: Woman and Justice*, 19(1–2): pp. 62–73.

Sheremata, Davis. (1997) "Rape that Wasn't: Wilfred Beaulieu's Sexual Assault Conviction was a Travesty, but the Rights of the Accused Count for Little with Justice Minister (Allan) Rock," *Alberta Report,* 24(25): pp. 28–31.

Tertullian. (1997) "On the Apparel of Women," in *The Ante-Nicene Fathers*, vol. 4, ed. Alexander Roberts and James Donaldson. Albany: Ages Software.

Van Dieen, Jodie. (1997) "*O'Connor* and Bill C–46: Differences in Approach," *Queen's Law Journal,* 23: pp. 1–65.

Verbug, Peter. (1996). "Guilty until Proven Innocent: A New Law will Deny Rape Counseling Records to Defendants," *BC Report,* 7(45): pp. 35–36.

Nine

RELATIONAL REMEMBERING: SUGGESTIBILITY AND WOMEN'S CONFIDENTIAL RECORDS

Sue Campbell

1. Defense Requests for Women's Confidential Records

In *Rewriting the Soul*, a study of multiple personality disorder and early memory science, philosopher Ian Hacking expresses a "fear" that "we have very little understanding of the workings of 'suggestion,' a word ... that so often stands for a question mark rather than for a clear idea" (Hacking, 1995, p. 255). Hacking's words are intended as a warning. Suggestibility appears in his work, as it now does on the public horizon, as a particular threat to the veridicality of memory. Thus it is also a threat to what Hacking reminds us is our "best vision of a human being" (Hacking, 1995, p. 267): someone whose actions and character are founded in the kind of self-knowledge that depends on a clear-eyed view of one's own past. If, as Hacking implies, we do not understand when or in what ways we are susceptible to influence, how will we avoid the harm to autonomous judgement, memory, and character threatened by suggestibility?

I want to interrogate the current widespread use of suggestibility as a social alarm about memory. As I will show below, the production of women's therapy records in sexual assault cases illustrates how the construct of suggestibility can be used to justify violations of confidentiality. I challenge the presentation of suggestibility as a generalized concern about the malleability of anyone's memory. In section 2, I argue that our current understanding of the "workings of suggestion" has been specifically shaped by a disturbing stereotype of women as especially susceptible to influence. Although our attention has been deflected from this stereotype by appeals to recent science, the direction of scientific research must itself be evaluated through understanding the forces that condition science as a social practice. I make this case in section 3. In section 4, I contend that we have failed to recognize and value the necessity of relationships to people's abilities to remember and understand the past well and with appropriate responsibility. We cannot look only to a laboratory science of memory in order to redress this failure, but must look as well to the natural settings in which people remember. Our abilities, skills, and experiences as rememberers are developed and continuously shaped within a wide range of personal, social, institutional, and political relationships that make possible, support, enhance, or distort our understandings of a personal past. Consequently, we must resist the current legal, scientific, and public tendency to equate the influence of relationships on memory solely with memory distortion.

Suggestibility is neither an abstraction nor a question mark; it is a concept animated—given meaning and specific causal efficacies—through its use in social practices. Access to women's therapy records stands as an example of what suggestibility now means in practice. Throughout the 1990s in Canada, defense counsel in sexual assault cases requested and often received access to a broad range of complainant's personal records, including psychiatric, counseling, and rape crisis center records, compromising therapeutic confidentiality and reinforcing women's persistent legal vulnerability as sexual assault complainants. The nearly routine request for personal records was unique to sexual assault cases and fear of therapists distorting women's memories through suggestion was a common reason for seeking access to personal records.

Distrust of women's therapeutic relationships is to some extent unsurprising. It was aggressively encouraged by the advocacy work of the False Memory Syndrome Foundation (FMSF) throughout the period of greatest ease of access to women's records. The FMSF claims that a certain phenomenon became epidemic in the 1980s and 90s: the practice among therapists of inappropriately suggesting to women that they may have been abused as children and yet may fail to remember the abuse. The foundation speculates that tens of thousands of women in therapy have consequently created pseudo-memories of abuse, developing new identities and lifestyles around memories that they think they have recovered and suffering from an iatrogenic psychopathology: "false memory syndrome." "False memory syndrome" is now part of a popular and legal discourse of skepticism when women claim to have recovered memories of childhood sexual abuse. (For a critical assessment of the work of the work of the foundation, including its claims about epidemic numbers see Pope (1996; 1997).)

It is important to recognize that in the period when suspicion of therapeutically contaminated memory was most influencing the practice of records production, few Canadian records cases actually involved recovered memories. In her excellent 1997 study of the discriminatory impact of records production, Karen Busby surveyed the forty cases referenced on Canadian legal databases where records were requested in the eighteen month period preceding Canadian Supreme Court deliberations about the practice in *A.(L. L.) v. B. A.* [1995] and in the companion decision *R. v. O'Connor* [1995]. The procedures for gaining access to records were laid out in *O'Connor* (see below). In only two cases, were complaints laid subsequent to purportedly recovered memory and in one of these "the evidence specifically indicated that the memories were restored" without therapeutic intervention (Busby, 1997, p. 166). (In addition to Busby's work, the impact of promoting this syndrome on records disclosure has been noted by various commentators including Bronitt and McSherry (1997) and Kelly (1997).) Nevertheless, the discourse of women's suggestibility activated by the FMSF clearly facilitated access to women's confidential records. Defense lawyers were blunt about their intent to use therapist influence on memory as a reason to demand records (see Fitz-James, 1995, p. 18):

> In cases where a rape complainant has gone to therapy, and the accused's position is "I'm innocent, she was never raped," you have to have those records to see whether or not the counselor was encouraging her false beliefs or solidifying them. ... We're talking about a kind of indoctrination here where a therapist encourages a belief in the victim, hardening the memories or filling in the blanks. These people have no concern about the presumption of innocence and the possibility of convicting innocent people ("Rock must modify court's rape ruling," A–16).

In seven of the cases Busby surveyed, suspected improper therapy influence was offered by the defense as a rationale for seeking records. Moreover, the threat of suggestive therapy critically affected assessments of the potential relevance of records in higher court decisions even when there was no evidence to bolster this concern.

In *A.(L. L.) v. B. A.* [1995], the complainant had continuous memory of a sexual assault that had occurred when she was six years old. Even though her memory was continuous, the defense sought counseling records partly to determine "the method of extracting the information from her during the 14 months she underwent sessions before going to the police" (Aboriginal Women's Council, *et al.*, 1996, p. 464). In *R. v. O'Connor* [1995], Bishop Hubert O'Connor, former principal of a native residential school, was charged with four sexual offenses involving four different women, all former students who were subsequently employed at the school under O'Connor's supervision. The women were ordered to authorize release of all residential school records and all medical, psychiatric, and counseling records that related to the incidents. The defense made no allegation of improper suggestive therapy. In using these cases to formulate procedures for records access, the Supreme Court majority on this issue employed therapeutic influence on memory as one of three examples to support its contention that the relevance threshold for records production to the court should be a low one. It stated that records "may reveal the use of a therapy which influenced the complainant's memory of the alleged events," referring to this as "the problem of contamination" (*R. v. O'Connor* [1995], para. 29). *O'Connor* and *A. (L. L.)* did involve claims about historic events. The majority concern about inappropriate therapy cannot, however, be grounded in the facts of these cases; nor do the cases leading up to *O'Connor* and *A. (L .L.)* support the court's concerns about memory influence.

In 1997, Parliament finally moved to restrict access to complainant records in sexual violence cases, affirming a woman's right and need to seek therapy after assault without thereby compromising the success of a claim against her assailant. Bill C–46, which amends ss.278.1 to 278.91 of the Criminal Code, balances the potential relevance of the records to the accused's right to make full answer and defense with both the equality and privacy rights of the complainant. It requires that judges provide written reasons for production or non-production of records, and singles out eleven assertions that are no longer sufficient in themselves to establish the likely relevance of a record including that the record relates to medical or psychiatric treatment, therapy, or counseling the complainant or witness has received or is receiving and that the record may relate to the reliability of the testimony of the complainant or witness merely because the complainant or witness has received or is receiving psychiatric treatment, therapy, or counseling. In *R. v. Mills* [1997], a decision again showing the influence of the FMSF, Belzil J., Alberta Court of Queen's Bench, declared C–46 unconstitutional. He reduced the issue of probative value of records to one of avoiding "recovered memory syndrome": "It is acknowledged that some therapists may 'contaminate' the process of recovered memory through suggestion, and the records would have to be examined in order to determine whether a recovered memory is valid" (*R. v. Mills* [1997] para. 34–35). The case did not involve an adult women and did not involve recovered memory.

Belzil's decision was reviewed by the Supreme Court and in *R. v. Mills* [1999] the Court reconsidered its earlier position, upheld C–46, and characterized the notion that "consultation with a psychiatrist is, by itself, an indication of untrustworthiness," as an "invidious" myth (*R. v. Mills* [1999] para. 119). Although this concession is important, I remain concerned that there has been little adequate analysis of our fear of suggestibility or how this fear has encouraged a restrictive and negative understanding of the influence of others on how we view and narrate a personal past. Post Bill C–46, the disclosure of women's personal records remains a matter of judicial discretion; there is no absolute or prima facie class privilege for therapy records. While there is a more stringent process of justification demanded of the courts, the legislation leaves unclear what judges should or will consider sufficient reason to examine a woman's records. We have reason to remain concerned about records production, since deep assumptions about the relevance of women's personal records may be intact. In my view, this will be likely if assessments of relevance have been supported by still prevalent stereotypes, or if there has been an inadequate critical examination of the considerations that have made the confidentiality of women's therapy relationships so easy to override.

In summary, we are, I contend, in the grips of an exaggerated concern about suggestibility, initiated by the FMSF as a specific problem of memory contamination in women's relationships with therapists. Increased requests for access to women's confidential records show that we need to understand the movement of suggestibility outside of contexts of recovered memory. However, that such requests have been largely confined to sexual assault cases shows that we also need to understand the continued firm attachment of concern about suggestibility to women's memories.

2. How the Defense Construct of "Suggestibility" Gets it Meaning

Our current worries about suggestibility reflect our concern about relationships of influence. The power of suggestibility to evoke social alarm depends on how we picture or represent these relationships. In the representations deployed in false memory writing, women are portrayed as dangerously susceptible to the power of a group of therapists who (deliberately or inadvertently) use suggestive techniques to implant false memories that become new self-conceptions for these clients. This is to model therapeutic influence on a classic representation of hypnotic power as a danger to the social order and it is to invoke a disturbing stereotype of women that traverses historical and contemporary debates.

As used technically in the context of hypnosis, hypnotic susceptibility or suggestibility "refers to the subject's level of responsiveness to test suggestions." These suggestions describe a "make-believe or counterfactual situation" that is to be

> treated by subjects as if it were really happening and is to lead to the occurrence of a congruent overt response. ... In short, suggestions implicitly invite subjects to suspend the tacit rules usually employed to differentiate imagined events from actual events, to define the ongoing situation in terms of imagined events and to enact behaviors implied by those imagined events (Spanos, 1986, p. 90).

Nicholas Spanos describes the situation of suggestibility as a shared project of imagining where what is to be imagined is under the control of one of the parties and enacted by the other. Hypnotic susceptibility (sometimes called "primary suggestibility") is tested through responses perceived by the subject as involuntary and is carefully distinguished by researchers and practitioners from gullibility (sometimes called "secondary suggestibility") (Gibson and Heap, 1991, pp. 48–49; Hilgard, 1965, pp. 273–274). That a person receives a high score on a test for hypnotic susceptibility gives no indication that he or she is gullible, dependent, weak-willed, or compliant. Nevertheless, the idea of one person's responses being controlled by another, derived from popular representations of hypnosis, has animated a long history of concern about suggestibility. In its present manifestation, this concern pays little attention to the technical notion of hypnotic susceptibility. Ernest Hilgard writes, "for assessment purposes we may define susceptibility as the depth [of hypnosis] achieved under standard conditions of induction, the more susceptible becoming more hypnotized than the less susceptible when common procedures of induction are followed" (Hilgard, 1965, p. 67). Items tested on suggestibility scales range from eye-closure to post-hypnotic suggestion, and responses are experienced as involuntary. Therapists are themselves often not careful to distinguish hypnotic susceptibility from other meanings of suggestibility. Most writers on hypnosis insist that the distinction is clear and justified on the basis of many kinds of experiments that have substantiated a lack of correlation between hypnotic susceptibility and others kinds of suggestibility. Therapists have also been affected by the current skepticism and have become somewhat uncertain as to whether they should respond to a charge of suggestive therapy. Therapists need to both understand the forces that are determining public alarm and to be clear about what they mean when they, themselves, use the term. (The arguments in this section draw on Campbell, 2001.) In this chapter, my interest is in suggestibility as a social alarm.

The link between hypnosis and suggestibility is clearly part of the public imagination. In their comprehensive psycho-legal history of hypnosis, Jean-Roch Laurence and Campbell Perry remark that "the general public tends to equate hypnosis with the notion of suggestibility, which is a polite way of characterizing a person as gullible and weak-willed" (Laurence and Perry, 1988, p. xiv). Their work makes clear that the public has often had excessive and ungrounded fears of hypnotic power related to particular views about the moral weakness of hypnotic subjects, especially women. If we take the popular conception of hypnosis as our model for thinking about suggestibility what moral fears are engaged?

It is worth noting right away that shared imagining is a feature not only of hypnosis, but of a variety of valuable make-believe activities. Children learn a wide range of social, motor, and cognitive skills through make-believe games initiated by adults and older children. From childhood on, friends and family help us achieve our objectives by staging preparatory imaginary scenarios that allow us to anticipate obstacles and formulate responses. Moreover, philosopher Kendall Walton has argued that our ability to participate in shared imaginings that we do not control is at the root of our response to the representational arts (Walton, 1990). We can thus think of many cases in which following the imagining of another is benign, pleasurable, and useful.

The overriding concern historically evoked by hypnosis, however, is one of excessive dependence: that the person following the imagining is too much under the power of the suggester. According to Laurence and Perry, the history of response to hypnosis is dominated by concerns about hypnotic power and the will: "From a very early period, there have been allegations that hypnosis ... could be used to sexually seduce women, or more generally, to abolish the willpower of those who submitted to it" (Laurence and Perry, 1988, p. xvi). This concern about the autonomy of the hypnotized subject is actually a complex grouping of three distinguishable worries, all of which are present in recent concerns about women in therapy. Although *A. (L. L.)* has received little commentary, it usefully illustrates our suspicion of therapy and I refer to it often in my discussion.

First, the implication between Spanos's contrast between imagined and actual events might make it look as if what is to be imagined is always false. In fact, situations with which we imaginatively engage may be true or untrue, likely to come about or unlikely. But we think of hypnotic subjects as gullible because we often picture them as accepting and enacting false or absurd suggestions about themselves. In transferring this concern to women in therapy, we may think that the therapist will implant ideas that are false, but will be believed, such as for example, that a woman has been abused when she has not been. *A. (L. L.)* was presented to the public as a case where the defense sought production "on the suggestion that counselors may have unwittingly coached her into developing false memories of abuse" (Vienneau, 1995, p. A–3).

Secondly, we worry about the effect of uncritical judgement on action. Laurence and Perry note that hypnosis is a situation in which one is "asked to set aside critical judgement without abandoning it completely" (Laurence and Perry, 1988, p. xiv). More precisely, the worry is that some feature of the suggestive circumstances, typically the authority of the suggester, will encourage a person to unwisely enact an imagining while at the same time rendering that person unable to properly evaluate whether they should do so. It may also simply be the need to take action. For example, social workers are sometimes instructed to be careful in speculating about a client's situation when that client is in crisis, to avoid saying, for example, "What would happen if you were to confront him about his abuse?" The worry is not that the client will develop false beliefs, but that the need to take some action may be so great that the client is rendered unable to evaluate the consequences of acting, even when it might be unwise for her to act. The concern about unwise action (action that is both unfortunate and uncritical) is central to the current alarm about the suggestibility of women's memories. Therapy is represented as seriously undermining women's critical abilities, and thus causing them to make precipitous false accusations.

Finally, we may fear that the projects and objectives a person takes to be important to who they are, their self-understanding and self-presentation, are too much under the control of another. Throughout their study, Laurence and Perry refer to this as the persistent concern that the hypnotized subject has become an automaton with no will of her own. In *A. (L. L.)* the complainant was presented by the defense as an instrument of the therapist's project rather than, as the record appears to show, a self-directing agent:

> The production order was made ... notwithstanding there being no evidence that information concerning the assault was "extracted by counselors from the Appellant". To the contrary, the Appellant's evidence is that she brought up the issue of reporting the assault to the police, a decision she came to once she developed the strength to do and the insight to realize that the assault was not her fault (Aboriginal Women's Council, *et al.*, 1996, p. 465).

Philosopher Diana Meyers has defined autonomy as a cluster of competencies including skills of self-discovery, self-direction, and self-definition. Moreover, like many contemporary theorists, she defends autonomy as relational, acknowledging that the relevant competencies "can only be developed in the context of social relationships, practices, and institutions" (Mackenzie and Stoljar, 2000, p. 17). It is evident that the Appellant in *A. (L. L.)* assessed her counseling as autonomy enhancing, an experience that supported her skills of self-discovery and self-direction. But understandings like Meyers, which are realistic in their acknowledgment of our relational embeddedness, compete with traditional ideals of autonomy that give "normative primacy to independence, self-sufficiency, and separateness from others" (Mackenzie and Stoljar, 2000, p. 8). Since the value of relations has been both central to women's lives and symbolically associated with the feminine, women have often been regarded and represented as less capable of self-direction than men.

Worries about who people become in their relationships with others are especially high for groups such as women who have been traditionally regarded as lacking autonomy. Unsurprisingly, throughout the history of public response to hypnosis, women were regarded as particularly suggestible. Laurence and Perry's study demonstrates that moral alarm about the hypnotist's power often took the specifically gendered form of doubt about women's moral character, interestingly, not only over their alleged innate weakness of will, but also their purported tendency towards hysterical pathologies, and their inclination to lie about sexual assault. Current concerns about women's suggestibility reanimate and repeat this stereotype.

Moral theorists have argued that stereotypes are not simply a matter of false belief or of over-generalization amenable to correction by pointing to facts incompatible with the stereotype. They are a deeper problem of moral perception, of which facts we are not even in a position to notice. Stereotypes have the power to organize our responses to the group represented in ways that cause us to look for confirming instances of the stereotype while being inattentive to examples that challenge our responses (Walker, 1998, chap 8).

Women have been recently represented in false memory writings, such as those of the FMSF, as extraordinarily susceptible, not only to therapist suggestion, but to general cultural influences, group dynamics, and their own fantasies of victimization. They become caught up in the idea that they might be incest survivors and are eager to play out this drama. Elizabeth Loftus and Katherine Ketchum, for example, in *The Myth of Repressed Memory: False Memories and Allegations of Sexual Abuse* (1994) create for their reader a picture of a "typical" meeting of an incest survivor's group where the women are competitively immersed in acting out distress. One woman is sitting and crying while she tells her story. "On the other side of the room a woman was beating the wall with an 'encounter bat' ... while another sat moaning in the corner her hands pressed against her ears, and yet another hunkered now in the middle of floor." The women in this recreation are meant to engage not our sympathy but our contempt. The authors comments: "no one ever told you to stop, grow up, behave yourself" (Loftus and Ketchum, 1994, p. 16). I find it disturbing that such representations can still affect our response to women's credibility. But it is important to see that they do as part of a tradition of representing women as missing a firm sense of self or individuality and thus as easily mesmerized.

The link to a history of worry about women and hypnosis is sometimes very explicit. In "Making Monsters," Richard Ofshe and Ethan Watters represent the (again) "typical" client of repressed or recovered memory therapy through the story of a thirty-eight year old frequently hypnotized woman who has come to believe she has been the victim of multiple rapes despite a family life everyone else had characterized as placid (Ofshe and Watters, 1993). Critics of the FMSF do not deny that someone could come to falsely believe that awful things have happened to them or be influenced to do so. Their concern is rather that this possibility is presented as typical of a certain sort of relationship between women and their therapists that is said to be extremely widespread, and that the depiction of suggestive influences is vividly and explicitly fashioned around the model of hypnotic susceptibility earlier discussed. Therapy clients are represented as lacking autonomy. Clients in "recovered memory therapy" are "blank canvasses on which the therapist paints"(Ofshe and Watters, 1993, p. 9). "[T]herapists prep these victims-in-training for key turning points in their therapy drama. Clients become sufficiently knowledgeable of the therapy's plot line that they can improvise their way through the next scene ... [they] discover that playing the sexual abuse victim is both a demanding and engaging role" (Ofshe and Watters, 1993, p. 9). Critical judgement is abandoned and the result is fantasy, false belief, damaged identity, and precipitous and harmful action: "Whatever doubts they may have are subordinated to the therapist's judgement, the images they have fantasized, the stories they have confabulated and the identity they have developed" (Ofshe and Watters, 1993, p. 10). "As a result of this therapy, adult children *will* eventually come to hold their parents responsible for imagined betrayal and *will* come to detest them for it" (Ofsche and Watters, 1993, p. 11, emphasis mine)

Ofshe and Watter's description plays on a long history of symbolization of feminine vulnerability to power that is well evidenced in Laurence and Perry's psycho-legal history of hypnosis. Janice Haaken describes the hysteric as someone with the crucial absence of "an ego that will resist the influence of various powerful stimuli. ... The hysteric it seems is captive to whatever appears in her field of perception, whether it be spirits, hypnotic suggestion, the rumblings of her own unconscious or the trivial preoccupations of everyday life" (Haaken, 1998, p. 166). Laurence and Perry provide a historical lens that allows us to see that however false memory syndrome is described, it is depicted as a hysterical pathology indebted to a history of representing women as without the will to resist influence and, consequently, as a danger to others through their false accusations.

In Loftus's and Ofshe's representations, the women are without individualized perspectives and lack the capacity for self-definition. The representation of women as lacking psychic integrity, ego boundaries, and individuality has been a particularly damaging and effective stereotype in the context of records production. It helps explain why the confidentiality of women's therapy relationships has been easy to override. First, confidentiality as a value depends on a respect for privacy. Traditional accounts of the value of privacy have been predicated on individuality and autonomy as key virtues. Philosophical and legal commentators have argued that the function of privacy is, variously, to protect our own point of view on our activities, to protect our ability to hold unpopular opinions and act without undue interference, or to give us a sense of moral self-ownership, a recognition of our capacity to shape our own lives. (See variously, Benn (1984), Gavison (1984), and Reiman (1984).) To represent women as without autonomous individuality has put them outside the range of considerations that typically engage people's defense of privacy. Secondly, women's lack of psychological boundaries constitutes a public danger that must be contained by overseeing their relations of dependence. There is thus a positive reason to override women's expectations of privacy.

I have analyzed suggestibility as a complex grouping of concerns about who we become and what actions we take through our relationships with others. When we are told to be worried about suggestibility, we have a responsibility to identify and disentangle specific kinds of concerns and to be alert to the forces and representations that socially shape our understanding of risk and of who is at risk. We must look realistically and carefully at the relationships in which problematic influence on memory is suspected. Finally, we must weigh our realistic concerns against the threat to important values that alarm about suggestibility encourages. In the next section, I offer a caution about how far our present reliance on science can aid in these projects.

3. Science and Suggestibility

From its inception in 1992, the FMSF's work has been supported by a very active Scientific and Advisory Board that has played a key role in legitimating the foundation and in spreading concern about memory influence. Loftus and Ofshe, previously quoted, are both prominent, long-time board members. Loftus is a well-known forensic psychologist, expert witness, and author whose research on memory malleability has had a substantial impact on how suggestibility is understood by both the public and courts. Her recent work has shifted from testing the effect of questions containing misinformation on the accuracy of eyewitness testimony to attempting to develop pseudo-memories about childhood in her research subjects by exposing them to the fake reminiscences of trusted family members.

Many of us have simply accepted that "the dominant discourse in the war over family recollections is a scientific one" (Haaken, 1998, p. 251; Raitt and Zeedyk, 2000, p. 145), in particular, that suggestibility is a problem that scientists are in the best position to define and study. This certainly seems to be the view of memory scientists who have been drawn into the false/recovered memories debates. Daniel Schacter writes: "The recovered memories controversy, though a complex affair that touches on issues of incest, family, social mores and even religious beliefs, is fundamentally a debate about accuracy, distortion, and suggestibility in memory" (Schacter, 1996, p. 251). We must be careful not to concede the legal construct of suggestibility to science. Scientists can provide valuable knowledge about the workings of memory, but only if we are confident of our ability and right to challenge the ways in which they frame problems and the special authority that they sometimes claim to have.

In the present context, we need especially to notice that the way scientists model suggestibility depends on emphasizing the effect of deceptive information from trusted others (including the experimenter) and inflames the particular concern that influence on memory inevitably leads to false belief. Suggestibility is standardly operationalized by scientists as "the susceptibility to error when given false information or asked questions designed to elicit false information" (Fivush, 1996, p. 152). In a simple and typical experiment on memory suggestibility, a subject will be shown a series of slides of a scene and then tested on her recall. The test questions will incorporate misleading information: for example "did the car go through the stop sign?" when the slide showed a yield sign. The subject's answering yes will be taken as evidence that memory is suggestible. This example is based on Loftus's earlier research into the misinformation effect on memory (see Campbell, 2001). In other words, the scientific meaning of suggestibility is modeled on a situation invariably characterized by misinformation and deception.

Haaken has argued that much scientific research on memory, "in its counterposing of the individual mind and the effects of the social field," expresses an implicit commitment to individualism. "Emotional and social variables are introduced as factors that weaken and impair memory. ... The potential for social influence to enhance or potentiate memory and the importance of group support in the preservation of collective forms of remembering are missing in this line of research" (Haaken, 1998, p. 51). If a background assumption on which experiments are designed is that memory is most accurate when there is no influence on it, this memory research will obviously overlook the possibility that relational support may be vital to our abilities as rememberers. Moreover, because the assumption is built into experimental design, it is itself not tested.

The difficulty with the scientific framing of suggestibility is not easy to see because scientists often represent their results as objective and value-neutral, as deriving from experiments carried out in carefully controlled circumstances designed to be unaffected by surrounding social and political biases and agendas. The artificiality of experimental design can itself lead to a certain criticism: namely, that because scientists study memory in a decontextualized manner, that is, outside the contexts in which remembering takes place, they therefore cannot give us much insight into these contexts. While it is true that science gives us limited insight into actual relational contexts of remembering, I do not attribute these limits solely to decontextualization. There is an additional level to the problem. Science is a social practice influenced by cultural ideals of individualism and autonomy in its study of memory. Scientific work on the suggestibility of memory does represent people as remembering in contrived relational contexts, portraying these relationships as wholly negative in their impact on memory.

Moreover, research like Loftus's exemplifies that scientific and legal practice are neither independent of each other nor of specific cultural influences like the FMSF. The work of the FMSF arose as a response to a legal problem—increased possibilities for women to institute criminal proceedings related to historic abuse. In Chapter 7 of *The Myth of Repressed Memory* (Loftus and Ketchum, 1994), Loftus explains how controversies over abuse memories motivated her to devise new kinds of experiments. The shift in Loftus's research, towards using authority figures to implant "false" childhood memories in her subjects, attempts to structure a scientific understanding of suggestibility specifically for legal use in cases alleging sexual abuse where the complainant has been in therapy. In doing so, it seems to imply that in dependency relationships, women are regularly deceived by those to whom they are vulnerable in trusting.

The generalized and gender neutral language of empirical psychology combined with its implicit commitment to individualism has allowed the discussion of suggestibility as a threat to memory accuracy to spread to contexts where recovered memories are not at issue, as, for example, to legal cases that involve continuous memory for sexual assault. Nevertheless, because of the impact of false memory advocacy on scientific practice, the threat also remains to some extent bounded by worry about contexts like therapy. Even a scientist like Schacter, who is committed to a balanced and non-alarmist assessment of current controversies, contrasts the indispensable value of the laboratory where "we can control the events" that influence the development of memories to therapy where "it is impossible to make controlled comparisons" (Schacter, 1996, p. 276). As Schacter's remarks make clear, therapy has now entered scientific writing as an unreliable contrast to a laboratory setting since there are no controlled comparisons. But his comments also intimate the extent to which we are devaluing knowledge about memory that is gained from contexts like therapy.

Thus finally, we need to be critical and cautious of claims to expertise that implicitly exclude or denigrate alternative sources of knowledge. Raitt and Zeedyk characterize the relationship between law and psychology as increasingly "strong and vibrant" (Raitt and Zeedyk, 2000, p. xiii). Both disciplines, for example, endorse a norm for good or hard evidence for a phenomenon: "evidence that can be measured quantitatively and recorded using replicable techniques" (Raitt and Zeedyk, 2000, p. 150). The authors are particularly concerned about the impact of shared legal and scientific norms on what perspectives can be heard and whose expertise counts. Psychotherapists, who know a great deal about individual memory experience and about the dynamics of remembering and forgetting that are difficult to model or test in the laboratory, will generally be regarded as less expert than those engaged in laboratory science. This bias has been evident and troubling, for example, in the difficult time clinicians and psychotherapists have had in gaining legitimacy for their knowledge of trauma related amnesias. Because scientists "who work in the laboratory usually consider these methods of inquiry superior and privileged and more successful than case histories or anecdotal reports," they are likely to reinforce rather than challenge this convergence of norms (Waites, 1997, p. 4). For example, Loftus has claimed that any therapist's reports of incest survivor's delayed recall, whatever the terminology used, shows a commitment to repression which is "essentially untestable" (Loftus and Ketchum, 1994, p. 31). One also often hears false memory advocates charge that support for repression is purely anecdotal (Loftus, 1993, p. 519; Ofshe and Watters, 1993, p. 5; Pendergast, 1995, p. 101). The devaluing and dismissal of therapists' understandings of particular cases must be seen as the contention that legal discourse should continue to endorse a certain view of knowledge and a certain view of who has knowledge.

In concluding my analysis of how our current legal and public understanding of suggestibility is being concretely shaped by social practice, I have argued that current memory science is often complicitous in representing relational contexts, such as psychotherapy relationships, as sources of memory distortion while devaluing the knowledge that arises from these contexts. I do not claim that scientists have little to offer an account of relational remembering. My sketch of a relational approach in the next section refers to a variety of theorists, including scientists, who share a common commitment to theorizing memory as a social competence.

4. Relational Remembering

I have used the debate about women's confidential records to show the damaging effects that our excessive fear of influence can have for women. Certain pictures of human relations are made vivid in false memory writings. The reinvigoration of hysterical feminine stereotypes, a history of alarm about hypnotic power, and the authority of science and law have converged to fan alarm about false claims and license violations of confidentiality while preempting a more careful investigation into the dynamics of relationships in which we remember a personal past.

A view of memory for personal events that puts it beyond the legitimate influence of others' perspectives erases the social conditions that make remembering a personal past possible. Such a view is not viable. What we can and do remember of our pasts and how we use memory to form a sense of self depends on an array of social resources. First, Maurice Halbwachs, one of the first important theorists of the social dimensions of memory, emphasizes the shared sets of interests, concerns, and ways of attending that characterize the various social collectives to which we belong (Halbwachs, 1950). Memory is inherently selective and what is salient for us will depend on interests and concerns that are seldom ours alone. Consequently, we often remember from a shared rather than an individual point of view.

Second, we are able to develop autobiographical memory only by articulating our experience, thus by interpreting it through culturally shared concepts and meanings, and by rehearsing it in relational contexts. The possibility of sharing our pasts is critical to our abilities to form and maintain memories. As psychotherapist and memory researcher Elizabeth Waites notes "social validation or devaluation can be a significant contextual factor in the retrievability of self-relevant memories. By discouraging or even forbidding rehearsal, an audience can have a profound effect not only on the organization but on the persistence of particular recollections" (Waites, 1997, p. 83). Sharing the past is also responsible for much of the meaningfulness of memories, of which the representational content is only a part. David Middleton and Derek Edwards refer to the organization of memories, their personal and social significance, and "their contexts and occasionings in the flow of ordinary experience" (Middleton and Edwards, 1990, p. 9). These social scientists argue that the multi-layered meaning of memory experience can only be accounted for by close attention to "the context of ideology and social action, collectivity and culture, and the everyday pragmatics of communication" (Middleton and Edwards, 1990, p. 9).

Third, contemporary identity theorists argue that we constitute ourselves as persons by creating a self-conception that is narrative in form (Schechtman, 1994). We come to think of ourselves as persisting subjects who have had experiences in the past, anticipate a future, and take certain experiences and actions to be our own, by interpreting events and actions through a series of stories about who we are. The response of significant others is necessary to our lives as narrators. We understand our experiences, characterize our actions, and develop our perspectives through our involvement in relationships with others and their perspectives on who we are and have become in relation to our past.

Finally, our lives as rememberers involve us in a vast range of skilled activities. We reminisce with others, remind them to do things, learn from our mistakes by recognizing when we are about to make them again, form habits and learn to break them, learn to concentrate and to ignore distractions, develop strategies to keep track of source information, learn whose interpretations of our past to rely on, and learn when we can and cannot trust ourselves as rememberers. Good memory requires skills of articulation, attention, judgement, and criticism that can only be developed in relationships with others. In my view, a particularly disturbing aspect of current alarm about suggestibility is our tendency to represent people, and especially women, as uncritical rememberers.

As Halbwachs understood, the family is a particularly important collective when we seek to understand memory skills as socially evolved and exercised. What we attend to as needing remembering and how this should be remembered, how we learn to relate memory and in what detail, and how we come to trust and doubt memory are the consequence of explicit socialization. It is in families that we are initially socialized as rememberers. It is also in the family that we develop an initial sense of who we are as individuals. In a meticulous presentation of the observations and conclusions of social and developmental psychologists, Waites describes how memory capacities are socialized from infancy. She discusses the importance of early attachment relations, for example, which, in her words, offer "an interactional schema for organizing memory." Attachment relations regulate attention, they provide "the emotional content that makes certain experiences memorable," they contribute the crucial "conceptual and linguistic categories" that we use to encode our experience, and they prescribe "the evaluations that help children differentiate between what should be remembered and what forgotten" (Waites, 1997, pp. 64–65). Our personal history and sense of ourselves as individuals evolves out of these interactions. In addition, as children we learn what counts as making things up and lying, which forms of deception are very bad and which are more acceptable or even tactful. Waites makes the important point, in response to the cultural myth of children as natural confabulators, that children's activities of make-believe and story-telling are themselves learned and practiced. We are no more unsocialized imaginers than we are unsocialized rememberers.

As older children and as adults, we continue to be self-constituting rememberers in the context of present relationships and through the impact of our individual relational histories on how we attend to our environment, with what interests, emotions, and judgements. Our interpretation of the past and our formation of a sense of identity through self-narrative activity are ongoing. If our circumstances provide us with adequate relational resources, we learn how to check our perceptions and interpretations of the past with others, how to contribute our perspectives to group recollection, and how to use our own memories to correct the memories of others. Our skills and capacities as rememberers are not separable from our autonomy competencies, our abilities to trust appropriately and our capacities for self-trust, all themselves socialized. We are, it is true, often under tremendous pressure as children and later as adults to remember both a personal and cultural past as those more socially powerful want it represented and our abilities to withstand these pressures and act as autonomous rememberers are lifelong developmental tasks that often require social support. We often deliberately seek out occasions where we can review and re-experience our past in the company of trusted interpreters.

The importance of others' interpretations of our past addresses one of the mechanisms by which our past comes to have new meaning, an issue that underlies much current alarm about women's suggestibility. How can we claim to faithfully and autonomously remember the past if others who were not even there can influence and change our memories? Hacking, for example, seems to take our common tendency to reinterpret the past as evidence of suggestibility or lack of autonomy. He is particularly concerned about women's tendency to review the past through new social categories like sexual harassment and child sexual abuse, fearing we will unable to resist the force of new stories of harm and victimization as a way to "reorder and reorganize" the past. Although Hacking positions himself as a skeptical spectator to the "memory wars," elsewhere I have argued that his book, *Rewriting the Soul*, does contribute to concern about the suggestibility of women's memory (Campbell, 1999). I now want to make some general comments about the evolution of meaning in memory before returning to briefly consider the particular context of therapy.

Experiences and actions can be described in a variety of different ways, many equally accurate, depending on our needs, interests, concerns, and the context in which we describe our experiences. Memory is not only selective in terms of what significance something has for us at the time of attending; how and what we remember also depends on the concerns, interests, and associations contributed by our present environment. Our understanding of the past, its significance to us, changes as we evolve new interests, gain knowledge, shift circumstances, and enter new relationships. Hacking grants that we do not always remember the same events in our pasts in the same way, that "there is no canonical way to think of our own past" (Hacking, 1995, p. 88). But he has too little to say about the significance of this for the moral agents that we become. In my view, he neglects our morally reflective, self-critical capacities as rememberers, claiming instead that "in the endless quest for order and structure, we grasp at whatever picture is floating by and put our past into its frame" (Hacking, 1995, pp. 88-89). Both the necessity and ubiquity of reflective memory change becomes particularly evident when we look at one of the most important social practices that memory supports, responsibility. Moreover, looking at this capacity displays the continuing importance of other's perspectives to how we remember and forces us to question how far excessive fear of memory influence is compatible with "our best vision of a human being" (Hacking, 1995, p. 267).

The social practice of taking responsibility for our actions requires that we can become aware of them as now fitting certain normative descriptions that we may have been unaware of at the time we acted. Moral learning and ongoing responsibility thus require shifts in the meaning of memory. I develop morally by coming to re-understand and re-experience a piece of behavior undertaken innocently as thoughtless and mean. I come to understand I was thoughtless because adults encourage or compel me to reflect on my behavior. The process of moral understanding is not one where I remember the experience in exactly the same way but merely describe it differently. If this is what I do, I have made little moral progress. Unless I can not only frame the experience through different concepts, but re-remember it experientially, now with shame or regret, for example, I could not develop as a moral agent affected by this re-remembering.

Philosopher Susan Brison, theorizing trauma and memory in the aftermath of rape and attempted murder, relates an example meant to capture Halbwachs insight into the impact of the social on the coding of experience and the subsequent critical reassessment of memory. She relates that after the first murder attempt:

> I recalled stories of Holocaust victims and heard my assailant speaking in what I later described as a "gruff gestapo-like voice" ... I framed my experience in terms of a genre with which I was familiar. I do not advocate appropriation of other's trauma narratives, however, as I am aware of the risks of misappropriation, especially of the Holocaust archetype (Brison, 1999, pp. 209-10).

Brison's point is that how we initially experience an event is socially mediated through available representations and that we must often reconsider their adequacy. What Brison experienced and then remembered and related as a gestapo-like assault, she now remembers somewhat differently, as involving her appropriation of trauma narratives belonging to others. Her understanding of this appropriation indicates that perspectives other than her own have provided motivation and resources for her reflection. Others' perspectives on events and behaviors may contribute new interpretive frameworks through which to re-remember our pasts and these frameworks may contribute towards a better understanding of the past and a more appropriate sense of ourselves.

Therapy is a context where many of us solicit the interpretations of another because we expect that person to be particularly skilled at noticing how we are living out our past in our relationships, beliefs, attitudes, and anxieties. Moreover, anyone who enters therapy does so believing that there are more adequate interpretive categories through which to understand the past. Finally, clients seek therapy in order to further their capacities for self-discovery, self-direction, and self-definition, that is, to increase their autonomy.

Most therapists clearly understand that they contribute new meanings and interpretive frameworks to their clients. Frawley O'Dea, for example, writes: "The questions we ask, the theories through which we filter data given to us by the client, our own personalities and predilections as professionals and people cannot help but contribute to the clients eventual understanding of herself" (O'Dea, 1999, p. 82). But some theorists have been unsure about how to respond to recent fears and criticisms about suggestibility. They have been concerned that "the charge of suggestibility cannot be avoided when the therapeutic task is recognized as one of the joint construction of meaning" (Brown and Burman, 1997, p. 13).

I believe that while therapists have reason to be concerned and an obligation to be vigilant about their influence on clients, the charge of suggestibility on the basis of joint construction of meaning should be resisted. It is instructive to return a final time to *A.(L .L.)*, as this was clearly a case where the complainant's counselors faced the "charge" of suggestibility. It is also obviously a case where the complainant's counselors contributed to the complainant's eventual understanding of herself and her past. The complainant came to remember her past differently as a consequence of her therapy. She came to remember it as involving an assault that was not her fault.

I have analyzed the current fear of suggestibility as a complex of worries focused on women's susceptibility to false belief, precipitous action, and loss of will and self-definition in their relationships with their therapists. Interestingly, if we understand autonomy in the way that Meyers does, this complex of worries is a point by point denial of women's autonomy: their abilities at self-discovery, self-direction, and self-definition. But the complainant in *A.(L. L.)* testified that she had never forgotten the abuse, had described it to others, had raised it herself in therapy, and had come forward when she heard that the respondent had assaulted someone else (Aboriginal Women's Council *et al.*, 1996, p. 455). She claimed, and there is no reason to disbelieve her, that her counseling was autonomy enhancing. She came to remember her past more accurately and she was able to take action that she considered right and necessary. To say that she remembered her past more accurately than when she held herself to be at fault is to express my own commitment to the view that some interpretations of the past are truer than others. We are not thereby committed to thinking there is only a single way to accurately describe or remember a past event.

A woman who has been sexually assaulted is often in a particularly vulnerable social position as a rememberer. Her memory of the assault is being influenced by a variety of different perspectives on the event, including that of her assailant and those of a culture that often discredits and blames victims. Even if she believed it happened, a victim may be discouraged from speaking about the assault or may be ashamed to do so, making it difficult for her to understand the experience and integrate it into her personal history. She may, in addition, be under cultural pressure to come to a distorted view of her own responsibility for the assault. Victims of sexual assault need social support to come to a reasoned and reflective view of their pasts and therapy is often a critical resource for them. Feminist interveners to *A.(L. L.)* and *O'Connor* argued that the production of women's records in sexual assault cases is discriminatory, permitting and facilitating the stereotype that women commonly fabricate sexual assault charges and conditioning their access to the law's protection "on legally sanctioned access to their private lives and disregard for their autonomy and dignity to a degree unparalleled in other criminal proceedings where credibility is an issue" (Aboriginal Women's Council, *et al.*, 1996, p. 460). When a woman's therapy records are produced to the court, this act expresses a dominant social perspective through which she is made to view the assault, one that makes her credibility the only issue. At the same time, the production damages her trust in a relationship that may be crucial to her ability to understand her past, regain her autonomy, and repair her sense of self. In *Mills*, the Supreme Court rightly concluded that not only a victim's privacy, but also her psychological integrity is at stake in protecting the confidentiality of her therapy records (*R. v. Mills* [1999] para. 85).

We can be denied many of the benefits of personal memory when we are denied appropriate opportunities or resources for understanding the past. We can be exploited, our self-concepts damaged, and our sense of responsibility undermined when relationships offer us faulty conceptual resources for understanding the meaning of our past or mislead us about when seeming memory should or should not be trusted. Obviously to point to the crucial social dimensions of successful remembering is in no way to deny that our understandings of the past may be harmfully distorted through our associations with others.

It is important, however, to notice that the lawyers and judges who were concerned about women's memory in the context of records spoke of memory influence solely in terms of notions like implantation and contamination. In other words, any influence on women's memory was thought of only in terms of memory distortion. While this contemporary concern about suggestibility appears to acknowledge social dimensions to remembering, it in fact endorses an implicit model of memory purity that suggests that when others influence our memory, they do so only harmfully. I have argued that this misconception is very widespread, affecting philosophical accounts of memory like Hacking's, court decisions about confidentiality, and scientific models of memory accuracy. It is shaped and exacerbated by an unacceptable stereotype of women's dependency itself related to a false ideal of autonomy as complete independence. We must resist this negative alignment of memory influence solely with memory contamination and work for a more balanced view of memory as an inherently relational capacity. A relational account of memory presents a deep challenge to theories of memory derived from controlled laboratory-style scientific experiments. It is central to providing an adequate and coherent account of our skills as rememberers and moral agents, of our "best vision of a human being." Finally, it is only in more fully understanding the complex social dimensions of personal memory, how memories are formed, supported, undermined, narrated, and tested in a variety of relational circumstances, that we can engage in an informed and intelligent conversation about influence.

Acknowledgments

I am grateful to Christine Koggel, Allannah Furlong, and Jan Sutherland for extensive and very helpful comments on this paper.

Works Cited

A.(L. L.) v. B (A.), [1995] 4 S. C. R. 536.

Aboriginal Women's Council, *et al.* (1996) "Factum for *A.(L. L.) v. Beharriell.*" In *Equality and the Charter: Ten Years of Feminist Advocacy Before the Supreme Court of Canada*, ed. Women's Legal Education and Action Fund. Toronto: Edmond Montgomery, pp. 451–467.

Benn, Stanley I. (1984) "Privacy, Freedom, and Respect for Persons." In *Philosophical Dimensions of Privacy: An Anthology*, ed. F. Schoeman. Cambridge: Cambridge University Press, pp. 223–243.

Brison, Susan. (1999) "The Uses of Narrative in the Aftermath of Violence." In *On Feminist Ethics and Politics*, ed. Claudia Card. Lawrence: University of Kansas Press, pp. 200–223.

Bronitt, S., and B. McSherry. (1997) "The Use and Abuse of Counselling Records in Sexual Assault Cases: Reconstructing the 'Rape Shield'?," *Criminal Law Review* (Camden), 8(2): pp. 259–291.

Brown, Laura S., and Erica Burman. (1997) "Editor's Introduction: The Delayed Memory Debate: Why Feminist Voices Matter. Feminist Responses to the 'False' Memory Debate," *Feminism and Psychology,* 7(1): pp. 7–16.

Busby, Karen. (1997) "Discriminatory Uses of Personal Records in Sexual Assault Cases," *Canadian Journal of Women and the Law,* 9: pp. 148–177.

Campbell, Sue. (2002) "Dependence in Client-Therapist Relationships: A Relational Reading of *O'Connor* and *Mills*." In *Personal Relationships of Dependence and Interdependence in Law*, ed. Law Commission of Canada. Vancouver: University of British Columbia Press, pp. 3–37.

———. (2001) "Memory, Suggestibility and Social Skepticism." In *Engendering Rationalities*, eds. Nancy Tuana and Sandra Morgen. New York: State University of New York Press, pp. 151–173.

———. (1999) "A Singular and Representative Life: Personal Memory and Systematic Harms," *Canadian Journal of Philosophy*, Supplementary volume 25, Civilization and Oppression: pp. 227–257.

———. (1997) "Women, 'False' Memory, and Personal Identity," *Hypatia: A Journal of Feminist Philosophy,* 12(2): pp. 51–82.

Criminal Code, R. S. C. 1985, c. C–46.

Fitz-James, M. (199 5) "Sexual Abuse Cases Raise Tricky Issues of Records Disclosure," *The Medical Post*, (12 September): p. 18.

Fivush, Robyn. (1996) "Young Children's Event Recall: Are Memories Constructed Through Discourse?" In *The Recovered Memory/False Memory Debate*, eds. Kathy Pezdek and William P. Banks. San Diego: Academic Press, pp. 151–168. Reprinted from *Consciousness and Cognition*, 3(1994): pp. 356–373.

Frawley-O'Dea, Mary Gail. (1999) "Society, Politics, Psychotherapy and the Search for 'Truth' in the Memory Debate." In *Fragment by Fragment: Feminist Perspectives on Memory and Child Sexual Abuse*, ed. Margo Rivera. Charlottetown, P.E.I.: Gynergy Books, pp. 73–90.

Gavison, Ruth. (1984) "Privacy and the Limits of Law." In *Philosophical Dimensions of Privacy: An Anthology*, ed. F. Schoeman. Cambridge: Cambridge University Press, pp. 346–402.

Gibson Hamilton B., and Michael Heap. (1991) *Hypnosis in Therapy*. London: Lawrence Erlbaum Associates, Ltd.

Haaken, Janice. (1998) *Pillar of Salt: Gender, Memory and the Perils of Looking Back.* New Jersey: Rutgers University Press.

Hacking, Ian. (1995) *Rewriting the Soul: Multiple Personality and the Sciences of Memory*. Princeton: Princeton University Press.

Halbwachs, Maurice. (1950) *La Memoire Collective*. Preface by Jean Duvugnaud. Introduction by Michel Alexandre. Presses Universitaires de France. English translation published 1980 as *The Collective Memory*. Introduction by Mary Douglas. New York: Harper and Row.

Hilgard, Ernest R. (1965) *Hypnotic Susceptibility*. New York: Harcourt, Brace & World, Inc.

Kelly, Katherine. (1997) "You Must be Crazy if You Think You were Raped: Reflections on the Use of Complainant's Personal and Therapy Records in Sexual Assault Trials," *Canadian Journal of Women and the Law,* 9: pp. 179–195.

Laurence, Jean-Roch, and Campbell Perry. (1988) *Hypnosis, Will and Memory: A Psycho-legal History*. New York: The Guilford Press.

Loftus, Elizabeth F. (1997) "Creating False Memories," *Scientific American* 277 (September). ACAADC@aol.com. 21 October 1997.

———. (1993) "The Reality of Repressed Memories," *American Psychologist,* 48: pp. 518–537.

Loftus, Elizabeth F., and Katherine Ketchum. (1994). *The Myth of Repressed Memory: False Memories and Allegations of Sexual Abuse*. New York: St. Martin's Press.

Mackenzie, Catriona, and Natalie Stoljar. (2000). "Introduction: Autonomy Reconfigured." In *Relational Autonomy: Feminist Perspectives on Autonomy, Agency, and the Social Self,* eds. C. Mackenzie and N. Stoljar. Oxford: Oxford University Press, pp. 3–31.

Meyers, Diana Tietjens. (1989) *Self, Society and Personal Choice*. New York: Columbia University Press.

Middleton, David, and Derek Edwards. (1990) "Conversational Remembering: A Social Psychology Approach." In *Collective Remembering*, eds. D. Middleton and D. Edwards. London: Sage Publications, Ltd., pp. 1–22.

Ofshe, Richard, and Ethan Watters. (1993) "Making Monsters," *Society*, March/April: pp. 4–16.

———. (1994) *Making Monsters: False Memories, Psychotherapy, and Sexual Hysteria*. New York: Charles Scribner's Sons.

Pendergast, Mark. (1995) *Victims of Memory: Incest Accusations and Shattered Lives*. Hinesburg, Vt.: Upper Access.

Pope, Kenneth S. (1996) "Memory, Abuse, and Science: Questioning Claims About the False Memory Syndrome Epidemic," *American Psychologist,* 51(9): pp. 957–974.

———. (1997) "Science as Careful Questioning: Are Claims of a False Memory Syndrome Epidemic Based on Empirical Evidence?" *American Psychologist,* 52(9): pp. 997–1006.

R. v. Mills. [1997] A. J. No.1036. (Alta. Q. B.), online: QL (AJ).

R. v. Mills. [1999] S. C. J. 68, online: Q L (S C J).

R. v. O'Connor. [1995] 4 S. C. R. 411, [1995] S. C.J . No. 98, online: Q L (S C J)

Raitt, Fiona E., and M. Suzanne Zeedyk. (2000) *The Implicit Relation of Psychology and the Law: Women and Syndrome Evidence*. London: Routledge.

Reiman, Jeffrey H. (1984) "Privacy, Intimacy and Personhood." In *Philosophical Dimensions of Privacy: An Anthology*, ed. F. Schoeman. Cambridge: Cambridge University Press, pp. 300–316.

"Rock Must Modify Court's Rape Ruling." (1996) Editorial. *The Toronto Star* (4 January): A–16.

Schacter, Daniel L. (1996) *Searching for Memory: The Brain, the Mind, and the Past.* New York: Harper Collins.

Schechtman, Marya. (1994) *The Constitution of Selves*. Ithaca: Cornell University Press.

Schoeman, Ferdinand, ed. (1984) *Philosophical Dimensions of Privacy: An Anthology.* Cambridge: Cambridge University Press.

Spanos, Nicholos P. (1986) "Hypnosis and the Modification of Hypnotic Suggestibility: A Social Psychological Perspective." In *What is Hypnosis?*, ed. Peter L. N. Naish. Philadelphia: Open University Press, pp. 85–120.

Stanton, Mike. (1997.) "U-Turn on Memory Lane," *Columbia Journalism Review*, (July/August): pp. 44–49.

Vienneau, David. (1995) "Court Opens Rape Records to Accused," *The Toronto Star* (15 December): A–3.

Waites, Elizabeth A. (1997) *Memory Quest: Trauma and the Search for Personal History.* New York: W. W. Norton and Co.

Walker, Margaret Urban. (1998) *Moral Understandings: A Feminist Study in Ethics*. New York: Routledge.

Walton, Kendall. (1990) *Mimesis as Make-Believe: The Foundation of the Representational Arts*. Harvard: Harvard University Press.

Yabko, Michael. (1994) *Suggestions of Abuse: True and False Memories of Childhood Sexual Abuse*. New York: Simon and Shuster.

Part Four

LAW

Ten

PSYCHOTHERAPIST-PATIENT PRIVILEGE: THE HISTORY AND SIGNIFICANCE OF THE UNITED STATES SUPREME COURT'S DECISION IN THE CASE OF *JAFFEE v. REDMOND*

Paul W. Mosher

"[T]here is obviously something revolting about the spectacle of a psychotherapist testifying to a patient's confidences in a criminal action in which the patient is the defendant."

(*People v. Stritzinger* [1983] pp. 521–522).

"It is said that certain relationships are by their very nature so confidential that it would be sheer sacrilege to violate them."

(Fisher, 1964, p. 623)

"[I]f a patient has a right to obtain [psychotherapy] services, he has a correlative right to the essential confidentiality of communication."

(Louisell, 1957, p. 746)

"There is no man so good, who, were he to submit all his thoughts and actions to the laws, would not deserve hanging ten times in his life; and he may well be such a one, as it were great injustice and great harm to punish and ruin."

(Montaigne, 1952, p. 480)

1. Introduction

In 1996, the United States Supreme Court established the psychotherapist-patient privilege in the Federal Courts in its *Jaffee v. Redmond* decision. This powerful decision was the culmination of a near half-century effort to establish the principle that communication between psychotherapists and their patients are in need of a very high level of protection, protection similar to that given to the communication between lawyers and their clients.

Unfortunately, many in the legal and psychotherapy professions have not sufficiently understood the significance of the Court's decision. Commentators have erred either in interpreting the decision too narrowly or too broadly. It is the purpose of this report to place *Jaffee* in historical perspective and thus to promote a balanced view of the decision's significance and meaning. Without a historical understanding of the origin of the new privilege established in *Jaffee*, it will be difficult to understand the likely evolution of this new development in the psychotherapist-patient relationship. The following points will be emphasized:

(1) The *Jaffee* decision represents a very significant affirmation by the Supreme Court of the undisputed necessity of "absolute" confidentiality for "psychotherapy" in general and for the psychoanalytic psychotherapies in particular.

(2) Despite the narrow reach (judicial proceedings) of the decision taken literally, the ramifications of the decision extend far beyond the courtroom.

(3) The *Jaffee* decision is not a statement of the Court's support for "health care" privacy. In fact, the decision reaffirms the Court's awareness of a distinction between the confidentiality needs of psychotherapy patients and the privacy needs of patients receiving other forms of health care.

(4) Although details of the new privilege are yet to be worked out, there is no doubt that the privilege applies to patients receiving psychoanalytic psychotherapy from psychiatrists, psychologists, and social workers.

(5) The decision clearly applies to psychoanalysis and to psychoanalytic psychotherapy, the requirements of which formed the basis of the original rationale for the privilege. Other therapies that have confidentiality needs distinct from those of ordinary health care may also be included.

2. What is a Privilege?

In the natural sciences, "truth" is determined by application of the experimental method and it is a fundamental assumption that each experimenter will report experimental results honestly. This assumption is so important that, without exception, falsification of evidence in scientific reporting is considered to be the most egregious violation of professional conduct imaginable.

In the law, the process of ascertaining "truth" is not the same. "Truth" is arrived at in a court proceeding by a judgment based on the weighing of all available evidence. Because of the importance of this most basic legal principle, it is fundamental to our system of justice that no person has the right to withhold any evidence from a court. The sacrifice of a person's privacy in giving all evidence was justified by Professor John H. Wigmore as follows:

> the sacrifice may be of his privacy, of the knowledge which he would preferably keep to himself because of the disagreeable consequences of disclosure. This inconvenience which he may suffer in consequence of his testimony, by way of enmity or disgrace or ridicule or other disfavoring action of fellow members of the community, is also a contribution which he makes in payment of his duties to society in its function of executing justice. If he cannot always obtain adequate solace from this reflection, he may at least recognize that it defines an unmistakable axiom. *When the course of justice requires investigation of the truth, no man has any knowledge which is rightly private* (Wigmore, 1961, vol. 10, p. 72, emphasis added).

It has long been recognized that the principle that no person may withhold any evidence from a court comes into conflict with society's wish to promote certain intimate or private relationships in which necessary information will be exchanged only in the absence of the threat that sometime in the future such information could be forced into public in a court proceeding. In *Jaffee*, examined in detail later, the Court wrote, "Without a privilege, much of the desirable evidence to which litigants such as petitioner seek access—for example admissions against interest by a party—is unlikely to come into being. This unspoken 'evidence' will therefore serve no greater truth-seeking function than if it had been spoken and privileged" (*Jaffee*, 1996, p. 9). Referring to *Jaffee* in its majority opinion in *Swidler*, the Court said, "In related cases we have said that the loss of evidence admittedly caused by the privilege is justified in part by the fact that without the privilege the client may not have made such communication in the first place" (*Swidler*, 1998, p. 8). Therefore, the rules regarding what information must be made available to courts have been modified to create certain very limited exceptions to the principle of "all available evidence."

These exceptions are called "privileges," meaning literally "private laws" which exempt certain "privileged relationships" from the general rules. Courts and legislatures have been very hesitant to establish privileges because each such exception detracts from the "truth seeking function" of the judicial system. When such a privilege is established, it is an expression of society's intention to allow an otherwise unacceptable restriction on judicial truth seeking, because a greater value is placed on the particular relationship that is protected by the privilege. Some typical examples of privileges recognized by courts include the lawyer-client privilege, the spousal privilege, and the priest-penitent privilege.

Beyond the value assigned to a particular class of relationships, the establishment of privileges has been seen by some commentators to be an essential component of human freedom in a free society because privilege laws regulate the power of the state to compel disclosure of confidential information by individual citizens. Additionally, some commentators have argued that privileges, rather than detracting from truth-finding, promote an increase in the ascertainment of truth because they may diminish the likelihood that a person who feels morally bound to keep silent will be forced to commit perjury in a court or other setting. This view is highly respected in European courts where the proclivity to compel witnesses to testify against their will is much weaker than in the United States.

Privileges may be established through either a series of court decisions (common law) or the action of legislative bodies. Once established, privileges become part of the "rules of evidence" and there are distinct and varying sets of such rules in each of the States and in the Federal Courts. Thus, in the Federal Courts privileges are a part of the Federal Rules of Evidence (FREs).

3. The Effects of Privileges Extend Far Beyond the Courtroom

In the narrowest technical sense, a privilege affects only the issue of whether confidential information may be subject to compelled disclosure in a court proceeding. It is not correct, however, to say that the effect of privileges is limited to such situations. Unlike other rules of evidence, privilege rules extend their effect to the behavior of citizens, and to the arrangements that citizens make, outside the courtroom, in a variety of settings.

> Most evidentiary rules affect only behavior in the courtroom. The rules determine whether a litigant may introducc certain evidence in at trial, but they have little impact on conduct outside the courtroom. Privilege rules are different. They affect prelitigation behavior such as the freedom with which patients divulge information to their physicians; they influence everyday activity such as the interaction between husband and wife. Privilege doctrines thus impact the conduct of citizens outside the courtroom to a greater extent than other evidentiary rules. While other evidentiary rules focus on the institutional legal objective of accurate fact finding, privilege doctrines promote extrinsic social values (Imwinkelried, 1994, p. 514).

During the House of Representatives hearings on the Proposed Rules of Evidence in 1972 the importance of privilege rules in the regulation of relationships outside the courtroom was discussed at length. In testimony, Justice Arthur Goldberg said, "The privileges which are involved here are designed to protect interpersonal relations which may never reach a courtroom. They may emerge in many other contexts" (Proposed Rules of Evidence, 1973, p. 144).

Specifically, the effects outside the courtroom of the psychotherapist-patient privilege have been recognized (Smith, 1980, p. 27, n. 168). They include promoting openness within the relationship and reciprocally reinforcing the commitment of the therapist to the ethical principle of confidentiality outside the relationship.

4. Privilege Rules Create Complications

A privilege may be qualified, that is, subject to certain additional rules that limit the situations to which the privilege applies. Two classes of qualifications that are important in understanding *Jaffee* are "exceptions" and "balancing tests." Privileges may also be undone by "waivers."

"Exceptions" are specific rules that spell out situations in which the privilege does not apply. For example, the lawyer-client privilege does not apply in a situation in which a client has consulted an attorney for the purpose of planning to commit a crime. Even though every privilege has one or more such exceptions, the term "absolute privilege" is often used to describe a privilege in which a specific set of narrowly described exceptions expresses the only ways in which the privilege can be set aside (Amann and Imwinkelried, 1997, p. 1021).

A "balancing test" is a qualification of a privilege that can weaken it considerably. In applying such a test, a judge may decide on a case-by-case basis whether the need for the evidence in the particular case at hand outweighs the individual's interest in retaining the privileged information. The lawyer-client privilege is not subject to such a balancing test, but the so called "executive privilege" of the President is subject to case-by-case balancing by a Court and is therefore considerably weaker (*Swidler*,[1998]; *U. S. v. Nixon* [1974]). Thus the lawyer-client privilege is often described as "absolute" while the executive privilege is not.

A "waiver" is a voluntary giving up of the privilege by the protected person or an inadvertent surrender that can occur as the result of the action of either party to the protected relationship. For example, the client, not the attorney, is the holder of the privilege in the attorney-client relationship. Therefore the client may "waive" the privilege by giving the attorney permission to disclose the protected information in court or elsewhere. An involuntary waiver of the protection of related information may occur if, even in error, some protected information from a relationship is released. Courts have varied widely in the extent to which they have insisted on this principle. The issue here is said to be one of fairness; that is, one cannot selectively use favorable information from a protected relationship while seeking to conceal unfavorable information by invoking a privilege (Marcus, 1986).

An additional basis for challenging a privilege arises when the privilege prevents a criminal defendant from exercising his or her Sixth Amendment constitutional right to confront an accuser and thus creates the need to balance the rights of the accused against the rights of the accuser. This "Confrontation Clause" argument has been used with varying success to challenge privilege claims (Smith, 1980, p. 55; Courville, 1998).

As a result of the complicated and controversial nature of privilege rules, these rules are frequently the basis of disputes. The fact that such cases are common does not indicate that the core protections in the privilege rules are in doubt: it simply means that the application of the rules "at the edges" is constantly being argued and thus the "contours" of the privileges are given shape.

5. The Physician-Patient Privilege

Because information disclosed by a patient to a physician in the course of obtaining medical care is often of a very private nature, physicians and some legal scholars have argued that society would be served by the establishment of a "physician-patient" privilege. In fact, many states have enacted some form of a physician-patient privilege, although in eleven states no such privilege exists (Slovenko, 1998, p. 22, ft 4). Because of the potential for misuse of such a privilege, the large number of exceptions in the widely varying rules of those states that do have the privilege is held by many authorities to render the "privilege" essentially meaningless (Slovenko, 1998, pp.16–34). Furthermore, as will be shown, no such "medical privilege" currently exists, or is likely to exist, in Federal Courts.

In an authoritative explication of the conditions under which a privilege could be justified, Dean Wigmore laid out a time-honored test, which consists for four questions; all of which must be answered in the affirmative to justify the privilege:

> (1) Does the communication originate in a confidence? (2) Is the inviolability of that confidence vital to the achievement of the purpose of the relationship? (3) Is the relation one that should be fostered? (4) Is the expected injury to the relation, through the fear of later disclosure, greater than the expected benefit to justice in obtaining the testimony? (Note, 1952)

Dean Wigmore applied these criteria to the physician-patient relationship and reached the conclusion that there could be little justification for a "medical privilege." His conclusion has been generally accepted by legal scholars (Note, 1952; Slovenko, 1960, p. 179; Slovenko, 1998, p. 18). On the basis of Wigmore's long honored and respected analysis, and the generally sieve-like privilege in those states where a medical privilege does exist, it has been almost a certainty that such a privilege will not be created in the Federal Courts. This fact should not be interpreted to mean that the Federal Courts do not hold privacy in the doctor-patient encounter to be an important societal value. In fact, the Supreme Court has supported the idea of medical privacy (*Whalen v. Roe* [1977]; Smith, 1986, p. 495). (However, not all commentators read *Whalen* this way: "the Supreme Court has specifically held that there is no federal constitutional right to informational privacy for medical records, casting further doubt on the idea that there might be a constitutional right to privacy applicable to psychotherapeutic communications" (Smith-Bell and Winslade, 1994, citing *Whalen*).) In any case, the federal courts have simply recognized that the needs for testimony are not outweighed by the need for medical privacy and thus have in effect acknowledged that the need for privacy for ordinary health care is at a lower order of priority than, for example, the priest-penitent relationship or the lawyer-client relationship.

6. The Practice of Psychiatry, Psychotherapy, and Counseling in the 1950s

Because the psychotherapist-patient privilege appeared in the 1950s, it is important to understand the relevant historical context. Terminology that is used in much of the subsequent writing on the subject reflects 1950s usage.

In the 1950s, psychiatrists in the United States generally fell into two groups, those who practiced psychotherapy for the most part and a larger group who concentrated on "somatic" (physical) therapies, often referred to as "neuropsychiatrists" (Muncie and Billings, 1951, p. 172). Furthermore, almost all psychotherapy in the United States was practiced by certain psychiatrists and a smaller number of psychologists; it was only later that the enormous expansion of the psychotherapy field brought in many psychologists and social workers (Davidson, 1956, p. 44). Beyond that, it is important to realize that, unlike the situation in the 1990s, psychotherapy in the 1950s was comprised almost exclusively of classical psychoanalysis and a less intensive form of psychotherapy based on the psychoanalytic approach known variously as "psychoanalytic psychotherapy," "psychoanalytically oriented psychotherapy," "psychodynamic or dynamic psychotherapy,"(Gabbard, 1990, p. 3) or just "psychotherapy."

Reflecting on the training of psychiatrists and the status of psychoanalytic practice in 1953, Dr. Robert Knight, President of the American Psychoanalytic Association wrote:

> The interweaving of psychiatric and psychoanalytic training ... has implications for both psychiatric and psychoanalytic practice. Stated roughly, those psychiatric residents who either do not aspire to psychoana-

> lytic training or are unable to obtain it settle for residencies in large psychiatric hospitals where the shock therapies are emphasized and where opportunities for psychotherapy are minimal. They have virtually no chance to learn how to conduct psychotherapy, and, if they go into office practice, usually set up for consultations and electroshock therapy. Those psychiatric residents who do aspire to and obtain psychoanalytic training learn to do both psychotherapy and psychoanalysis and veer away from the shock therapies. The result may be to bring about an ever greater cleavage between practitioners of the so-called physiological therapies on the one hand and practitioners of the psychological therapies on the other. Also, among the doctors obtaining both psychoanalytic and psychiatric training, there is a marked tendency for the distinctions between psychoanalysis and psychotherapy to become obscured.
>
> It is my impression from talking with many analytic colleagues that the "pure" psychoanalyst, one who does only classical psychoanalysis, is a much scarcer individual at present, and that many analysts would privately admit that they are treating a number of patients with modified analytic techniques, or even with psychotherapy, and have relatively few patients with whom they employ a strictly classical technique (Knight, 1953).

So while it is generally the case today in the mental health professions that the term "psychotherapy" refers to a wide variety of nonphysical methods of treating a person with a mental disorder, in the 1950s the term "psychotherapy" usually referred to treatment that was being carried out using "psychoanalytic principles." It is the very unusual relationship upon which such treatment is based which led to the idea that "psychotherapy" was somehow different from "health care" and that a privilege for the psychotherapy patient was a necessity in order for the relationship to exist (Slovenko, 1960, pp. 186, 184 n 35).

Courts and legal scholars have recognized that professionals and others engage in helpful verbal interactions with clients that do not fit the definition of psychotherapy for which a privilege was being considered. Thus, legal writers, until recently, differentiated "psychotherapy," (which mental health professionals would call "intensive psychotherapy") from "counseling" (which mental health professionals might refer to as "supportive psychotherapy," some forms of "short term therapy," or "behavior therapy"). This distinction is supported by authoritative texts for general physicians as well (see, for example, *Allred v. State* [1976], pp. 418–419, 419 n 20).

Although the psychotherapy "turf" was being disputed throughout the 1950s by psychologists and others, the original term for the "psychotherapist-patient privilege" was the "psychiatrist-patient privilege" because in the 1950s basically only psychiatrists were engaged in the practice of psychotherapy. There was never an indication that this privilege was proposed because of some special characteristics of mental patients or because of some other aspect of psychiatric practice and there is no indication that there would have been any suggestion for a differentiation of "psychotherapy" from medical care had it not been for the special nature of the therapist-patient relationship in psychoanalytic treatment (Fisher, 1964, p. 616). In 1954, the American Medical Association, the American Psychiatric Association, and the American Psychoanalytic Association approved, and published, a joint resolution which stated, in effect, that only "psychiatrists" could carry out "psychotherapy," which was defined as a "medical treatment" (American Medical Association Committee on Mental Health, 1954).

7. Special Nature of the Relationship Between Psychoanalytic Psychotherapist and Patient

Psychoanalysis brought to the study of mental disorders the concepts that these disorders were rooted in early (childhood) experiences, that the memories of these experiences and the emotions associated with those memories were often not conscious, and that the treatment of the disorders required the uncovering of these experiences, memories, and emotions. It is important to understand that this viewpoint is quite different from the view of "neuropsychiatry," which might take the "cause" of an illness to be some present disturbance in the "brain."

As described by Freud and subsequent authorities, the patient in psychoanalytic treatment is instructed to engage in a very unusual mode of communication with the therapist, which is described by the fundamental rule of psychoanalysis. This rule states simply that the patient must, to the best of her ability, try to speak out loud to the analyst every thought that comes to mind without regard to rationality, relevance, propriety, or obligations to others to maintain secrecy. Called free association, this technique allows the analyst to establish a set of connections among various "mental contents" that may not be obvious to the patient. The resulting unveiling of every inner thought is a "technical" necessity for the treatment to succeed and it can take place only in an atmosphere of complete trust. Rationales for a privilege for psychotherapy patients allude to this special mode of communication, and the complete trust that it requires, as the basis for the privilege, even though many commentators in the 1950s did not specifically mention psychoanalysis; probably because, as noted above, the terms psychotherapy and psychoanalytic therapy were virtually synonymous in that era.

Psychoanalysts have recognized the hazards of disclosure of the information that they obtain in the treatment of their patients and it has been long-recognized in the legal world that many psychoanalysts and, to some extent other psychotherapists, keep no written records of their patients' communications to them. "The world of psychiatry is not like the world of law or medicine. ... Even if there is a record, it would not pass muster under the business-records exception to the hearsay rule, which allows the admission of records only when they have a high degree of accuracy and are customarily checked as to correctness. ... Psychotherapy is concerned with the tension between inner reality and the outside world. The law is concerned with the outside world, i.e., with objective facts, that which is called truth" (Slovenko, 1975, p. 190). As the trend toward the loss of confidentiality throughout health care has accelerated recently, the American Psychoanalytic Association has explicitly recommended to its members in Practice Bulletin #2, "Charting Psychoanalysis" that no written record should be kept of daily sessions (American Psychoanalytic Association, 1994). The profession currently holds that such records are not needed for good psychoanalytic care despite assertions to the contrary in earlier times (Saul, 1938). The existence of this Practice Bulletin (not yet, but on its way to becoming a standard of care) is another factor differentiating psychoanalytic practitioners from other groups of psychotherapists who have less stringent confidentiality concerns.

It is very important, however, to be aware of the way in which the evolution of support for the privilege is intertwined with a confidential-psychoanalytic-confessional model of psychotherapy based on "free association." Over the decades that the privilege has gained acceptance, the field of psychotherapy has changed; many therapists now practice forms of "psychotherapy" which arguably do not fit within the same set of criteria upon which the privilege is based and might better be called "supportive therapy" or "mental health counseling." On theoretical grounds, some current forms of mental health treatment, such as behavioral methods, specifically and explicitly disclaim any interest in "the mind" or other internal subjective constructs (for example, Hofmann and Spiegel, 1999, p. 4). Furthermore, there are many psychiatrists who practice little psychotherapy at all. "Psychiatrists are now often called 'hydraulic doctors'—they raise and lower dosages; they are less and less 'the listening and talking doctor,' The 'P' word is no longer psychoanalysis, but Prozac. Rapidly fading are the days of free association, dream analysis, and an exploration of one's past history. *This change in the practice of psychiatry very much undercuts the argument distinguishing psychiatry from medicine in regard to privilege*" (Slovenko, 1998, p. 45, emphasis added). This fact, which has only started to gain recognition among legal commentators, is certain to become the cause of future disagreements about the scope of the psychotherapist-patient privilege and is discussed below.

8. Origins of the Proposal for a Psychotherapist-Patient Privilege

The concept of a psychotherapist-patient privilege was born of the realization that the relationship between a physician and a patient on the one hand, and the relationship between a psychotherapist and a patient on the other, are fundamentally different when the method of psychotherapy employs techniques derived, in a general sense, from the psychoanalytic method of encouraging disclosure of all thoughts without restraint.

In the landmark Illinois case, *Binder v. Ruvell* [1952], a prominent psychiatrist, Dr. Roy Grinker, refused to testify in a case in which information about a patient of his, not actually a party to the case, was sought by one side in an Illinois court. In that case, and despite the fact that Illinois had no physician-patient privilege, Judge Harry M. Fisher ruled that the information given by a patient to a psychiatrist practicing psychotherapy was protected from disclosure. "The [relationship between the psychiatrist and his patient]" said the judge, "is unique and is not at all similar to the relationship between physician and patient. ... His sphere of inquiry necessarily covers every experience of the patient. ... In fact, what he seeks to do is to bring back to the conscious memory of the patient things forgotten but which lie dormant in the subconscious mind" (*Binder v. Ruvell* [1952], p. 1241). The opinion of the Court made reference to a clearly Freudian model of psychotherapy. In both the brief submitted by the psychiatrist and the decision of the court, the similarity of the psychotherapist-patient relationship and the confessional nature of the priest-penitent relationship was noted (*Binder v. Ruvell* [1952], p. 1242). Furthermore, Judge Fisher analyzed the new privilege in terms of the four elements proposed by Wigmore to justify privileges and concluded that Wigmore's criteria were met.

Binder v. Ruvell is the first significant judicial recognition of a need for different standards of confidentiality for "psychotherapy" and "medical care" and it thus marks the point at which legal thought on these two issues began to diverge. It is perhaps no coincidence that this development occurred only two years after the director of the Federal Bureau of Investigation (Hoover, 1950) published a widely noted opinion piece in a leading medical journal asking physicians, in effect, to report subversive activity to the government, an initiative protested by the American Psychoanalytic Association and the American Psychiatric Association (Slovenko, 1958, p. 49). Over the ensuing fifty years, there has been a gradual erosion of the confidentiality of ordinary health care information as health care has become more complex and bureaucratized. Already by the early 1980s, an article in a leading medical journal said: "Medical Confidentiality, as it has traditionally been understood by patients and doctors, no longer exists ... it is a decrepit concept. ... Psychiatrists have tacitly acknowledged the impossibility of ensuring the confidentiality of medical records by choosing to establish a separate, more secret record" (Siegler, 1982, p. 1518). However, society's awareness of the need to safeguard information generated in psychotherapeutic relationships has increased. Commentators have appreciated that the inability or unwillingness in some circles to differentiate certain "psychotherapy" from ordinary medical care has led to a failure to provide the special protection that certain forms of psychotherapy require.

In a widely cited authoritative book on the subject, the authors of *Psychiatry and the Law* (Guttmacher and Weihoffen, 1952) argue that on policy grounds the "psychiatric patient" has a special need for protection. In explaining the need for a privilege for "psychiatric patients" the authors were clearly speaking of psychoanalysis or psychoanalytic psychotherapy:

> The psychiatrist must insist on very personal data, and must explore the relationship of the patient's acts to his basic drives, which can only be adequately revealed by his deepest and most secret thoughts and feelings. This is true not only in psychoanalysis but in all psychotherapy. [i.e., psychoanalytic psychotherapy] The possibly neurotic nature of even such patently criminal acts as forgery or theft cannot be determined without exploring their patient's attitudes and behavior in regard to masturbation, homosexuality, etc.
>
> What is more, the patient's statements may reveal to his therapist much more than the patient intends or realizes. The psychiatric patient confides much more utterly than anyone else in the world. He exposes to the therapist not only what his words directly express; he lays bare his entire self, his dreams, his fantasies, his sins, and his shame. Most patients who undergo psychotherapy know that this is what will be expected of them, and that they cannot get help except on that condition. It is extremely hard for them to bring themselves to the point where they are *willing to expose the dark recesses of their mind to the psychiatrist*; often patients have undergone therapy for a year or more before they begin to reveal anything significant. It would be too much to expect them to do so if they knew that all they say—and all that the psychiatrist learns from what they say—may be revealed to the whole world from a witness stand (Guttmacher and Weihoffen, 1952, p. 272, emphasis added).

During the subsequent 1950s the idea that a patient in such a situation needed special protection took hold, and the concept of a "psychiatrist-patient" privilege was under active discussion (Perkins et al., 1954; Stern, 1958; Hollender, 1960).

In 1960, an influential law review article, in a detailed fleshing out of the decision in *Binder v. Ruvell*, argued that unlike the ordinary health care situation, the psychotherapist's relationship with his patient fully satisfies Wigmore's criteria (Slovenko, 1960). The article made reference to "the fundamental rule," "speaking every thought," and quoted a judge who said, "Psychotherapy by its very nature is worthless unless the patient feels assured from the outset that whatever he may say will forever be kept confidential" (Slovenko, 1960, p. 203).

In this article, Ralph Slovenko reversed a view expressed two years earlier in which he had supported a balancing approach to the "medical" privilege as a recognition of the general predisposition of courts to avoid extending privileges (Slovenko, 1958). In 1960, he said, "[f]rom the view point of the psychiatrist, it is important to assure patients that the confidentiality of their relations with their psychiatrist is absolute, and not subject to exception at the discretion of the judge" (Slovenko, 1960, p. 198).

In that same year, 1960, the Group for the Advancement of Psychiatry (GAP) issued a report entitled "Confidentiality and Privileged Communication in the Practice of Psychiatry." The GAP report included this frequently quoted passage:

> Among physicians, the psychiatrist has a special need to maintain confidentiality. His capacity to help his patients is completely dependent upon their willingness and ability to talk freely. This makes it difficult if not impossible for him to function without being able to assure his patients of confidentiality and, indeed, privileged communication. ... There is wide agreement that confidentiality is a sine qua non for successful psychiatric treatment. The relationship may well be likened to that of the priest-penitent or the lawyer-client. Psychiatrists not only explore the very depths of their patients' conscious, but their unconscious feelings and attitudes as well. Therapeutic effectiveness necessitates going beyond a patient's awareness and, in order to do this, it must be possible to communicate freely. A threat to secrecy blocks successful treatment (Group for the Advancement of Psychiatry, 1960, p. 92).

The GAP Report concluded with the following proposal under "Model Statute for Privilege of the Psychiatrist-Patient Relationship": "The confidential relationship and communication between psychiatrist and patient shall be placed on the same basis as regards privilege, as provided by law between attorney and client" (Group for the Advancement of Psychiatry, 1960, p. 112).

Despite its elegant simplicity, the GAP proposal fell short in the eyes of legal scholars and psychoanalysts. In particular, criticism was leveled at the fact that it would be impossible, under such a law, to specify what a "psychiatrist" is because such practitioners are licensed as "physicians" without any legal recognition of their specialty status. In addition, several differences between kinds of exceptions that might make sense in the lawyer-client and the psychiatrist-patient relationship were recognized (Saltzburg, 1984). Consequently, in the State of Connecticut, a committee was formed under the auspices of the Connecticut District Branch of the American Psychiatric Association and Connecticut Mental Health Association. This committee included members of the District Branch as well as lawyers from the community and legal scholars from Yale Law School. The committee's work resulted in the enactment of a "psychiatrist-patient" privilege statute in Connecticut (Goldstein and Katz, 1962). That Connecticut law forms the basis of the Supreme Court's proposal a decade later for a psychotherapist-patient privilege.

Notable in the Connecticut statute is that it applied in "civil and criminal cases, in proceedings preliminary thereto, and in legislative and administrative proceedings." The privilege covered communication of patients to psychiatrists and also communications between patients and persons working under the "supervision of the psychiatrist" including psychologists and social workers; it did not protect psychotherapy patients of psychologists who were being seen by the psychologist in an independent practice. The law spelled out three specific exceptions to the privilege: (1) proceedings to hospitalize a patient, (2) court ordered psychiatric examinations, and (3) a balancing test where, in a civil proceeding, a patient has introduced his mental condition into a case. After the enactment of the Connecticut law, GAP withdrew its earlier proposal and substituted the new law as a "better model" (Slovenko, 1998, p. 68, n. 7). Subsequently, as we shall see below, several states enacted similar laws.

In 1961, an Advisory Committee to the Supreme Court recommended that the Court formulate rules of evidence for the federal courts. A draft of proposed FREs was submitted in 1969 including Article V, "Privileges." Article V proposed nine privileges, among which was Rule 504, a psychotherapist-patient privilege closely modeled on the Connecticut Law and the new GAP model statute. Rule 504 referred to a "psychotherapist" rather than a psychiatrist, and the Rule defined the practitioner covered by the privilege in terms of both professional license and function: a "psychotherapist" was a licensed physician or psychologist engaged in the "diagnosis or treatment of a mental or emotional condition, including drug addiction." Exceptions to the privilege in Rule 504 were essentially the same as those in the GAP/Connecticut law. The accompanying Advisory Committee Note explained the fact that no privilege would be proposed for the "physician-patient relationship": "an assurance of confidentiality is essential to effective psychotherapy, but not essential to most medical care" (Smith, 1986, p. 521).

The Advisory Committee note reads, in part, as follows:

> The rules contain no provision for a general physician-patient privilege. While many states have by statute created the privilege, the exceptions which have been found necessary in order to obtain information required by the public interest or to avoid fraud are so numerous as to leave little if any basis for the privilege. ... The doubts attendant upon the general physician-patient privilege are not present when the relationship is that of psychotherapist and patient (Smith, 1986, p. 521).

It then quotes at length from the GAP report cited above and the Slovenko analysis of the privilege(s) in the light of Wigmore's analysis (Slovenko, 1960).

In 1972, the proposed new FREs were submitted by the Supreme Court to Congress for approval. Unexpectedly, the proposed FREs, and particularly Article V dealing with privileges, got caught up in a political firestorm related to the Watergate scandal (Imwinkelried, 1994). Full-blown hearings took place in both the House and Senate. Testimony for and against proposed Rule 504 was heard. Significantly, proposed Rule 504 was opposed by both the American Medical Association and the American Bar Association. The most controversial proposed rule, however, had to do with the Watergate-related Rule 509 which created a broad "government privilege."

Ultimately, Congress decided to eliminate all the proposed privileges, including Rule 504, from the FREs and to substitute instead a new single rule, Rule 501, which uniformly applied to both criminal and civil cases (Graham, 1996, p. 508). This rule in effect sent the issue of specific privileges back to the Courts and held that the Courts should develop privilege rules in "the light of reason and experience," the process by which the common law ordinarily evolves.

The decade of the 1960s thus marks a nodal point in which the development of the Federal psychotherapist-patient privilege was set on a dual path. On one path, the privilege was seen as analogous to the absolute and relatively inviolate attorney-client privilege as proposed by Slovenko in 1960 and the original GAP Report. On the alternate path, as manifested in the Connecticut Statute and the proposed Federal Rule 504, the privilege was seen as somewhat analogous to the physician-patient privilege with its many exceptions and loopholes, its poor standing among legal scholars, and its dismal prospects for adoption in the Federal courts. The decision by Congress to reject Rule 504 (among others) and instead to return the development of the privilege to the courts allowed the privilege's dual ancestry to continue to play out.

9. Rationale for a Psychotherapist-Patient Privilege

Several justifications have been offered for the psychotherapist-patient privilege. The most significant are the "utilitarian" (also called "instrumental" or "classical") basis and the "privacy" (also called "humanistic," "autonomy" or "modern") basis. [An additional basis, now considered by some to be anachronistic, is "professional honor." Subsumed under this rationale is a profession's obligation to maintain confidentiality on an ethical basis. "Thus, in practice, professional honor, or ethical obligations is an important basis for privileges" (Smith, 1986, p. 479).] "The traditional utilitarian justification for the psychotherapist-patient privilege derives from an essentially Freudian model of psychoanalysis" (Harvard Law Review Association, 1985, p. 1542). This justification holds that a patient either will refuse to seek treatment or will refuse to "free associate" (fully disclose) once in treatment unless secrecy is guaranteed. In other words, without the privilege the treatment cannot take place and the sought after evidence will not come into existence. Thus, the loss of evidence in the truth-seeking process caused by the privilege is minimal.

Other commentators have held that the privilege is essentially a "privacy" issue; that is, disclosure of sensitive information revealed by the patient in the course of psychotherapy would be an invasion of the patient's "privacy rights" (Harvard Law Review Association, 1985, p. 1545) or constitutional "privacy interest" (Smith, 1980; Smith, 1986, p. 495; Courville, 1998, p. 203). In fact, at least three different "constitutional" bases for a privilege have been considered. Two of these are based on the Fourth and Fifth amendments, providing protection against unreasonable search and self-incrimination, respectively. Each of these would apply in only a small number of cases and so are seen as not being an adequate basis to support the privilege. The third, the so-called constitutional "privacy right" would be much more general in its application and therefore is often referred to as simply the "constitutional rationale" for the privilege (Courville, 1998, p. 203). The distinction between these approaches is important because the utilitarian basis tends to narrow the scope of the privilege to psychoanalytic therapies requiring "free association" while the privacy basis tends to expand the range of psychotherapy treatment modalities covered to include any treatment in which very sensitive information is disclosed. It is much more difficult to distinguish the supposed privacy justification for psychotherapy not based on "free association" from the non-privileged (federal) privacy needs of the physician-patient relationship. Furthermore, advocates of the "privacy" rationale have had difficulty specifying a "bright line," which could differentiate those helping relationships in which a privilege is supportable from the vast number of other such psychotherapy-like relationships in which such a privilege could not be supported because of the judicial system's concerns about the loss of evidence. Thus, advocates of the privacy basis are, in effect, forced to fall back on what again becomes a utilitarian rationale. In any case, as will be seen, the new privilege that has been created is based on the utilitarian justification.

Both rationales are seen by commentators as having particular strengths and weaknesses. The utilitarian rationale gains strength from the ability of courts to so define the privilege as to avoid case-by-case balancing which would severely weaken the privilege (*Jaffee v. Redmond* [1996]). "Operating under the assumption that certainty favors absolute rules over ad hoc standards, scholars commonly state that privileges justified by the traditional justification should be cast as absolute rules, and that privileges justified by the privacy rationale should be qualified by the case-by-case balancing of privacy against the need for evidence. The notion that the type of justification employed governs the choice between rules and standards is, however, overly simplistic" (Harvard Law Review Association, 1985, p. 1487). Nonetheless, the utilitarian basis is subject to empirical testing: can it be shown that strict confidentiality is really essential for the relationship? Such tests have yielded weak or inconclusive or mixed results (Courville, 1998, p. 197). However, the passages quoted above illustrate that the predominant view among professionals is that confidentiality is indispensable to the conduct of at least some forms of psychotherapy. The privacy rationale, being based on a predicated constitutional right would not be subject to such empirical testing. Yet, case-by-case balancing against other judicial considerations, such as a "compelling state interest" in obtaining the information would seriously weaken a privacy based privilege (*Whalen v. Roe*, [1977]; Courville, 1998, p. 212).

10. The Supreme Court Has Been Particularly Hesitant to Create New Privileges

From the time that President Ford signed the legislation containing the new FREs on January 3, 1975 until the 1990s, the federal courts have been very hesitant to create new privileges. The Supreme Court recognized the existence of only the lawyer-client privilege and the spousal privilege. Some federal courts held that the intent of Rule 501 was actually to prevent the development of any new privileges beyond the ones that existed in common law prior to 1975. The Supreme Court declined to create an academic privilege, a reporter's privilege, an accountant's privilege, or a state legislator's privilege. This very strict interpretation of Rule 501 has been in accord with the conservative position asserted by Justice Frankfurter. Therefore, the creation of a new privilege is not only unusual; it signifies a very notable recognition by the Supreme Court of a most important societal need (Amann and Imwinkelried, 1997, p. 1020).

Psychotherapist-patient privilege cases have arisen in several federal districts since 1975 and have been decided with varying results, mostly in the negative (Klein, 1998, p. 723). However, at the state level, all fifty states have recognized (mostly through legislation) the privilege. The dual ancestry of the privilege is illustrated by the fact that in some states the privilege is a replica of the attorney-client privilege while in others it is patterned on the rejected Federal Rule 504. (Eleven states equate the privilege with the attorney-client privilege. Five others have minor modifications. Twenty-one states have rules that follow the proposed Rule 504. Four states combine the privilege with that of physicians or mental health professionals. Four states recognize a privilege for psychiatrists only. One state recognizes a physician-patient privilege without specifically mentioning psychotherapists (Klein, 1998, p. 720).)

Thus the answers to questions regarding the status of a Federal psychotherapist-patient privilege, whether such a privilege should be recognized under Rule 501 and what kind of privilege should be established, were uncertain when the Supreme Court accepted to hear *Jaffee v. Redmond* in 1995. The specific issues in the case were (1) should a psychotherapist-patient privilege be recognized in the federal courts and (2) if so, should the privilege be extended to apply to the psychotherapy patients of social workers? Details of the facts in the case have been described elsewhere (Amann and Imwinkelried, 1997; Klein, 1998).

11. The Supreme Court Creates the Psychotherapist-Patient Privilege

To the surprise of both participants in the case and legal experts, in a very powerful seven to two decision, the Court ruled that the communication of a psychotherapist-patient relationship is privileged under Rule 501. The Court further ruled that the privilege should extend beyond the patients of psychiatrists and psychologists and should also include the patients of social workers (*Jaffee v. Redmond* [1996]). Several important aspects of the Court's decision are worthy of comment.

The majority opinion sustained the decision of the appellate court in holding that the information in the psychotherapist-patient relationship is protected by a new privilege. However, the majority went far beyond the appellate court in holding that the new privilege was not subject to a balancing test and is therefore absolute in the same sense that the attorney-client privilege is so described.

The majority opinion makes no direct reference to "psychoanalysis" or to "psychoanalytic psychotherapy," referring instead only to the generic terms "psychotherapy" and "psychotherapist." However, the Court's awareness that all psychotherapy may not be within the scope of the privilege is signaled by the opening sentence of Justice Scalia's dissenting opinion which refers specifically to "psychoanalytic counseling" (*Jaffee v. Redmond* [1996], dissent, 1). It is also of note that the briefs submitted to the Supreme Court by the petitioner in *Jaffee* attempted to argue that the patient, Officer Redmond, was not receiving "psychoanalysis" and on that basis was not entitled to the privilege (Flaxman, 1995). In the reply brief submitted by the petitioner, the argument was advanced that "The Record Fails to Show that Respondent Received 'Psychoanalytic Psychotherapy'" (Flaxman, 1996).

In the appellate court's explanation of its support for the privilege, weight was given to both traditional justifications for the privilege: the utilitarian/instrumental and the privacy rationales. However, in the Supreme Court's majority opinion, the court rested squarely on the utilitarian/instrumental basis (Amann and Imwinkelreid, 1997, p. 731) and virtually ignored the privacy justification, other than to comment on the appellate court's juxtaposition of the privacy considerations with the balancing need for evidence (Courville, 1998, p. 210).

Reaction to *Jaffee* in the legal community has been decidedly mixed.

Critical commentators particularly faulted the Court's reliance on the existence of a psychotherapist privilege in each of the fifty states, because these privileges had been created by state legislatures rather than by decisions in state courts. The critics pointed to the requirement, under Rule 501, that new privileges should evolve as a matter of common law. Some commentators tried to assure the legal profession that *Jaffee* was not a signal that the Court was ready to create additional new privileges (Imwinkelried, 1997, p. 36). Others suggested that *Jaffee* indicates the Court's willingness to create additional Federal privileges under Rule 501 such as a parent-child privilege or even an accountant-client privilege (Ricafort, 1998; Molony, 1998). Commentators, who had for years held a skeptical attitude toward the privilege, viewed the decision in that same skeptical light implying that it changed nothing (Shuman & Foote, 1999; Slovenko, 1997). In particular, despite his having played a major role in the sequence of events which led eventually to the *Jaffee* decision (Slovenko, 1960), Slovenko lost confidence in the value of the privilege by the mid-1970s when he wrote: "The concept of privilege, while it may offer a sense of security, should be abandoned as a means of determining whether disclosure of communication in psychotherapy should be required ... privilege is, in the case of psychotherapy, an unnecessary and misleading claim" (Slovenko, 1974, p. 672).

12. Questions Raised by the *Jaffee* Decision

Unlike other well-known privileges such as the attorney-client and spousal privileges, the psychotherapist-patient is of relatively recent origin and lacks the thorough analysis and understanding that would accompany privileges with hundreds of years of cultural history.

Privilege rules are the subject of intense debate and it comes as no surprise that commentators have claimed that the court's decision in *Jaffee* raises more questions than it answers (Josephson, 1998). In considering these questions, however, one should not lose sight of the fact that the question, which was answered with great clarity by the court, is that question regarding whether psychotherapy that requires the kind of disclosure to the therapist that is essential in psychoanalytic treatment will be privileged. That question was answered in the affirmative. Undoubtedly, a torrent of opinion will be heard in law review articles and court decisions centered on questions that have to do with the unresolved "contours" of the privilege. The fact that this debate is taking place should not distract from the reasonable certainty of the privilege's application in psychoanalysis and psychoanalytic psychotherapy, modalities that are clearly within the privilege when practiced by psychiatrists, psychologists, and social workers.

However, the lack of clarity in specifying which types of treatment are to be considered "psychotherapy" severely undermines the Court's stated intention of creating a privilege that will be "predictable" for patients so that a patient in other forms of "psychotherapy" or "counseling" will know in advance that utterances to her therapist/counselor are within or outside the privilege: "As we explained in *Upjohn*, if the purpose of the privilege is to be served, the participants in the confidential conversation 'must be able to predict with some degree of certainty whether particular discussions will be protected. An uncertain privilege, or one which purports to be certain but results in widely varying applications by the courts, is little better than no privilege at all'" (*Jaffee* [1996], majority, p. 15). A commentator added, "certainty may require the Court to draw a bright line as to whom the privilege applies. … In *Jaffee*, the Court emphasized the need for a predictable privilege; however the psychotherapist privilege will not be predictable until more of its contours (especially to whom it applies) are defined. District courts have little to guide them in their application, and as a result, may look to the law of the states in which they sit [and] ...inevitably more conflict will develop" (Fulkerson, 1997, p. 422).

Of course, the most significant question raised by the court's decision is the scope of the privilege. As if to suggest that the court somehow intends that the privilege should be diluted and/or weakened by future developments, some commentators have pointed to footnote 19 of the Court's majority opinion, which appears at the following point in the opinion:

> A [i.e., Rule 501] rule that authorizes the recognition of new privileges on a case-by-case basis makes it appropriate to define the details of new privileges in a like manner. Because this is the first case in which we have recognized a psychotherapist privilege, it is neither necessary nor feasible to delineate its full contours in a way that would "govern all conceivable future questions in this area." However, it should be remembered that unlike Proposed Federal Rule 504, which included three specific exceptions, the privilege established by the court under rule 501 presently has no exceptions at all. It is clearly the court's intention that the exceptions and scope of the privilege should be determined in the same way that the privilege, itself, was established; under rule 501's concept of "reason and experience" (*Jaffee* [1996] majority, n. 19).

The court, however, has tended to view proposed Rule 504, itself, as a significant part of the "experience" in this matter and therefore it is the belief of some legal scholars that the exceptions to the privilege that the Court will be prepared to sustain will be similar to those actually spelled out in Rule 504, with the possible addition of a child-abuse reporting provision now supported in some form in all fifty states (Jordan, 1984; Imwinkelried, 1998; Klein, 1998, p. 722). Nevertheless, the statement in footnote 19 of the majority opinion that: "we do not doubt that there are situations in which the privilege must give way, for example, if a serious threat of harm to the patient or to others can be averted only by means of a disclosure by the therapist" anticipates possible support for a so-called "duty to protect" or "dangerous patient" exception according to some commentators. (Looking to the states for guidance, the following exceptions are listed by one writer: hospitalization, twenty six states; court ordered examination, twenty seven states; patient-litigant exception twenty nine states; child abuse cases, fourteen states; homicide and violent crime trials, four states; all crimes, two states; controlled substances, one state (Cantu, 1998, p. 383). However the conflicting requirements in some states to report child abuse cases may not be listed as a specific exception in the privilege statute.) Others have pointed out the confusing potential of this footnote in that it really does not state an exception to the privilege as much as a description of a situation in which the privilege per se is not at issue (Harris, 1999).

A second question not answered by the decision, and one which has been alluded to throughout this chapter, is the need to define the part of the spectrum of "psychotherapies" and "psychotherapists" to which the privilege actually applies. From the earliest days in which the need for a "psychotherapist" privilege has been recognized, the utilitarian justification has stressed the special considerations that apply to and derive from the special theoretical and technical aspects of Freudian psychoanalysis (unconscious, free association, and need for "complete trust"). However, as mentioned earlier, since the early 1950s when the privilege was first proposed, the general usage of the terms "psychotherapy" and "psychotherapist" has changed greatly. No longer the dominant paradigm among non-physical methods of treating mental disorders in the United States, psychoanalytic treatment is now a very influential but minority subset of a much larger "industry." Furthermore, many of the newer forms of mental health counseling, particularly those influenced by behaviorist schools of psychology, such as "behavior therapy," and to a lesser extent "cognitive-behavior" therapy, explicitly disavow the importance of the unconscious, childhood experience, and uncovering of lost memories. Therefore, although these therapies may deal with highly personal and potentially embarrassing material from a patient's current life, it is difficult to support the instrumental justification for a privilege in these treatments in the same sense that it is difficult to support a broad "medical privilege" for health care in general, which often deals with the same kind of sensitive matters.

As noted above, one approach to this dilemma, the differentiation of "psychotherapy" from "counseling," provided a way to distinguish that kind of interaction which would generate information within the privilege from that which would not (*Allred* [1976]). However, the clear waters of *Allred* have been seriously muddied by a recent confusion of terminology that has crept into the legal literature and that now treats the two terms as either functionally synonymous or treats the term "psychotherapy" as a subset of a larger set of interactions generally called "counseling." The entangling of these terms has been immeasurably heightened by the *Jaffee* court because the majority opinion, while explicitly addressing the issue of a psychotherapist-patient privilege, repeatedly (six times) refers to the interaction as "counseling sessions" when clearly intending to refer to "psychotherapy"! In his dissent, Justice Scalia used the term "counseling" in the following phrases: "psychoanalytic counseling," "psychotherapeutic counseling," (two instances) and "psychological counseling"(two instances). The extension of the privilege by the Court to include social workers and the use of the term "counseling" could support a rationale for an expansion of the privilege to unacceptable bounds.

As early as 1957, the troubling prospect of the undue extension of the privilege was recognized. One authority sympathetic to the privilege wrote: "society cannot afford to subordinate the needs of judicial administration to a never-ending expansion of the confidential communication privileges to embrace a multitude of additional relationships" (Louisell, 1957, p. 743). Forty years later, the same problem is unsolved:

> Without strict, judicially-imposed standards regulating the application of the psychotherapist privilege, the inevitable efforts to broaden it will eviscerate the time-honored rule that "privileges are to be narrowly construed" ... the Court's reasoning suggests that a "psychotherapist" privilege extends to those who perform psychotherapy, irrespective of professional affiliation. However, what constitutes "psychotherapy" remains unclear ... Nothing in the Court's analysis indicates that the privilege could not also extend to licensed family therapists, licensed professional counselors, employee assistance professionals, registered nurses, chemical dependency counselors, pastoral counselors, or even volunteer domestic violence and rape counselors. Thus, when applying *Jaffee* to novel claims of psychotherapist privilege, federal courts will confront inevitable difficulties (Archer, 1997, pp. 358, 360–362).

This issue is further complicated by the fact that a small sub-segment of the counseling profession actually employs psychoanalytic methodology in its approach using a technique which is, in fact, called "Psychoanalytic Counseling" (Patton and Meara, 1992; Patton et al., 1997).

Organizations of professional counselors have not hesitated to take a cue from *Jaffee* to advocate not only for a privilege extended to "counselors," but also for extension of third party reimbursement for "counseling sessions" with their members. Extension of the privilege to the patients of all currently licensed mental health practitioners would not even come close to recognizing a privilege as wide spread as the attorney-client privilege. Thus, even a very broad expansion of the privilege would not contribute a comparable loss of potential evidence as caused by the lawyer-client privilege in a nation with so many more lawyers than psychotherapists. (There are between 900,000 and one million attorneys in the United States. "There are approximately 30,642 psychiatrists, 56,000 psychologists, and 81,000 psychiatric social workers practicing mental health counseling today" (Winick, 1996, p. 264).) Earlier commentators have been concerned that expansion of privileges could lead to calls for their total abolition (Saltzburg, 1980, p. 602). Most recently, the decision of the Supreme Court to extend the privilege to include social workers' psychotherapy communications with clients has led to broadening of the professional groups covered in the "Uniform Rules of Evidence," a set of model rules created by academics and others (NCCUSL, 2002) and which have some influence in the development of state statutes (Aronson, 2001, p. 599).

Additionally, while most psychoanalysts steadfastly refuse to discuss or disclose identifiable information about their work with patients outside of the treatment situation itself (and the very limited ambit of professional consultation), most treatment of mental illness today is conducted with a great deal of public disclosure by other therapists. In particular, counseling or "treatment" carried out under so-called "managed care" requires frequent discussion of the patient's material with a "case manager" who usually is not a professional colleague governed by the same ethical confidentiality constraints as the counselor or therapist, and who may enter sensitive information into networked computer systems:

> The big secret these days is that what patients tell therapists [in managed care programs] is no longer confidential. Managed care companies demand detailed accounts of patients' workplaces, family problems, love life, addictions, suicidal ideation, episodes of anger, and so on. These data are required to substantiate the diagnosis and treatment plan at a remote site where case managers sit at computers. The information, which includes case assessments, mental status exams, and progress reports, comes in by telephone, fax, and mandatory written reports and questionnaires. Everything is entered on the computer; written reports may be microfilmed for future reference. Almost all behavioral health companies file material by the patient's health insurance number, which is usually the same as his or her social security number.... Furthermore these companies are constantly merging and expanding (Pomerantz, 1999, p. 3).

Patients and counselors working in the managed care environment (eighty five percent of all employment based third-party reimbursed "behavioral healthcare" care in 1998) are clearly aware that this disclosure is taking place. Furthermore, to a very large extent, the counseling conducted under managed care programs fails to resemble the "psychotherapy" upon which the utilitarian justification in

Jaffee is based: "Managed care defines and treats mental illness in terms of the ability of a person to function, while traditional mental health care is concerned with long-term treatment of underlying illness. Mental health is becoming geared toward the needs of larger populations rather than those of individual patients in one-to-one meetings" (Tuttle and Woods, 1998, p. 6).

13. Subsequent Developments

The *Jaffee* privilege clearly has a dual ancestry. In part the privilege stems from the highly respected attorney-client privilege with its absolute nature and centuries of legal analysis. This origin can be traced to the 1960 article by Slovenko and to the original proposal in the 1960 GAP report noted above. The other ancestor is the physician-patient privilege with its many exceptions and loopholes, and its absence from the federal courts and the courts of eight states. That lineage traces from the 1962 Connecticut Statute and the subsequent similar Supreme Court proposal in Rule 504 with its stated exceptions, particularly the exception for the so-called "patient-litigant." In its *Jaffee* opinion the Supreme Court appears to have inclined in the direction of the attorney-client model with an emphasis on the privilege's absolute nature. Subsequent legal decisions have inclined somewhat in the same direction.

As *Jaffee* has found its way into the workings of the lower Federal Courts, the "contours" of the new privilege have begun to emerge. For a more detailed discussion of those underlying decisions which are considered of most significance see the review article on developments since *Jaffee* by Melissa Nelken (2000).

Generally, in applying *Jaffee*, the lower courts have taken a very broad approach to the definition of a psychotherapist and psychotherapy, extending the privilege to cover verbal treatment of mental disorders by a wide range of licensed psychotherapists. Rather than distinguish among specific psychotherapeutic modalities, the courts have included within the privilege "marriage counseling records," and Employee Assistance Plan Counselors but not unlicensed alcoholism counselors (Dubbleday, 1985; Nelken, 2000, p. 9).

Among the possible exceptions to the privilege, the most discussed are (1) the "dangerous patient" exception, (2) the "crime-fraud" exception, and (3) the so-called "mental condition at issue" or "patient-litigant" waiver.

The dangerous patient exception actually comes down to a question of whether in carrying out an ethical or legal obligation to warn or protect an intended victim of a dangerous patient (either with or without the patient's consent) the psychotherapist thereby causes the privilege to be "waived" or lost. To date, the Federal appellate courts have been divided on this issue, but it appears that because of the Supreme Court's intent to establish a predictable privilege, the courts and legal scholars are now inclined to hold that issuing such a warning does not affect the privilege. Thus, even though the information revealed may be used to protect an intended victim from harm, that or other confidential information cannot be used against the patient in a subsequent court proceeding (Harris, 1999; Nelken, 2000, p. 33).

One Federal Appellate Court has considered the question of whether the privilege is lost if a patient consults a psychotherapist for the purpose of committing a specific crime or fraud. Reasoning by analogy with the attorney-client privilege, the court found that, as in the well known crime-fraud exception to the attorney client privilege, the privilege is lost under similar circumstances. However, the Court took particular care to spell out that such an exception applies only in the case of a specific intended crime and would not undermine the privilege in the case of a career criminal who was seeking therapy to improve his or her efficiency in committing crimes in general (Nelken, 2000, p. 40; *In re Grand Jury* [1999]). This decision gains additional significance because it exemplifies the way the courts may use the analogy of the time honored attorney-client privilege in seeking out the "contours" of the newer privilege.

Perhaps the most controversial issue that the courts have struggled to resolve is the so-called "at issue waiver." Before *Jaffee*, courts that had ruled on the issue tended to take the position that if a person entered his mental condition into a claim or defense, he thereby waived the right to keep privileged any records of prior or current psychotherapy (West, 1998). In essence, this view represented the carrying over of a similar principle from the physician-patient privilege where the courts had ruled that a person must not use the privilege as both a "sword and a shield," such as when entering a claim for a physical injury and then refusing to allow access to the records of medical examinations. Such analogizing to the physician-patient privilege represented a major weakening of the psychotherapist-patient privilege because it meant that any person in psychotherapy would risk exposure in court of some or all confidential information when raising any claim that involved any kind of mental distress. Immediately following *Jaffee* several lower courts continued to follow this line, but a contrary trend has been evolving in which some courts are now beginning to rule, again using the analogy to the attorney-client privilege, that the privilege is not lost in such a case unless the patient specifically intends to use the psychotherapy as part of a claim or defense or to introduce testimony of the psychotherapist (McDonnell, 2001). This trend is consistent with the Supreme Court's holding that the privilege should be absolute and again strengthens the analogy with the attorney-client privilege (Gott, 2001).

Outside the judicial system *Jaffee* has begun to have significant impact as well. In the past three years, the United States Federal Government has been acting under a Congressional mandate to create a Privacy Rule for the protection of all medical records in order to provide a reasonable level of protection as the federally mandated computerization of most health transactions takes place. The new Privacy Rule, which goes into effect in April 2003, has the full force of Federal Law (Department of Health and Human Services, 2000). Although many groups submitted suggestions and pleas for special protection of particular parts of the record, such as HIV-AIDS data, mental health information, and genetic information, the government decided in the end to offer no special protection to any subset of medical data with a single exception: psychotherapy notes. Under the rule, psychotherapy notes are extended very stringent protection and information in such notes may not be disclosed (unless the disclosure is required by law) by the psychotherapist without the patient's specific written authorization. Of particular importance is the provision that no insurance policy may require a patient to sign such an authorization. In other words, insurers will have access only to the very specific information needed for claims processing and may no longer demand access to any additional private information. In its setting forth of the rationale for this very strong protection, the Department of Health and Human Services referred specifically to and relied on the principles enunciated by the Supreme Court in *Jaffee*: "Generally, we have not treated sensitive information differently from other protected health information; however, we have provided additional protections for psychotherapy notes because of *Jaffee v. Redmond* and the unique role of this type of information" (Department of Health and Human Services, 2000, 82652).

14. Conclusion

The Supreme Court's decision in *Jaffee v. Redmond* is the culmination of a near half-century effort to gain recognition in the federal courts for a testimonial privilege for psychotherapy patients. The psychotherapy patient has been given protection analogous to that provided to legal clients and religious penitents. Furthermore, the decision has ramifications that extend beyond the courtroom situation and points the way to further steps for psychotherapists to take to bring their conduct and the conduct of others into line with the new privilege right of their patients. Yet the *Jaffee* privilege rule, as is the case with all privilege rules, raises new questions that will be the subject of debate over the coming years. These questions have to do with the "contours" of the privilege with respect to exceptions and waivers, the types of psychotherapy covered by the privilege, and the classes of psychotherapists whose patients are protected. Coerced waiver-like blanket authorizations of disclosure, which were typically required in the past by third party insurers and Federal programs as a precondition to obtaining confidential psychotherapy, now appear to be improper and are becoming illegal.

Acknowledgments

My thanks to the many people who made helpful comments and suggestions, especially: Jerome Beigler, M.D., Norman Clemens, M.D., Edward J. Imwinkelried, Esq., Marjorie Karowe, Esq., Barry Landau, M.D., Melissa Nelken, Esq. Particular thanks to Christine Koggel for her extensive editorial assistance and suggestions.

Works Cited

Allred v. State. [1976] Alaska, 554 P.2d 411.

Amann, D. M., and Imwinkelreid, Edward J. (1997) "The Supreme Court's Decision to Recognize a Psychotherapist Privilege in *Jaffee v. Redmond*," 116 S. CT.

———. (1996) "The Meaning of 'Experience' and the Role of 'Reason' Under Federal Rule of Evidence 501," *University of Cincinnati Law Review,* 65: pp. 1019–1049.

American Medical Association Committee on Mental Health. (1954) "Resolution on Relations of Medicine and Psychology," *Journal of the American Medical Association,* 156: p. 72.

American Psychoanalytic Association (1994) *Practice Bulletin #2: Charting Psychoanalysis.* URL = http://www.apssa.org/pubinfo/pract21.htm.. Published as American Psychoanalytic Association (1997). "Charting Psychoanalysis," *Journal of the American Psychoanalytic Association,* 45: pp. 656-672.

Archer, M. S. (1997) "All Aboard the Bandwagon!: The Uncertain Scope of the Federal Psychotherapist-Client Privilege in the Aftermath of *Jaffee-Redmon*d," *Journal of Urban and Contemporary Law,* 52: pp. 355–374.

Aronson, R. H. (2001) "The Mental Health Provider Privilege in the Wake of *Jaffee v. Redmond*," *Oklahoma Law Review,* 54: pp. 591–612.

Beigler, Jerome S. (1984) "*Tarasoff v.* Confidentiality," *Behavioral Science and the Law,* 2: pp. 273–289.

———. (1978) "Psychiatry and Confidentiality," *American Journal of Forensic Psychiatry,* 1: pp. 7–20.

———. (1971) "The 1971 Amendment of the Illinois Statute on Confidentiality: A New Development in Privilege Law," *American Journal of Psychiatry,* 129: pp. 87–91.

Binder v. Ruvell. [1952] (Civil Docket 52 C 25 35, Circuit Court of Cook County, Ill., June 24, 1952) reported in full: *Journal of the American Medical Association*, 150: pp. 1241–1242.

Cantu, D. A. (1998) "When Should Federal Courts Require Psychotherapists to Testify About Their Patients? An Interpretation of *Jaffee v. Redmond*," *University of Chicago Legal Forum,* 1998: pp. 375–394.

Davidson, H. A. (1956) "The Structure of Private Practice of Psychiatry," *American Journal of Psychiatry,* 113: pp. 41–44.

Department of Health and Human Services (2000) "Standards for Privacy of Individually Identifiable Health Information; Final Rule," *Federal Register,* 65: pp. 82461–82510.

Dubbleday, C. J. H. (1985) "The Psychotherapist-Client Testimonial Privilege: Defining the Professional Involved," *Emory Law Journal,* 34: pp. 777–826.

Fisher, Harry M. (1964) "The Psychotherapeutic Professions and the Law of Privileged Communications," *Wayne State Law Review,* 10: pp. 609–654.

Flaxman, K. N. (1996) *Reply Brief for Petitioner in* Jaffee v. Redmond.

———. (1995) *Brief for Petitioner in* Jaffee v. Redmond, November.

Fulkerson, M. B. (1997) "One Step Forward, Two Steps Back: The Recognized but Undefined Federal Psychotherapist-Patient Privilege," *Missouri Law Review,* 62: pp. 401–424.

Gabbard, Glen O. (1990) *Psychodynamic Psychiatry in Clinical Practice.* Washington: American Psychiatric Association.

Goldstein, Abraham S., and Jack Katz. (1962) "Psychiatrist-patient privilege: The GAP Proposal and the Connecticut Statute," *American Journal of Psychiatry,* 118: pp. 733–739.

Gott, R. M. (2001) "The Evolving Treatment of 'Garden-Variety' Claims under the Psychotherapist-Patient Privilege," *Journal of Trial & Appellate Advocacy,* 6: pp. 91–105.

Graham, Michael H. (1996) *Handbook of Federal Evidence*, 4th Edition.

Group for the Advancement of Psychiatry. (1960) "Confidentiality and Privileged Communication in the Practice of Psychiatry," *GAP Report 45*: pp. 89–112.

Guttmacher, Manfred S., and Henry Weihoffen. (1952) *Psychiatry and the Law*, New York: Norton.

Harris, G. C. (1999) "The Dangerous Patient Exception to the Psychotherapist-Patient Privilege: the *Tarasoff* Duty and the *Jaffee* Footnote," *Washington Law Review,* 74: pp. 33–68.

Harvard Law Review Association. (1985) "Developments in the Law: Privileged Communications," *Harvard Law Review*, 98: pp. 1450–1666.

Hofmann, Stefan G., and D. A. Spiegel. (1999) "Panic Control Treatment and Its Applications," *Journal of Psychotherapeutic Practice and Research,* 8: pp. 3–11.

Hollender, Marc H. (1960) "The Psychiatrist and the Release of Patient Information," *American Journal of Psychiatry*, 116: pp. 828–833.

Hoover, J. Edgar. (1950) "Let's Keep America Healthy," *Journal of the American Medical Association*, 144: pp. 1094–1095.

Imwinkelried, Edward J. (1997) "A New Threat to Plaintiffs' Discovery Rights?" *Trial,* 33: pp. 36–43.

———. (1994) "An Hegelian Approach to Privileges Under Federal Rule of Evidence 501: The Restrictive Thesis, the Expansive Antithesis, and the Contextual Synthesis," *Nebraska Law Review,* 73: pp. 511–523.

In re Grand Jury (Gregory P. Violette) 183 F.3d 71 (1st Cir. 1999)

Jaffee v. Redmond. [1996] 116 S. Ct. 1923.

Jordan, J. S. (1984) "The Psychotherapist-Patient Privilege, the Child Abuse Exception, and the Protection of Privacy Through the Fifth Amendment," *Whittier Law Review,* 6: pp. 1033–1053.

Josephson, G. D. (1998) "Couching the Law of Privilege: The Supreme Court Recognition of Psychotherapist-Patient Privilege," *Whittier Law Review*, 19: pp. 533–557.

Klein, J. S. (1998) "'I'm Your Therapist, You Can Tell Me Anything': The Supreme Court Confirms the Psychotherapist-Patient Privilege in *Jaffee v. Redmond,*" *Depaul Law Review,* 47: pp. 701–741.

Knight, Robert P. (1953) "The Present Status of Organized Psychoanalysis in the United States," *Journal of the American Psychoanalytical Association,* 1: pp. 197-221.

Louisell, David W. (1957) "The Psychologist in Today's Legal World: Part 2," *Minnesota Law Review,* 41: pp. 731–750.

———. (1956) "Confidentiality, Conformity and Confusion: Privileges in Federal Court Today," *Tulane Law Review,* 21: pp. 101–124.

Marcus, R. L. (1986) "The Perils of Privilege: Waiver and the Litigator," *Michigan Law Review,* 84: pp. 1605–1655.

McDonnell, E. E. (2001) "Certainty Thwarted: Broad Waiver Versus Narrow Waiver of the Psychotherapist-Patient Privilege After *Jaffee v. Redmond,*" *Hastings Law Journal,* 52: pp. 1369–1390.

Molony, T. J. (1998) "Is the Supreme Court Ready to Recognize Another Privilege? An Examination of the Accountant-Client Privilege in the Aftermath of *Jaffee v. Redmond,*" *Washington & Lee Law Review,* 55: pp. 247–286.

Montaigne, Michel Eyquem de. (1952) "Of Vanity." In *The Essays of Michel Eyquem de Montaigne*, volume 25 of Great Books of the Western World. Robert Maynard Hutchins, editor-in-chief, Charles Cotton, transl. Chicago: Britannica, pp. 457–486.

Muncie, W., and E. G. Billings. (1951) "A Survey of Conditions of Private Practice Throughout the United States and Canada," *American Journal of Psychiatry,* 108: pp. 171–172.

NCCUSL (2002) The National Conference of Commissioners on Uniform State Laws, URL = http://www.nccusl.org/nccusl/default.asp. Model Rule is at URL = http://www.law.upenn.edu/bll/ulc/ure/ev503.htm.

Nelken, Melissa L. (2000) "The Limits of Privilege: The Developing Scope of Federal Psychotherapist-Patient Privilege Law," *The Review of Litigation,* 20: pp. 1–43.

Note. (1996) "The Supreme Court—Leading Cases," *Harvard Law Review,* 110: pp. 287–295.

Note. (1962) "Functional Overlap Between the Lawyer and Other Professionals: Its Implications for the Privileged Communications Doctrine," *Yale Law Journal,* 71: pp. 1226–1273.

Note. (1952) "Confidential Communication to a Psychotherapist: A New Testimonial Privilege," *Northwestern Law Review,* 47: pp. 384–389.

Note. (1951) "Regulation of Psychological Counseling and Psychotherapy," *Columbia. Law Review,* 51: pp. 474–495.

Patton, Michael J., et al. (1997) "The Missouri Psychoanalytic Counseling Research Project: Relation of Changes in counseling Process to Client Outcomes," *Journal of Counseling Psychology*, 44: pp. 189–208.

Patton, Michael J. and Naomi M. Meara. (1992) *Psychoanalytic Counseling*. Chichester, England: Wiley.

People v. Stritzinger [1983]34 Cal.3d 505, Kaus, J. (Otto M.. Kaus) Concurring and Dissenting.

Perkins, R. M., et al.(1954) "Summary of Symposium on Privileged Communications," *American Journal of Psychiatry,* 111: pp. 13–21.

Pomerantz, Jay M. (1999) "Behavioral Health Matters—Is Confidentiality Still Protected Under Managed Behavioral Health Care?" *Drug Benefit Trends,* 11: pp. 2–56.

Proposed Rules of Evidence. Hearings before the Special Subcommittee on Reform of the Federal Criminal Laws of the House Com. On the Judiciary, 93rd Cong. 1st Sess.(8 February 1973).

Ricafort, N. M. (1998) "*Jaffee v. Redmond*: The Supreme Court's Dramatic Shift Supports the Recognition of a Federal Parent/Child Privilege," *Indiana Law Review*, 32: pp. 259–295.

Saltzburg, Stephan A. (1984) "Privileges and Professionals: Lawyers and Psychiatrists," *Virginia Law Review,* 66: pp. 597–651.

Saul, Leon. (1938) "Psychoanalytic Case Records," *Psychoanalytical Quarterly,* 8: pp. 186–190.

Shuman, Daniel W., and W. Foote. (1999) "*Jaffee v. Redmond*'s Impact: Life After the Supreme Court's Recognition of a Psychotherapist-Patient Privilege," *Professional Psychological Research and Practice*, 30: pp. 479–487.

Siegler, Mark. (1982) "Confidentiality in Medicine—A Decrepit Concept," *New England. Journal of Medicine,* 307: pp. 1518–1521.

Slovenko, Ralph. (1998) Psychotherapy and Confidentiality. Springfield, Ill.: Thomas.

———. (1997) "The Psychotherapist-Patient Privilege," *American Journal of Psychoanalysis,* 57: pp. 63–73.

———. (1975) "On Testimonial Privilege," *Contemporary Psychoanalysis,* 11: pp. 188–205.

———. (1974) "Psychotherapist-Patient Testimonial Privilege: A Picture of Misguided Hope," *Catholic University Law Review,* 23: pp. 649–673.

———. (1960) "Psychiatry and a Second Look at the Medical Privilege," *Wayne State Law Review,* 6: pp. 175–203.

———. (1958) "The Physician and Privileged Communication," *Journal of the Louisiana State Medical Society,* 110: pp. 39–53.

Slovenko, Ralph, and G. L. Usdin. (1961) "The Psychiatrist and Privileged Communication," *Archives of General Psychiatry,* 4: pp. 431–444.

Smith, S. R. (1986) "Medical and Psychotherapy Privileges and Confidentiality: On Giving With One hand and Removing With the Other," *Kentucky Law Review,* 75: pp. 473–557.

———. (1980) "Constitutional Privacy in Psychotherapy," *George Washington Law Review*, 49: pp. 1–60.

Smith-Bell, M., and William J. Winslade. (1994) "Privacy, Confidentiality and Privilege in Psychotherapeutic Relationships," *American Journal of Orthopsychiatry,* 64: pp. 180–193.

Stern, Harold R. (1958) "The Problem of Privilege: Historical and Juridical Sidelights," *American Journal of Psychiatry*, 115: pp. 1071–1080.

Swidler and Berlin and James Hamilton v. U. S. [1998] S. Ct. 97–1192.

Tuttle, G. M. and Woods, D. R. (1998) *The Managed Care Answer Book For Mental Health Professionals*. Bristol, Penna.: Brunner/Mazel.

U. S. v. Nixon. [1974] 418 U. S. 683.

West, A. P. (1998) "Implying Plaintiffs' Waivers of the Psychotherapist-Patient Privilege after *Jaffee v. Redmond*," *University of Pittsburgh Law Review,* 59: pp. 901–929.

Whalen v. Roe. [1977] 429 U. S. 589.

Wigmore, John H. (1961) *Evidence in Trials at Common Law*, (McNaughton rev.). New York: Little, Brown.

Winick, Bruce. (1996) "The Psychotherapist-Patient Privilege: A Therapeutic Jurisprudence View," *University of Miami Law Review,* 50: pp. 249–265.

Eleven

RESPONDING TO DEFENSE DEMANDS FOR CLIENTS' RECORDS IN SEXUAL VIOLENCE CASES: SOME GUIDANCE FOR RECORD KEEPERS

Karen Busby

1. Introduction

In early 1993, I was working on a case for the Women's Legal Education and Action Fund (LEAF). Someone suggested that we should read the *Osolin* case, a decision from the British Columbia Court of Appeal that was being appealed to the Supreme Court of Canada. It was a horrible case. The seventeen-year old complainant was abducted from her home, wearing only her underwear, by two men she had met earlier in the day. She had not invited them to her home. They drove her forty miles to a remote cabin, tied her to a bed, shaved her pubic hair, and repeatedly sexually assaulted her. She escaped in the middle of the night and was found by the police disoriented and wandering at the side of a highway wearing a nightgown. One man pleaded guilty, but the other contended that he thought she was consenting and the case went to trial. He was convicted and appealed his conviction. But it was not the brutality of the sexual assault or even the ludicrousness of the consent defense presented by the defendant that shocked us about the case. Rather it was his request to cross-examine the complainant on information he found in her psychiatric files. How did the defendant get the files? What use could he and his lawyer make of them? What effects would such a practice have on complainants and record keepers?

Osolin and his lawyer had obtained the complainant's files simply by asserting that since she was under psychiatric care she might not be a competent witness, that is, she might have memory or perceptual problems that made her testimony unreliable. Once they were in possession of the files, it was clear that she was competent. But the defense now contended that they should be able to cross-examine the complainant about the information contained in the records. For example, they learned from the records that the complainant did not always have a good relationship with her parents. This fact, according to the defendant, might show her motive to lay the complaint, perhaps that she needed an excuse to explain to her parents why she stayed out all night. Also, her psychiatrist had written on the file that "she is concerned that her attitude and behaviors may have affected the man to some extent and is having second thoughts about the entire case" (*R. v. Osolin* [1993], para. 92). The defendant contended that he should be able to cross-examine the complainant about inconsistent prior statements, in particular whether she had ever told anyone that maybe she did consent to the events that evening.

It was too late for LEAF to participate in the *Osolin* case but we found out through the Ontario Coalition of Sexual Assault Centres and the Canadian Association of Sexual Assault Centres (CASAC) that they knew of other situations where the defendants in criminal cases had sought complainants' counseling records. More research revealed that defense lawyers had been encouraging each other to try this tactic, which one lawyer described as "whacking the complainant" (Schmitz, 1998, p. 22), as early as 1988. Moreover, we discovered that they were seeking not just counseling records but also every other possible personal record, including records from child welfare agencies, prisons and other corrections bodies, schools (including residential schools), doctors and hospitals, employers, the immigration department, victims' advocates, and abortion clinics.

Records access in criminal cases has now become a primary concern for feminist service providers and other record keepers. Many have taken measures, primarily through modifying record keeping practices, to alleviate this concern (Downe, 2000). In this chapter, I will review the Supreme Court of Canada's decisions and Parliament's legislative initiatives on records disclosure and then briefly consider some of the effects these practices have had on record-keepers. I will then turn to my main focus: the relatively narrow issue of whether and how those who keep records, especially counselors and therapists, should alter their record making and retention practices in light of the continuing uncertainty about when the defense (and therefore the defendant himself) can obtain possession of a complainant's records in criminal prosecutions. In particular, I will consider three issues. Do counselors have an obligation to create evidence? Should counselors stop keeping records? And what can record keepers do to minimize the impact of their records in criminal proceedings?

2. The Supreme Court of Canada's Record Disclosure Decisions

The Supreme Court of Canada released the *Osolin* decision in 1993. It stated that once defendants had access to complainants' personal records they should be free to use them for cross-examining on motive to fabricate or on prior statements about the events. The Court's judgment was, in effect, an invitation to defense lawyers across Canada to do whatever they could to access records, including making groundless assertions about complainants' competency.

Over the next few years, LEAF, working in a coalition with CASAC, the Aboriginal Women's Council of BC, and the DisAbled Women's Network, worked to develop legal responses to the now burgeoning defense requests for access to complainants' personal records. The coalition's position when this issue went to the Supreme Court of Canada was:

> until the devaluation of women and children, their word and their integrity are addressed instead of reinforced by the law, the disclosure of complainants' personal records is so likely to reinstate sexism in the administration of criminal law, to deter reporting, to distort the fact-finding process and to violate victims' integrity that affirmation of complainants' constitutional rights ... requires that *no personal records be disclosed in any sexual offense proceeding* (Women's Legal Education and Action Fund, 1996, p. 443, emphasis added).

In December 1995, the Supreme Court of Canada, in its controversial *O'Connor* decision, endorsed the practice of giving defendants in sexual violence cases the right to obtain access to complainants' personal records on the ground that they were relevant to the defense in a wide range of circumstances, mainly concerning the complainant's credibility. As in most of the records disclosure cases, the vote on the Court was close: five of the judges (the majority) voted for disclosure whereas four judges (the dissent) voted against. The majority, whilst ignoring the arguments put forward by the feminist coalition, went so far as to hold that such access was part of a defendant's constitutional fair trial rights. It described numerous situations, to be described in more detail later, where records access would be justified and not a single concrete example of a situation where access would not be permissible. In contrast, the dissenting judges stated that records should be disclosed in rare cases only. Following this decision, many criminal defense lawyers considered it a professional obligation to seek all possible personal records in sexual violence cases.

A little more that a year after the *O'Connor* decision, the Supreme Court of Canada, in the *Carosella* case, stayed indecent assault charges against the defendant, a high school teacher, on the grounds that rape crisis center records of a counseling session held just prior to the complainant's report to the police had been destroyed and that therefore his fair trial rights had been irreparably compromised. The center, whose employees had been involved in numerous time-consuming records applications, had developed a policy of destroying all files where there might be "police involvement" unless a subpoena had already been served. The difference between the reasoning of the majority of judges and the dissent (again a 5/4 split) could not have been more stark. The dissent stated that third parties have "no obligations to preserve evidence" and while the center's policy "could perhaps be seen as questionable, the Court did not need to determine if it was appropriate" (*R. v. Carosella* [1997], para. 145). However, the majority decision described the center's policy as "high handed" and "an obstruction of the course of justice" (para. 40). Since the majority described the center's actions using the same language as the criminal offense of obstruction of justice and since the outcome of the case was a stay of the charges against *Carosella*, the twisted implications of this decision are that record-keepers who destroy records for the purpose of avoiding disclosure risk incurring criminal charges against themselves as well as having those against the defendant dismissed.

It is interesting to contrast the *O'Connor* and *Carosella* outcomes with how Canada's Supreme Court treats records created in a lawyer-client relationship. In the *McClure* case (2001), the defendant faced both criminal and civil proceedings alleging sexual violence. In the criminal proceedings, he sought lawyer-client records from the lawyer representing the complainant in the civil action to establish that the complainant's motive in going to the police was to extract a monetary settlement from the defendant. The lower court applied the *O'Connor* test and held that since the record might contain information on motive to fabricate, which is sufficient grounds to access a file, the lawyer's file should be released to the defendant. The Supreme Court of Canada reversed this decision and held that lawyer-client privilege could only be infringed if the defendant satisfied four conditions: the information was not available from any other source; a reasonable doubt as to his guilt could not be raised in any other way; the evidence sought related to core issues going to the guilt of the accused (and not just, for example, the credibility of the complainant); and, there existed a genuine risk of wrongful conviction. This case established that the threshold for release of lawyers' records (traditionally protected by privilege) is far higher than the simple relevance threshold for other records set in *O'Connor*.

The *O'Connor* and *Carosella* cases were utterly disastrous for women and children who have been sexually violated and especially for those who seek to rely on the criminal justice system to call their abusers to account. These decisions reinforce traditional beliefs about the credibility of those who have been sexually assaulted. These beliefs have animated the prosecution of such cases for centuries and, additionally, they now operate to separate women from the support systems that have developed to help women understand and challenge this form of oppression.

In response to pressure from feminists across Canada, Parliament passed amendments to the *Criminal Code*, commonly known as Bill C–46, in May 1996. This legislation was designed to reduce defendants' access to complainants' personal records in two significant ways. Most notably the legislation established that a number of defense assertions concerning the relevance of records would be insufficient to support a records application. The list included many of the grounds approved earlier by the Supreme Court of Canada in *O'Connor* and *Carosella* (for example, the defense could not get the record simply because it might contain information about her sexual or psychiatric history, as these grounds were now considered insufficient). As well, Parliament, unlike the Supreme Court of Canada, required lower court judges to seriously consider the impact of records disclosures on complainants' equality rights, including their willingness to report offences and to get assistance in the aftermath of an assault. Bill C–46 did not completely deny defendants' access to all personal records and therefore fell short of the position advocated before the courts and Parliament by feminist organizations. Nonetheless, feminist organizations did support the bill as the minimal acceptable protection for complainants.

Although defense lawyers immediately challenged the constitutionality of Bill C–46, the Supreme Court of Canada upheld the law in the 1999 *Mills* case. Canadian feminists were relieved that the bill was upheld but were disappointed that the Court stripped the "insufficient assertions" section of substantive meaning. Feminists had argued that the list of assertions insufficient to establish likely relevance meant that a records application asserting these grounds should always fail. However the Court held that this provision "does not entirely prevent an accused from relying on the factors listed, but simply prevents reliance on *bare assertions* of the listed matters, where there is no other evidence and they stand on their own" (*R. v. Darrach* [2000], para. 118, emphasis in original). Thus the provision became an evidentiary rather than a substantive provision: if the defendant can establish a case-specific evidentiary or informational foundation to suggest that the assertions are relevant, then the judge can order that the records be released. This interpretation of the bill significantly increases the likelihood that records will be released to the defendant. Moreover the Court does not repudiate any of its earlier cases (like *Osolin*, *Carosella*, or *O'Connor*) and therefore a judge who wants to release records can still find ample judicial authority to justify release.

As noted already, Bill C–46 does not bar defendants from making applications to produce records. The Bill leaves considerable discretion in the hands of the trial judge to weigh the rights of the defendant, the complainant, and society. However given that the historic balance, especially in sexual violence cases, has been to take special care in protecting defendants against deluded or malicious women, many judges will continue to exercise this discretion in favor of the defendant. The attitudinal change which Bill C–46 requires, if our experience with thirty years of attempting to change judicial attitudes around the use of sexual history evidence is a reliable indicator, will be neither quick nor widespread. Moreover, as almost no assertion concerning the relevance of the records is categorically barred as an impermissible assertion, lower court judges continue to have many grounds upon which to justify the release of records. Post *Mills* research has shown that records production applications continue to be successful (Busby, 2002). As *Shearing* (2000), the most recent Supreme Court of Canada decision on records, has established, once a record is in the defendant's hands, courts are reluctant to limit the defendant's ability to cross-examine the complainant based on information found in the record. Thus no reassurances can be given to complainants that their records will not get into the hands of defendants which means record keepers must remain attentive to this possibility when they create records.

While this chapter will focus on the use of personal records in criminal cases, I should mention that these records have also been sought in civil cases and cases before administrative boards. The *Ryan* case, a Supreme Court of Canada decision issued about the same time as *Carosella,* involved a civil suit for damages by a seventeen-year old plaintiff patient against the defendant psychiatrist who had been criminally convicted of indecently assaulting her. He sought her post-assault psychiatric records on the issue of the extent to which her difficulties were caused by his conduct. The Court held that her psychiatric records were only protected by a partial privilege giving permission for parts of the records to be disclosed to the defendant's solicitor and to expert witnesses on the condition that use be for the sole purpose of the litigation.

3. Effects on Record Keepers

The practice of seeking personal records in criminal cases has created numerous other problems for record keepers, especially counsel counselors and therapists, as well as complainants. A recent study (Downe, 2000) determined that, since the *O'Connor* decision, more than fifty per cent of sexual assault counseling centers have had their records subpoenaed, and most of these centers have had records subpoenaed more than once. While Bill C–46 permits both complainants and record keepers to appear with a lawyer in court to argue why records ought not to be released, such appearances are expensive and time-consuming. Record keepers have appeared in court to formally oppose disclosure of their records in fewer than half of the cases even thoughtheir presence at the courthouse while the application is being argued is usually required because a subpoena will have been issued. Many counselors tell stories of spending days in courthouse halls under subpoena waiting to be called. A British study on medical doctors' experiences as expert witnesses in sexual violence cases found that all doctors spoke of how shocked they felt at the behavior of defense counsel when they first appeared as a witness in court. Doctors comments included, "You feel very attacked and insulted," "The court experience is the most awful thing that I think I've ever experienced," and "If I had the choice, I don't think that I'd ever do it again" (Temkin, 1998, p. 839). To avoid having to appear in court, some record keepers (including doctors, social workers, and prison officials) have simply handed over files to the police, Crown Attorneys, or defense lawyers either upon request or of their own initiative without the complainants' consent (Busby, 1997; Oleskiw, 1999). Fortunately, Bill C–46 now precludes the Crown and the police from disclosing to the defense any records it receives in this manner. However, as Bill C–46 does not impose any non-disclosure requirements on record keepers (although such practices would obviously violate other ethical, professional, and statutory obligations), those who freely disclosed directly to the defense prior to Bill C–46 might continue to do so. The Supreme Court of Canada recently affirmed in the *Shearing* case that once the defendant has the record, regardless of how it was obtained, cross-examination should be permitted in most cases.

The Court's *O'Connor* and *Carosella* decisions and developing record disclosure guidelines, if not by design then certainly by effect, have undermined the work of sexual assault centers and counselors and other therapists across the country. Some counselorshave faced the dilemma of whether to suggest postponing counseling until criminal court proceedings are complete, a process which usually takes a year at least. As group counseling records have also been sought, some counselors now exclude from group counseling anyone who may become a complainant. Record keepers have also been excluded from the courtroom during hearings since they might eventually be called to testify. Thus they cannot be present in court to provide support for the complainant.

Perhaps most insidiously, the Supreme Court of Canada cast a pall over the work of counselors and therapists when, in both the *O'Connor* and the *Carosella* judgments, it credited the belief that counselors and therapists use improper therapy techniques to help their clients conjure up accounts of abuse. Sue Campbell has observed:

> what I shall call "false memory discourse" has activated potent stereotypes of women as emotionally unstable and easily manipulated. These gendered stereotypes have combined with growing public uncertainty about the reliability of autobiographical memory to allow for an extraordinarily fluid use of false memory discourse, enabling defence lawyers to call into question the credibility of women who bring complaints of sexual harm before the courts (Campbell, 2002, p. 3).

In a culture characterized by substantive inequalities, which in the context of sexual violence lead to internalized self doubt or self blame or diminished expectations and self esteem, coming to terms with the harms of that violence does require that women understand practices of inequality. Not mentioned in false memory discourse, as Campbell points out, is that understanding the harms of sexual violence requires rethinking the social and cultural frameworks through which they have been disguised. Counseling and therapy that assists in this understanding will lead to a re-remembering of the past, that is, a new contextualization of certain relationships and behaviors. Thus, in using the broad brush of improper therapy techniques, the Court has discredited the transformative effects that understanding inequalities in personal relationships can have on the perception women have of their lives.

4. Is There an Obligation to Create Evidence?

Record keepers who work in forensic investigation or law enforcement are responsible for collecting and analyzing evidence for criminal cases. Thus, a doctor who is involved in gathering rape kit evidence in a hospital emergency room is responsible for collecting evidence and may (or may not) be responsible for patient care, such as giving information on contraception or STDs (Temkin, 1998). A social worker evaluating a child both gathers evidence about the abuse and works out a safety plan. A psychiatrist engaged in assessing whether someone is a dangerous offender is specifically charged with gathering and evaluating information for presentation in court and may have little, if anything, to do with the person's treatment. But aside from these situations, which are well understood by those who have forensic and law enforcement functions, most record keepers have no obligation to create, or even to collect, evidence for criminal prosecutions.

There are good reasons why counselors, therapists, and others who work with complainants after an assault should not take on the task of collecting evidence. Unless they have been trained in evidence gathering, they probably would not do a thorough job collecting information that is required for a criminal prosecution. Taking on a law enforcement task is incompatible with the job of therapy and counseling. The former involves a focus on "what exactly happened?" and "how can you corroborate your story?" whereas the latter considers issues like "how do you feel about what happened?" and "where do you want to go from here?" A counseling session in which the counselor's task was to get something akin to a police statement, with a detailed and nuanced chronology of the events giving rise to the charge, would be profoundly alienating to many clients. While some details of the assault could be discussed from time to time at different counseling sessions, a thorough description at one time is unlikely. In my three year stint as a rape crisis counselor, the only callers who ever wanted to give precise, detailed accounts were men who took evident pleasure in describing (what invariably was their fantasy about) a sexual assault of a woman.

Some judges (although not all) operate under serious misapprehensions about what counselors do. For example, in the *Carosella* case, the complainant gave evidence that her reason for going to the sexual assault center was simply to figure how to make a complaint to the police. I would hazard a guess that the file notes in question in *Carosella* would have contained only a summary of a routine discussion on how to make a report to the police. Yet the majority stated, even though the trial record contained no evidence to support this assertion, that the counseling notes were "the first detailed account of the alleged incidents." Additionally, they surmised that the notes "may have revealed the state of the complainant's perception and memory. They might have revealed that some of the complainant's statements resulted from suggestions made by the interviewer" (*R. v. Carosella* [1997], para. 46). These egregious comments were pure speculation by the Court as there was no evidence on the record that the complainant had memory or perceptual problems or that the decision to report was anything other than the complainant's idea.

Consent is the most common defense in sexual violence cases involving complainants who are more than sixteen years old. Counselors have no reason to raise the issue of consent with clients (except, possibly, as discussed later, when discussing blame) and therefore even if the client describes the incidents giving rise to the charge, the counselor probably will not make any notes, much less detailed precise notes, on consent-related facts that may be relevant in a criminal prosecution. For example, in the *Fletcher* case [1993], the complainant had agreed to go out with her former boyfriend to discuss their break-up. He drove her home but she stated that she did not want him to come in. She got ready for bed in the bathroom and when she went to the bedroom she found him hiding behind the door. She testified that he sexually assaulted her and then left. The police statement did not contain as detailed an account of the incident as the one the complainant gave in oral testimony at the preliminary hearing. The defendant argued that certain nuances were very important to the issue of consent. In particular: did he try to remove her bathrobe or pull off her bathrobe? Did he just push on her legs or did he try to force them apart? Did she call to her roommate or scream out to her roommate? Subsequently, the defendant argued that he required access to sexual assault counseling records to examine them for additional accounts of the assault. However, it is doubtful that either the complainant/client or the counselor, especially in the aftermath of a break-in and some kind of assault, were concerned with the precise details of what had happened and the notes would have provided no assistance in this regard. Nonetheless, the judge accepted the defendant's argument and held that the records were relevant because they might contain a prior statement.

Some lawyers advise record keepers that more notes are better notes. This advice may be good when the record keepers are documenting the process of recovery of memories or when, like the emergency room nurse, the child welfare worker, or the forensic psychiatrist described earlier, they are collecting and evaluating evidence. This is not good advice, in my view, if the concern is that the notes might be used in a criminal prosecution to discredit a complainant. If there are statements on the file about the events giving rise to the charge, for example, it is much more likely that the file will be ordered disclosed to the defendant. Furthermore, the general rule in criminal prosecutions (with some narrow exceptions) is that prior statements by a witness about the events are not admissible if they are consistent with the testimony being given. Prior statements are only admissible if they are inconsistent with previous statements. (Although it must be mentioned that some defense counsel have argued that they need therapy notes to see if memories have been scripted, a scenario more likely, they have argued, if the story is told in precisely the same way each time it has been recorded.) Thus, in the *Fletcher* case, the notes probably could not have been used in court if they had only mentioned that the defendant had pulled off (not just removed) the complainant's bathrobe and forced apart (not just pushed on) her legs, and that she had screamed (not just called) to her roommate. Detailed notes will not help complainants; yet the fact that they are on file increases the likelihood that they will be released to the defendant for review.

While record keepers do not have a general obligation to create evidence that can be used in criminal proceedings, the law is clear that, once the record is made, it should not be destroyed. Similarly once a record has been made, it should not be changed as an adverse inference can be drawn when records are changed after the fact. If necessary, a note can be written explaining why a record should be changed but the original notes should be left intact and not crossed out, torn out, or otherwise altered. As noted earlier, the Supreme Court of Canada stated in the *Carosella* case that criminal charges may be dropped against the defendant if a third party record has been destroyed, and, in an ironic twist, those who are responsible for destroying the record can also be subject to obstruction of justice charges. This rule not only applies to documents that have been subpoenaed but, as the *Carosella* case makes clear, it applies to all documents that might be subject to a disclosure order. Therefore, while it is prudent for all record keepers to have a policy on records retention and destruction, the intent of such a policy cannot be to avoid record disclosure applications.

5. To Record or Not Record

Ever since defendants started making record disclosure applications many record keepers, especially those who are involved in counseling have had to consider whether they should stop making records at all. In my view, as I will discuss below, it would be a mistake to stop making records altogether. Nonetheless, the decision is complicated and one for record keepers to make themselves.

The failure to keep notes can interfere with the provision of services. Memory is imperfect and the counselor who can not remember what was discussed in previous sessions will not be effective. In some situations, co-workers need to rely on the notes of others for information. For example, all staff at a battered women's shelter need to know if a client is suicidal or if her partner poses a heightened or particular risk. On the other hand, sometimes minimal notes with little, if any, identifying information are all that is required. Many crisis line callers simply need information and the worker will not even know the caller's name. The only record that may be kept of calls like these are number of calls and duration (to assist in determining needed resources) as well as the general nature of the information sought (so that the center can ensure that all workers are up-to-date on the kinds of information being sought by callers). So, notwithstanding anything else I say, the underlying question all record keepers need to ask is "what notes do I/we need to make in order to provide the best service?"

The failure to keep notes could bring record keepers into conflict with other responsibilities, although the potential for conflict will vary depending on the nature of the record keeper's work. Certain professional bodies have clear and specific recording protocols and failure to meet these requirements can result in disciplinary action. Medical doctors, for example, must document symptomatology, diagnosis, treatment, and referral information. Nurses chart, often by the minute, what is happening with their patients. Most schoolteachers are required to write regular observations of students' academic progress and social behavior. Government employees at sexual assault programs, especially if they are not autonomous centers but part of a larger organization like a hospital or community-based health center, have run into serious disagreements with management or the boards of their institutions over the issue of how detailed records should be. Certain records need to be kept to meet the demands of funding organizations. Usually these demands are minimal involving questions such as, how many people were seen and how long was the meeting? But some funders, especially in a fee-for-service regime, will want to know what the problems and the justification for a particular action are.

Moreover, the failure to keep records makes it difficult to do proper research on violence against women. For example, sexual assault centers were key to documenting and identifying the prevalence of wife assault and sexual abuse of children by fathers, uncles, and brothers. Their logs have been an invaluable source of information on questions such as: have you heard of other assaults by a particular man? How many complainants make reports to the police? How many women are dropping charges because of records applications? The failure to keep records will mean that we will lose valuable archival information on male violence against women.

Finally the failure to keep notes can leave a record keeper vulnerable to charges of negligent work. Any counsel counselor or therapist who has ever been threatened with a lawsuit by a former client should be able to take solace in good notes documenting the process.

6. Minimizing the Impact of Records in Criminal Proceedings

There are three ways a record keeper can minimize the impact of their records in criminal proceedings: establish confidentiality; avoid creating a "prior statement"; and understand the defense rationales for seeking access and, to the extent possible, avoid making notes that can be used for these purposes. These suggestions may keep some records out of defendants' hands or minimize the use that can be made of the records. However, they may be inconsistent with the note keeper's requirement and they are not a foolproof guarantee that records will not be obtained by defendants to discredit a complainant. Therefore some record keepers might find it helpful also to keep in mind that any note they make might be seen by the defense, including the defendant himself.

A. Establish Confidentiality

A record that is not made in the expectation that it will be kept confidential is less likely to be afforded protection from disclosure. Record keepers and clients should be clear about what information will be recorded, the purposes of the record, and who will be permitted to see the record. It should also be clear, preferably in writing, that the record will be kept in strict confidence and not released except by consent or where the law requires disclosure. In some circumstances, it may be advisable for record keepers to warn clients that the records may be released directly to a judge and to the defendant in sexual violence proceedings so that clients can make their decisions in light of this possibility. (This advice may deter some women from seeking counseling until after a criminal prosecution is complete, or it may result in women not making reports to the police. In my view these are decisions that women should make themselves, understanding that no reassurances can be given about the likelihood of a court ordering that the record be released.) Record keepers may also tell clients whether they (or the institutions they work for) are prepared to resist records application by, for example, hiring a lawyer or working with clients' lawyers.

Finally, clients must be aware that their consent to use of the records by a third party may reduce the likelihood that the record will still be considered to be confidential and that upon release to a third party, other legal disclosure obligations will arise. For example, if the complainant agrees to release records to the police or to the Crown, these agents will then be obliged to disclose the record to the defendant. Release to other third parties, especially if they are connected to the government, like a criminal injuries board or victim/witness services may also trigger Crown disclosure obligations. In the *Chisolm* case (1997), the defendant argued that the teenage complainant did not have a privacy interest in matters such as her relationship with her parents, her drug and alcohol usage, her school performance, her interaction with boyfriends, her sexual history, or her criminal conduct and court involvement because she had discussed these matters with the expert psychologist retained by the Crown. The judge accepted that the complainant's expectation of privacy had been diminished and ordered that her counseling records, for matters unrelated to that assault, be produced to the defendant.

B. Avoid Creating "Prior Statements"

If there are inconsistencies between a record and the complainant's testimony in court, the record can be used at trial, in some circumstances, to discredit the complainant. The records used most often to discredit witnesses in this way are statements to police or evidence given in another proceeding, like the preliminary inquiry. However, notes made in a variety of situations can be used in this way, like counseling notes, student or employee misconduct reports, child welfare records, and complainant's own personal diaries, journals, letters, and other writings.

For example, consider the ambiguities in the psychiatrist's note in the *Osolin* case that "she is concerned that her attitude and behaviors may have affected the man to some extent and is having second thoughts about the entire case." What does "concerned" mean? Could it mean that the seventeen-year old complainant was angry for having been subjected to a barrage of suggestions by defense counsel that she consented? Or, that she was trying to believe the world would be a safe place if only she had done the right things? Why was she having second thoughts? Is it because she thought she was to be blamed for what happened or, because, just prior to this session, she had been cross-examined over a period of days at the preliminary inquiry and did not want to go through the ordeal again at trial? The complainant, who may have learned of this note for the first time when cross-examined about it, probably would have been so confused that she would not remember anything about that session, the statement, or the reasons for making it. The defense intended to use the statement to insinuate that she led the men to believe that she was consenting to sex. My point here is not that the psychiatrist erred in writing the note he did, but rather that the note is ambiguous and therefore can be used for the defendant in cross-examination to support discrediting innuendos about the complainant's conduct. Since the defense only has to raise a reasonable doubt about whether she consented, this statement can be a powerful tool. As the discussion earlier on the *Fletcher* case shows, inconsistencies on matters unimportant for the record keeper's purposes may, nevertheless, give legal leverage for access to the file (which, in itself, is problematic for the complainant) and then may be used to raise doubts about the complainant's credibility.

Record keepers can take steps to minimize the likelihood that the record keeper's notes can be used against the complainant at trial by taking care not to create a prior statement, that is, a statement that can subsequently be attributed to the complainant as her own statement. Records are less likely to be considered as a prior statement of the complainant, and therefore less likely to be used in court to discredit her account, if:

(1) The record only contains part of a narrative, or, as is more likely, is not concerned with recording the event giving rise to the charges with precise accuracy, in which case the incompleteness of the narrative should be noted. For example, the account could be prefaced with the disclaimer such as "some, but not all, of the events that occurred included."

(2) Specific quotes are not attributed to the client but rather her statements are paraphrased. Where possible, avoid quotes and use paraphrases.

(3) Notes are not made at the same time the account was given. Generally speaking, only notes that are made at the same time as statements were made can be used to discredit a complainant. However, in some cases, notes made immediately after the interview or session have been used as prior statements.

(4) The record is not reviewed by the client/complainant at the same time it is made. If a client reviews a record at a later date, the date of this review should be noted.

(5) The record is not signed or otherwisc acknowledged by the client. If there is a good reason, have a client sign or acknowledge only that portion of the record that needs to be acknowledged. For example, write it on a separate page.

A concrete example helps demonstrate some of the problems with prior statements and how they may be minimized in record keeping. A sixteen-year old student admits in a session with a school guidance counselor that she frequently lies to her parents and she describes to the counselor some concrete incidents of lying. She is concerned that she is now lying to others and that lying is becoming a habit. The student and the counselor come to a specific written agreement during the next session. In my view, such a statement will be very damaging to the student if it is used in court, an event that might happen years later, to demonstrate that she has a history of lying. The counselor and perhaps the student need to examine ways to minimize the potential harm of the statement. For example: does the agreement have to be in writing and signed or can it simply be an oral contract? If the reasons for lying are apparent (for example, maybe this is one of the methods she has resorted to in order to survive in a troubled household), can these reasons be noted, with the qualifier that, perhaps, this explanation is only a partial one? Does the agreement need to contain details of, or even a reference to, the lying incidents or the student's concern that the problem might be getting worse? Can it just focus on the future rather than the past? Does the counselor need to keep notes during the session or can all notes be made after the session?

7. Know What the Defendant is Looking For

In the *Mills* case, the Supreme Court of Canada stated that a complainant's constitutional privacy and equality rights must yield to a defendant's right to obtain information contained in a record if that information might bear directly on his right to fully defend himself. If record keepers know what information the defendant is looking for, they may be able to keep notes that either do not include this information or, if this is not feasible, record it in such a way as to minimize its value to the defendant. I have reviewed all of the records applications in which reasons for decision were issued in the sixteen month time period between *O'Connor* and the passage of Bill C–46 and the twelve month period immediately after the bill became law to determine what rationales are given in court by defense lawyers to get records. There are eighty cases and, in almost all of them, the defendant asserted more than one rationale for disclosure (Busby, 2001). My findings are described below with some illustrative examples. The rationales were accepted by judges in about half the cases but my data does not permit predictions about when a particular assertion is likely to be accepted.

My research only covers the formal reasons for disclosure presented by the defendant, which were noted in the judges' reasons for decision. While there are anecdotal accounts of complainants dropping charges because they did not want the defendant to see their personal records, it is difficult to determine whether and how often the defendants' motive for making a records application is to intimidate the complainant into dropping charges, or how often complainants react this way. In at least seventy one percent of records applications, the complainant and the defendant were related to each other (and at least a third of these cases involved fathers and daughters) and, in all of the other cases, the complainant and the defendant were involved in some kind of personal or professional relationship. Therefore, it would not be surprising to learn that the unstated reason of some, even many, defendants' applications is to intimidate the complainant into refusing to stay involved in the prosecution.

A. Generic Applications

In a few of the cases where the defendants' rationales for access are available, the request could best be characterized as a smorgasbord. In the *Pritchard* case, for example, the defendant stated:

> the purpose of this Application is to seek evidence (1) to confirm that the complainant T. K. had valid medical reasons for seeking two adjournments of the Trial (2) that there has been no further abuse of drugs in the five years since the offence date (3) to confirm her testimony from the preliminary hearing and/or the Trial previously held as to (4) why she moved to the Fraser Valley (5) injuries sustained by the alleged attack upon her (6) any alleged trauma attendant to the Court appearances (7) her non attendance in Court and any other relevant facts that might assist the defense (8) her history as a prostitute (*R. v. Pritchard* [1996], para. 9).

In the *J. C. B.* case, the defendant already had the complainant's victim impact statement and had cross-examined her about records at the preliminary inquiry. He then sought a number of other records. In granting the defendant's request, the judge stated:

> There are a number of examples I can point out, by which the accused might be able to use the information: the mental condition of the complainant on the night of the incident, at the Preliminary Inquiry, and/or at trial; her expressed hatred toward men following the incident; her anger, whether it existed before the incident, whether it affected or affects her reliability or testimonial capacity; that the incident was central to her thoughts throughout 1996, which would have included the time of the preliminary inquiry, and will also include the trial; that something similar happened before, and whether this experience influenced her and her reporting regarding this incident; that whereas she says sometimes she's not in reality, whether she was in reality at the time of the incident, at the time of the Preliminary Inquiry, and/or at the time of the trial; that whereas she says she is on and off medication, whether she was on medication at the time of the Preliminary Inquiry. There is a variety of purposes for which the accused may use the information regarding the complainant's recollection: testimonial capacity; credibility; competence on the night of the alleged incident, in which she indicates she consumed substantial alcohol, had been involved in sexual relations with a man. Her statements indicate her treatment and counsel counseling occurred before and after, although not at the time of the incident. She says in her statements she had flashbacks

> when drinking, and she was drinking at the time of the incident (*R. v. J. C. B.* [1997], para. 24).

If this judge's assessment as to when records might be relevant is correct, few records of any sort would ever escape defense scrutiny!

The *Pritchard* and *J. C. B.* cases are particularly egregious cases of sweeping defense and judicial rationales for disclosure following *O'Connor* in asserting that the record may contain information concerning the unfolding of events underlying the criminal complaint, may reveal the use of therapy which influenced the complainant's memory of the alleged events, or may contain information that bears on the complainant's credibility. After the *Carosella* decision, defendants added that the record may contain a prior statement, may assist in the preparation of a cross-examination, or may disclose other witnesses.

B. Incompetency

Defendants claimed, in more than half the cases, that the complainant may be an incompetent witness, that is, that she may have memory or perceptual problems making her evidence unreliable. Witness incompetency applications involving adults are very rare in other criminal cases. However, these claims in sexual violence cases are not surprising given that the Supreme Court of Canada has stated that records should be produced if they may have a bearing on complainants' "perception of events at the time of the offense and their memory since" or if they might reveal that the "use of therapy may have influenced the complainants' memory" (*R. v. O'Connor* [1995], para. 29). In only two or three of the eighty cases I reviewed for one study on records practices was it clear that the complainant's testimony was based on recovered memories. Otherwise, it was not possible to determine the number of cases in which the complainants may have had illnesses or disabilities that affected memory or perception because defense lawyers made such assertions so frequently, where they appeared to be completely without foundation, that the calculation would be misleading.

In some cases judges recognized just how spurious the defense claims were and refused the requests, but other judges did not. For example, the evidence filed in support of the records application in the *Mills* case shows that the twelve to thirteen year old complainant made a statement to the police and charges were laid in June, eleven months after the events giving rise to the charges had occurred. From August to October, she sought counseling from an organization that assists families in crisis and was followed by a family support worker. In September, the police could find only one page of her original police statement and this page did not disclose an offence but only the events of the earlier part of the evening. The complainant therefore prepared a second statement. Upon receiving the second statement, the defendant sought the family counseling records stating in his affidavit that "her statement contained more details and extensive facts than previously complained of. I understand that this has been very much due to the complainant being assisted in *recovering memory* by [the social worker]" (*R. v. Mills*. Supreme Court of Canada Record [1999], emphasis added).

No basis for the defendant's belief that the complainant had recovered memories was put forward and it appears groundless. Nor did he mention that the material portions of the original statement seem to have been lost by the police. Yet, on the basis of this affidavit, the family counseling records were ordered to be produced to the defendant. In an affidavit in support of a subsequent application to disclose hospital records, a legal secretary opines that based on her review of already disclosed social worker's notes, the complainant may be "delusional and may suffer from an acute psychosis" (*R. v. Mills*, Supreme Court of Canada Record [1999]). This opinion is not one a legal secretary is qualified to give. Yet when the judge heard the second records application, he again failed to comment on the insufficiency of the evidence and simply stated that the hospital records were likely relevant and ordered that they be produced.

C. Alcohol and Drug Use

Records which might reveal alcohol or drug (ab)use, at times other that the time of the events giving rise to the charges, were sought in about thirty per cent of the cases. This information is used to challenge the complainant's credibility in different ways. The defense may try to show that because of the abuse the complainant has developed significant memory difficulties. Drug and alcohol use may also be used by the defense to discredit the complainant on a general basis, particularly if it has led to other problems (like job loss) for the complainant or if the drugs used were illegal.

D. Motive

Use of records to find evidence of the complainant's motive to fabricate the charge is asserted in almost every records application. Specific motives include: dislike of the defendant or of men in general, retaliation for being placed in care or conversely in order to be taken away from home, to gain advantage in a custody battle, to force the settlement of a civil claim, to seek revenge, to avoid discipline, and to explain the loss of virginity or the presence of a sexually transmitted disease.

E. General Credibility

In half the cases, the defendants wanted records to see if they contained information on discreditable conduct that could impugn the complainant's general credibility or trustworthiness as a witness. Many of these general credibility claims were "fishing expeditions" in the hope that something would be found. Sometimes they were more specific, such as claims that records would show withdrawn claims of sexual violence against others, recorded incidents of lying, particularly to those in authority, involvement with the police, or misconduct at school or work. In one case, after the judge and the defendant had seen the complainant's victim impact statement, the judge ordered disclosure of victim services records for several reasons, including that they might provide information on "her expressed hatred toward men following the incident; her anger, whether it existed before the incident, whether it affected or affects her reliability or testimonial capacity" (*R. v. J. C. B.* [1997], para. 24).

F. Sexual History and Sexual Abuse History

Defendants requested information on sexual history or sexual abuse in about thirty per cent of the cases. They wanted to know whether there was history of prostitution or sexually transmitted disease, or information relating to loss of virginity, or promiscuity. Women and girls are still often required to give sexual history evidence in sexual violence cases and therefore the records might reveal the identity of sexual partners. Information on sexual abuse by others was sought to investigate the source of sexual knowledge, to identify the possibility of distorted sexual perceptions, to explain overreactions and misinterpretations of "innocent" advances, and to examine the possibility of what the defense has called "blurring" (that is, that the complainant has been abused but she is confused about who abused her).

G. Contemporaneous Disclosure

Various records, including child welfare, school and medical files, and diaries, have been ordered disclosed to show that the complainant failed to tell someone about the assault very shortly after it happened. This rationale is troubling because it is based on the faulty assumption that one who has been assaulted would share this information shortly afterwards to another person. Moreover, in order to demonstrate that something does not exist in a file requires disclosure of the whole file for review. This reasoning makes the further problematic assumption that the record keeper would have noted the disclosure. For example, in the *Whitehorse* case, the judge ordered disclosure to the defendant of the complainant's psychiatric records on the grounds that,

> the notes of Dr. DeCoutere ought to be disclosed because the complainant in her statement to the police indicated that she had disclosed the alleged

> abuse to a psychiatrist in 1983 but that the psychiatrist was only interested in knowing whether she enjoyed the sex and whether she was jealous of the accused's wife. The documents reviewed do not address the points mentioned by the complainant in her statement to the police and therefore go directly to her credibility (*R. v. Whitehorse* [1997], para. 10).

If a psychiatrist had, in fact, asked a teenager if she had enjoyed a sexual assault by her teacher, he may have thought it unwise to include a reference to this discussion in his notes. In any event, the connection between the psychiatrist's notes and the complainant's credibility in these circumstances is extremely tenuous.

H. Other Rationales

Other rationales asserted by defendants for access to records include: to show that because her grades had not fallen nothing traumatic could have been occurring in her life; to obtain the names of those who might have information about the case; and, with respect to government records, because they were the only contemporaneous records still in existence in an historic abuse case and might have assisted the defendant in piecing together events.

8. Conclusion

Using a complainant's personal records is the most recent tactic in a centuries-old tradition of discrediting sexually violated women and children on the ground that they are malicious or delusional. Because of the pervasiveness of these beliefs in legal thinking on sexual violence law, a class denial of defense access to these records is unlikely to become law in the foreseeable future. We can expect that many judges will continue to order the release of records to defendants and that defendants who obtained access either by order or some other means will then cross-examine complainants on the contents of these records. In light of the fact that notes and records of all kinds may be used in a manner not intended by the writer, record keepers must be cognizant of how their notes may be distorted in court to the detriment of their clients. Record keepers must consider their record keeping practices with a view to minimizing the impact they can have when a defendant seeks access to them.

Acknowledgments

I would like to acknowledge Colleen Stewart's invaluable research assistance and the financial support from the Legal Research Institute of the University of Manitoba and the Law Foundation of Manitoba. As well, the Gender, Law and Sexuality Institute at Keele University, Keele, England provided me with a most collegial atmosphere in which to complete this paper. Finally, for more than a decade I had the privilege of working with the Women's Legal Education and Action Fund (LEAF) on many sexual violence cases and law reform projects.

Works Cited

Busby, Karen. (2002) "Assessing the Impacts of Bill C–46 and C–49 After *Darrach, Mills* and *Ewanchuk*: A Review of Lower Court Decisions," Work in progress.

———. (2001) "Third Party Records Cases Since *O'Connor*," *Manitoba Law Journal,* 27: pp. 355–373.

———. (1997) "Discriminatory Uses of Personal Records in Sexual Violence Cases," *Canadian Journal of Women and the Law/Revue Femmes et Droit*, 9: pp. 148–177.

Campbell, Sue. (2002) "Epistemic Dependence in Client-Therapist Relationships: A Relational Reading of *O'Connor* and *Mills*," In *No Person Is an Island: Personal Relationships of Dependence and Interdependence in Law,* ed. Law Commission of Canada. Vancouver: University of British Columbia Press, pp. 3–37.

Downe, Pamela. (2000) "Preliminary Report: Record Keeping Practices of Sexual Assault Centres in Canada," Unpublished Study.

M. (A.) v. Ryan. [1997] 1 Supreme Court of Canada Reports 157.

Oleskiw, Diane. (1999) "Health and Counsel Counseling Practitioners: New Reasons to Maintain Confidentiality," *The 1996 Isaac Pitblado Lectures: The Expanding Frontiers of Liability & Responsibility*. Winnipeg: Law Society of Manitoba, pp. 215–227.

R. v. Carosella. [1997] 1 Supreme Court Reports 80.

R. v. Chisolm. [1997] Ontario Judgments No. 1816 (Q/L).

R. v. Darrach. [2000] 2 Supreme Court Reports 443.

R. v. Fletcher. [1993] British Columbia Judgments No. 2787 (Superior Court) (Q/L).

R. v. J. C. B. [1997] Prince Edward Island Judgments No. 26 (Supreme Court) (Q/L).

R. v. McClure. [2001] 1 Supreme Court Reports 445.

R. v. Mills. Supreme Court of Canada Record [1999], Court File # 26358.

R. v. Mills. [1999] 3 Supreme Court Reports 668.

R. v. O'Connor. [1995] 4 Supreme Court Reports 411.

R. v. Osolin. [1993] 4 Supreme Court Reports 595.

R. v. Pritchard. [1996] British Columbia Judgments No. 1768 (Supreme Court) (Q/L)

R. v. Shearing. [2002] Supreme Court of Canada 58.

R. v. Whitehorse. [1997] Nova Scotia Judgments No. 431 (Supreme Court) (Q/L).

Schmitz, Cristin. (1998) "Whack Sexual Assault Complainant at Preliminary Hearing," *The Lawyers' Weekly* (27 May): p. 22.

Temkin, Jennifer. (1998) "Medical Evidence in Rape Cases: A Continuing Problem for Criminal Justice," *Modern Law Review,* 61: pp. 821–848.

Women's Legal Education and Action Fund. (1996) "Factum of the Aboriginal Women's Council *et al. O'Connor v. The Queen,*" *Equality and the Charter: Ten Years of Feminist Advocacy Before the Supreme Court of Canada.* Toronto: Emond Montgomery, pp. 427–448.

Twelve

CONFIDENTIALITY, HUMAN RELATIONSHIPS, AND LAW REFORM

Nathalie Des Rosiers

"None can be so true to your secrets as yourself."

Sa'Di, Gulistan (1258)

"He that communicates his secret to another makes himself that other's slave."

Baltasar Gracian, *The Art of Worldly Wisdom* (1647)

"How can we expect another to keep our secret if we have been unable to keep it ourselves?"

La Rochefoucauld. *Maxims* (1665)

"It always hurts when you lose a secret."

Elie Wisel, *The Testament* (1981)[1]

1. Introduction

The four quotations just cited relate to the themes explored in this chapter: the role that secrets play in the definition of the self; the vulnerability experienced when expressing them; the barriers that we erect between ourselves in order to protect our secrets; and finally the loss suffered when we are revealed without our consent. Indeed, the conflicts surrounding the issue of whether to tell or not tell someone else's secrets and of whether one should be compelled to disclose other people's secrets have preoccupied philosophers and socio-legal scholars for centuries. When should one tell other peoples' personal stories? Should one ever be obliged to relate what one knows? Why do we have concepts such as confidentiality? What does it mean in our society to protect expectations of confidentiality? What role does a concept such as confidentiality play in the development of human relationships? How do we devise rules that respect and enhance the role that confidentiality may play? What is the role of law vis-à-vis the various conflicts raised by the idea of confidentiality? These are the questions discussed in this chapter.

I approach the idea of confidentiality as an aspect of human relationships.

Although the analysis of confidentiality may be well served by a rights based or even property based discussion or a conceptualization around the idea of privacy, I believe that an analysis based on the functional role of confidentiality in the development of human relationships could open new vistas in the public debate (Koggel, 2000; Campbell, 2002).

My thesis is the following: a "relationship" approach to the issue of confidentiality emphasizes the role that confidentiality plays in the development of relationships rooted in trust. There is great value in protecting supportive relationships where people can reveal themselves to others. If we were to take seriously the value of such relationships in our society, we might question several aspects of our current legal framework. I will criticize both the hierarchy established between caring relationships with respect to their entitlement to the protection of confidentiality and the way in which we adjudicate and decide that values such as the search for the truth may trump claims of confidentiality in relationships.

The chapter is divided into three sections. I first situate the relationship approach in the context of a law reform agenda by describing briefly the experience and mandate of the Law Commission of Canada (Section 2). I then explore the idea of confidentiality as an aspect of human relationships (Section 3) to then critically assess the way in which the current legal framework understands the functions and role of confidentiality in human relationships (Section 4).

2. Relationships and Law Reform

In this section, I want to situate a "relationship" approach in a broader framework of debates about the appropriate methodologies for law reform. I will discuss here briefly the reasons that supported the development of a "relationship" approach by the Law Commission of Canada. When it was created in 1997, the Law Commission was mandated to develop a multidisciplinary approach informed by an analysis of the context in which law is lived and applied (*The Act Respecting the Law*, 1977, Preamble). In addition, the Law Commission of Canada *Act* suggests an approach to law reform that is innovative, consultative, and accessible to all (Law Commission of Canada, 1997, Preamble). Early in the work of the Commission, it became clear that a research program based solely on legal categories would be unresponsive to such an ambitious mandate. Therefore, the Commission committed itself to two fundamental methodological undertakings: it would study "law as lived" and would engage Canadians in the process of renewing law.

The Commission's first Annual Report was indeed entitled "The Living Law" and it contained the following statement: "But law comprises more than the rules produced by public officials. Most living law arises in everyday human interaction" (Law Commission of Canada, 1998). The Law Commission's first President, Professor Roderick Macdonald, also explained: "Our aim is to see, from as many different perspectives as possible, how Canadians actually experience the law—not just the law written in the statute book and applied by public officials, but the law of their everyday lives." (Macdonald, 2002, p. 1).

If the law as lived was to be the focus of law reform, it was necessary to embark on a process that would enable us to fully understand this living law. It was accordingly necessary to seek out and ask the public to articulate its needs for reform. The theme of the 2000 Annual Report, *Engaging Canadians*, suggested the development of new consultation methods. Engaging Canadians in the renewal of law became the mission of the Law Commission and has been the driving force behind its consultation and research methodologies (Des Rosiers, 2001).

To study "law as lived" and to "engage Canadians in the renewal of law" required analytical tools that encompass not only the static description of the law in the statute and casebooks but also the dynamic forces that shape its day-to-day practice and reframing. The conceptual tools to be used to frame the law reform approach had to incorporate two aspects of the reality of the law as lived. First, law is experienced in the context of relationships between human beings, and not only as aspects of an isolated legal personality. Second, relationships are not only shaped by the expectations and aspirations of human beings, but are lived through the experience of the differences in power that they hold. The Commission decided to use "relationships" as a central focal point of its research agenda. It was a way to respond to some of the criticisms of past law reform approaches that had appeared too bureaucratic and myopic (Macklin, 1993, pp. 395, 400). It was also a way not only to keep the law up to date, but an attempt to some extent to rethink it (Des Rosiers, 2000). The Strategic Research Agenda is organized around the concept of human relationships; that is, personal relationships, social relationships, economic relationships, and governance relationships rather than around criminal law, administrative law, or constitutional law. From the beginning, therefore, an effort was made to conceptualize the mandate in a way that more closely reflected the way people see their own lives: not as a function of the criminal law but rather as a function of their economic and social relationships with others. This exercise proved very successful since it helped ensure that abstract legal categories were transcended in order to search for a more subtle, complex, and nuanced understanding of the social fact of relationships and of the role of law in managing them. Questioning the role of criminal law in society and its ability to influence the conduct of people is certainly a good first step toward reform. However, it is intriguing to start with social relationships and then to measure the impact of the criminal law on them. It may be possible to discern other cultural, religious, or economic mechanisms that have just as great an impact on social relationships as law. For example, the use of drugs may not be deterred by criminal law if it is part of the cultural expectations of the school setting. Any law reform that failed to take into account this cultural setting would not be successful. Law studied outside of its context becomes abstract and disconnected from the society it should serve.

Ultimately the question for the Law Commission of Canada was did the law create the appropriate conditions for people to engage in and develop healthy relationships or did it, conversely, undermine healthy and productive relationships? Did law support the establishment of non-exploitative relationships or did its impact in reality serve to reaffirm the exercise of power within relationships? Many of these questions have been the focus of socio-legal scholarship for the past few decades (for a comprehensive survey of Canadian writing on these issues, see Sheehy, Boyd, and Bouchard, forthcoming). The Commission's role is often to integrate this knowledge and translate it for decision-makers and the general public, to allow for change in its many forums to take place. The Commission, therefore, has the mandate to recommend legislative changes but can also suggest changes to policies, guidelines, and nomination procedures, or simply to engage the general public in broader discussions about the values that are promoted by our laws.

Certain conclusions have emerged from the relationship approach: in both the personal and economic relationships themes, our studies identified the exclusionary role that law has played. In attempting to promote certain personal relationships (such as marriage) and certain economic relationships (such as full time employment), it has marginalized and ignored the needs of other relationships. Non-conjugal relationships are invisible in law (see Law Commission of Canada, 2001), and other marginalized work similarly does not benefit from adequate health and safety protection (see a description of current work of the Law Commission of Canada on this subject at: URL = http://www.lcc.gc.ca). Law has often been under-inclusive in its support of personal relationships. In other words, a designed hierarchy among relationships is dangerous: it is often under or over inclusive and certainly may produce unintended detrimental effects.

In the context of social and governance relationships, we have learned that communities are legitimate places of governance and dispute resolution (see the description of the Communities Project of the Law Commission of Canada that has informed the approach toward Restorative justice at: URL = http://www.lcc.gc.ca/en/themes/sum.asp#communitiesproject). In a way, the work of the Commission has sought to recognize that governance occurs outside of governments and that respect for the human capacity to self-regulate must be at the center of our approach (Des Rosiers, *Governance and the Citizen*). This respect for human agency and for the existence of a plurality of modes and sites of governance is designed to reveal issues of power by allowing for a broader look at all the ways in which governance and dispute resolution are exercised.

It also suggests that we ought to recognize that governmental institutions play a relatively modest role in the way in which law is lived by citizens. Respect for human and community agency as well as recognition of the plurality of modes and sites of governance can be said to be the lessons of our social and governance relationships themes.

Finally, the Commission has tried to explore how the law has often ignored certain human needs. In its report on child abuse in institutions, *Restoring Dignity: Responding to Child Abuse in Canadian Institutions* (Law Commission of Canada, 2000), the Commission examined the needs of victims not only in terms of compensation but also in terms of recognizing other needs such as acknowledgment of the wrong done, accountability, and commitment toward a strategy of prevention. The Commission attempted to understand how victims articulate their needs for justice without assuming that the way in which the legal system has framed them is adequate. My analysis of the relationship aspects of confidentiality is informed by these preliminary conclusions.

3. Confidentiality in Relationships

The focus on relationships will be used here to study the issue of confidentiality and in particular the support that law can give to the issue of confidentiality in a therapist-client relationship and other relationships that seek to provide a "safe haven" for people (for the creation of "sanctuaries" as a path to healthier societies, see Bloom, 1997).

In my view, using "relationships" as a focal point is helpful for enriching our understanding of why our rules surrounding disclosure, privilege, and the right to privacy ought to be critically assessed. This is not to say that another focal point such as analyzing confidentiality through a rights based approach (such as the constitutional acknowledgment of a right to privacy) ought not to be pursued. Indeed, many would argue that relationships cannot flourish outside of a context in which people have ownership of their ideas, of their body, and of their self. There is a link between the claim for a "room of one's own" and a more developed right to privacy. In a review of two biographies of the poet Edna St. Vincent Millay, Cristina Nehring suggests this poignant need for privacy "however modest … however, indeed symbolic … for a soul pining for a 'room of her own'" as an explanation for the poem *Bluebeard*:

> Look yet again:
> An empty room, cobwebbed and comfortless.
> Yet this alone out of my life I kept
> Unto myself, lest any know me quite:
> And you did so profane me when you crept
> Unto the threshold of this room tonight (Nehring, 2002, p. 79).

It is not only wanting a room of one's own in the Virginia Wolfe sense, but also resenting the intrusions into this room. Many would say that this need for privacy is particularly important for people in vulnerable positions who do not have access to a symbolic "room of their own." It could very well be that the protection of such a core of privacy must be linked to any approach that aims at supporting the development of healthy relationships. For some, the protection of privacy may allow for self-revelation and the emergence of self-trust. Trudy Govier, in the Preface of her book, *Dilemmas of Trust*, makes the link between self-trust, that may require a measure of privacy, and interpersonal trust: " I argue that there are close logical parallels between self-trust and interpersonal trust, and that self trust is essential for personal autonomy" (Govier, 1998, p. vii).

My point is to discuss confidentiality as a relational concept, as an aspect of relationships, almost in a "contract" voice, that is, keeping promises made to someone, as opposed to focusing on privacy as a right or even as property. However, I am mindful of the importance for relationships of maintaining a core of privacy as a right, a privacy related to the ownership of one's ideas, of one's personal information, and of one's concept and image of self that allows for the development of healthy relationships. One of the issues will be whether the vulnerability in allowing someone into this precious room of one's own is what ought to be counted in discussing the relational aspect of confidentiality (in chapters in this volume, Campbell and Koggel make this point for victims of sexual violence who are in therapy). Sharing intimate details of abuse, problematic behavior, an addiction, bizarre fantasies, or strong emotions all create vulnerability in the one who tells. The issue of how law reflects this vulnerability is one of the aspects discussed in this chapter.

Our understanding and experience of confidentiality is shaped by how it has manifested itself in different relationships. Consider the following examples:

(1) Two lovers exchange stories about their childhood. One retells a story of incestuous abuse that explains why she hates being touched in a certain way.

(2) Friends speak about their relationships with their children. One of them explains how he finds it difficult to control his anger when his son swears because it reminds him that he felt saved by God in a boating accident.

(3) A six year old coming out of the car driven by her older seventeen year old sister blurts out: "Amy says that I cannot tell you what happened to the car." Answer from parent: "Oh yes, you can."

(4) A psychologist examines a young boy and determines that he suffers from attention deficit disorder and upon reading such report the teacher

concludes that the child is not very smart and that his failure to understand has nothing to do with bad teaching but everything to do with his intellectual capacity.

(5) A family law lawyer hears the story about how one of her clients has had several affairs, one of them with the wife of one of her friends.

(6) A publisher receives a manuscript written under a "nom de plume." If the identity of the author were revealed, he would make more money and save his publishing company.

(7) A therapist counsels a woman who relates abuse by a partner. The woman explains how she felt that she could predict his behavior, how she felt the need to push him by her words in order to be struck because that was the way her parents related to her (for the description of the ambivalent feelings confided to a therapist by a woman who started feeling guilty after being cross-examined on her charge of sexual violence and started to think that she had brought it on herself, see Busby, 1997, and Campbell and Koggel, this volume).

(8) A man describes to his therapist his secret desires for the young daughter of his partner. He is struggling with many issues of alcohol addictions and poor self-esteem.

(9) A man exaggerates for the benefit of his friends his sexual exploits because he is trying to fit in. He goes too far and relates a story about sexual tourism in Thailand that he has read on the Internet but wrongly associates with himself.

(10) A priest receives the confession by a serial killer of his past murders and of his desires to pursue his vendetta against society.

All these stories, fictional and real, told through movies, novels, and anecdotes shape our understanding of confidentiality in relationships. We know that life is about experiencing conflicts of many kinds, among them loyalty and moral conflicts. We often value confidentiality in relationships as an element of creating a place of repose, a safe place that allows for the true expression of self to be related to another. We value the trust that must support the continuing life of a relationship. However, we worry about keeping secret information that would save others, in particular, children. My purpose is more to explore the first point, that is, the social value of relationships being experienced as safe places for the sharing and divulging of information about ourselves. In the next section,

I will relate such explorations to the way in which the legal system responds to the balancing of interests raised in these various conflicts.

I argue that confidentiality is experienced in the context of expectations of intimacy, understood in a broad sense, and of trust. Expectations of confidentiality, and their fulfillment, provide essential needs for the development of human beings. Providing in such a way for the development of healthy and safe human interaction is a social good. My argument can be summarized in two main points. First, relationships rooted in trust are essential to human development. Second, trust is fostered by the fulfillment of expectations, such as confidentiality, within relationships. The argument suggests that the breach of expectations of confidentiality is not only a breach of one aspect of a relationship, but also of the very premise for trust in relationships, in the particular relationship itself and also in other relationships more generally. In other words, and to take a simplistic example that I will seek to refine throughout this paper, when I promise my seven year old daughter that I will not reveal that she has a crush on the neighbor's son, I allow her to create a safe place of revelation for herself in the context of a relationship. I allow her to experience trust in relationships, not only in her relationship with me but potentially in all of her relationships with adults and friends. Revealing even such—to our eyes—inconsequential information is a breach of the trust and of the relationship. It questions the value of trust in relationships and jeopardizes further trusting not only in me but also in other relationships in which she is and will be involved.

A. Relationships Rooted in Trust are Essential to Human Development

It seems trite to say that the experience of trusting others is essential to personal growth. We accept such statements because we know that the inability to completely trust others has been labeled a mental illness and that withdrawal from society often comes from the inability to trust. Most books about child rearing indicate the importance of creating the ability for the child to trust and love. We know that sexual abuse of children has long lasting effects because it involves betrayal and may prevent children from trusting adults and other people (see Finkelhor and Browne, 1985, p. 530; Herman, 1992). Much scientific literature speaks to how abuse by authority figures prevents victims from trusting others, and in particular any figure in authority, including police and judges (see Law Commission of Canada, *Restoring Dignity*; Wolfe, Jaffe, Jetté, and Poisson, 2002). Rehabilitation and healing are often generated by the re-establishment of trusting relationships with the self and with the rest of the world (Herman, 2002; Bloom, 1997). As Trudy Govier puts it: " For all of us, ... it is impossible to cope in this world without trust (1998, p. 4)." She points out that trust is also essential in everyday activities such as work, commerce, and travel. It is essential to the very survival of our institutions. Finally, much has been said about the demise of trust in our democratic institutions and how the inability to trust undermines meaningful democratic participation (Des Rosiers, *Governance*; more generally, the Strategic Agenda of the Law Commission of Canada on Governance Relationships).

This is not to say that healthy skepticism is not a useful skill. Unmindful trust is not what is advocated here. Different people have different relational aspirations and are more or less trusting. They may need further reassurance before they can trust others. The point is simply that when it is impossible to trust the words of others, it is impossible to function in society. Therefore, fostering trust is a worthwhile endeavor and one that has often been recognized and assumed by our governance institutions.

Supportive relationships occur in many sectors of our lives: within the traditional helping relationships of doctor-patient, lawyer-client, parent-child, therapist-client, social worker-client, and spiritual advisor-believer, but also in other corners, among friends, between siblings or coworkers. Indeed, friendship is often defined by its capacity to elicit confidences and create a space of acceptance. In the words of Trudy Govier: "Much of the joy of friendship derives from the ability to divulge our feelings without having to keep up a front or pretend. When we reveal intimate feelings to friends, we can be ourselves and relax, trusting the other to keep them confidential" (Govier, 1998, p. 25). She adds that this practice allows for the moral and psychological growth of individuals: the non-threatening dialogue allows one to accept being straightened out by a friend and to confront the incoherence of one's ideas. Sandra Bloom makes a similar point; she suggests that it is only by creating "sanctuaries," places of safety where people can heal, debrief, make sense of their experiences, and reveal themselves without fear that "sane societies" will emerge (Bloom, 1997, pp. 208-226). Very importantly, she adds that there will never be enough therapists to help all the traumatized people in society and that we ought to encourage the development of various safe forums: "We must begin to create naturally occurring, healing environments that provide some of the corrective experiences that are vital for recovery" (Bloom, 1997, p. 117).

Personal relationships may be places of safety for people to engage in self-discovery and self-reflection. There are many reasons why some relationships do not provide such opportunity: violence, exploitation, fear, dishonesty, and immaturity certainly prevent the establishment of a "sanctuary." However, the failure of keeping promises or of acting with loyalty may also deprive a relationship of the potential of becoming a safe haven.

B. Trust is Fostered by the Fulfillment of Confidentiality Expectations Within Relationships

If trust is necessary to our development, how can we increase our supply of trust? Trudy Govier suggests eight criteria that promote "trustworthiness":

> honesty (truth-telling), sincerity as opposed to hypocrisy, promise-keeping, keeping confidences and other forms of loyalty, reliability (performing expected tasks, keeping appointments), dependability, competence (as pertinent to the context role) and concern for others (non-manipulativeness) (Govier, 1998, pp. 126 f.).

There is no doubt that trust is often based on past experiences (Govier, 1998, p. 8). More importantly for my purposes is the reference to the "keeping of promises" and the experience of "loyalty and keeping confidences" as indicators of trustworthiness. Both ideas require further reflection.

Our ability to trust is context specific. We may require more or less evidence depending on the type of relationship involved. This point is important because it makes the expression of specific expectations and the fulfillment of such expressed expectations so significant in an analysis of trust. The demand for secrecy by my seven years old daughter is case specific. She wants protection for this particular revelation. She may not be as crushed if I describe to my friends that she has chosen karate over ballet or that she desperately wants a dog as a birthday present. Because she has specifically expressed her need for confidentiality, the failure to abide by such a demand requires explanation.

Expectations that are expressed demand that they be acknowledged if we are to build trust. The law knows that well: it is no surprise that expressed wording in a contract will be respected in the legal system on the theory that one could not "trust" a legal system that would not support reasonable reliance by parties on the terms of their understanding. Expressed aspirations of confidentiality should be considered like any other promise made. Respecting promises and keeping confidences are ways of increasing the supply of trust in society.

What about implicit expectations of confidentiality? Is the protection of "loyalty" in all our relationships a worthwhile objective? Would it be reasonable to always expect confidentiality in our relationships. Should relationships be presumed to be based on an exclusive sharing of information? Might an analysis of a number of other relationships reveal similar implicit expectations of confidentiality? In general, implicit terms of contracts are often given life because they correspond to the reasonable expectations of parties. There is no reason why expectations about confidentiality ought not to be subject to the same analysis. Therapists will certainly argue that it is reasonable for a client to expect confidentiality. The canons of professional codes of ethics, the practice and demeanor of therapists, even the way in which their offices and their business practices are conducted can lead one to expect that confidentiality is promised by the relationship.

But one may go further than this: my final question is: do all relationships raise expectations of confidentiality? When speaking or communicating with someone, do we generally expect that our information will be kept within the purview of that relationship? Do we expect that expanding the network of sharing the information requires permission? Our privacy laws (at the federal level, see the *Privacy Act* of 1985 with respect to information disclosed to governments, and the recent *Personal Information Protection and Electronic Documents Act*, 2000, which extends that protection to information collected through commercial activities; the *Access to Information Act*, 1985, also protects the confidentiality of information collected by governments) are often based on such presumptions: citizens who share data about themselves to governments expect that such data will not be shared with others unless they explicitly agree. Many other relationships, lawyer-client being one of them, are similarly constructed: all conversations within the lawyer-client relationship, even mundane or non-prejudicial ones, are supposed to be confidential. Does such expectation extend to other less regulated relationships? Do we expect that what we tell our friends, our neighbors, or our family ought to be treated as confidential information? Does my daughter expect that all our conversations should operate under the same oath of secrecy? My point here is that such questions matter if we want our laws to enhance the ability of citizens to trust one another.

However, it is not only in personal relationships that trust and confidentiality are expected. Indeed, many other relationships are equally marked by the necessity or the promise of confidentiality: A consumer may expect confidential treatment with regard to his or her credit line, but also with regard to the nature of his or her purchases. An explorer may consider his mining development plans secret and may expect the investor who is privy to those plans not to use them for his personal profit. Internet users may also want to keep their names and addresses secret and expect that Yahoo, Sympatico, or any other Internet service provider will not divulge their identity (for further exploration of the range of interdependencies that are created within relationships, see Law Commission of Canada, 2002).

There is a link between building trust in our society and the respect that we ought to give to confidentiality within relationships. It is not that such a link has escaped the legal system, but it has sought to weigh the loss of confidentiality against other losses, such as the loss of accessing the truth for the purpose of the application of criminal or civil law. It is somewhat interesting to reflect on the presumption embedded in the laws that regulate the disclosure of information to governments and now to commercial organizations (*Personal Information Protection and Electronic Documents Act*, 2000), that the information provided ought not to be disclosed without permission, and to contrast such a presumption with the treatment that our courts may give to other even more explicit expectations of confidentiality between friends or between a therapist and her client. In the next section, I will develop the argument that valuing relationships built on trust may lead to different calculations of the pros and cons of forcing disclosure.

4. Assessing the Current Legal Framework

Expectations of confidentiality exist in many types of human relationships, but the law recognizes and protects confidentiality in very few of them. There is a high level of complexity in the rules surrounding the balancing of confidentiality, the search for truth, privilege, and the duty to disclose. Nevertheless, the legal order can be said to be organized along two main ideas: first, that only in certain relationships defined by law is the confidential nature of communications entitled to respect and second, that the law's differentiation among relationships is accompanied by an instrumental assessment of the value of each relationship in comparison with the value of the "search for the truth" or other societal goals.

A. Differentiation Among Relationships

The law presumes that everyone owes a general duty to give evidence relevant to the matter before the court, so that the truth may be ascertained. However, at times, the law permits certain exceptions when it can be shown that they are required by a "public good transcending the normally predominant principle of utilizing all rational means for ascertaining truth" (*Trammel v. U. S.* [1980], p. 50; cited in *M. (A). v. Ryan* [1997]).

Some relationships have benefitted from greater protection because they are associated with the public good. The reasons advanced to outweigh the basic presumption of participation in the search for the truth resemble closely the ones discussed in this chapter, that is, the value that we ought to give to helping relationships such as that between lawyer and client. Indeed, the ideas put forth by philosophers such as Govier (building trust in relationships) and psychotherapists such as Bloom (creating sanctuaries) have resonance for legal scholars. For example, the lawyer-client privilege is said to be one that is required by the public good. It is rooted in a desire to allow for the full expression by the client of his or her legal situation (safe sanctuary). It is also grounded in an expectation of trust in the lawyer (Lauzière, 2002). As well, it is surrounded by a series of rules that prevent abuse by preventing lawyers, for example, from putting forth witnesses that they know will lie. Even, in the context of a lawyer-client relationship, highly valued by the justice system, there is still a concern for the search for the truth.

Another relationship that has benefitted from special protection is the husband-wife relationship. Although its history is rooted in discriminatory beliefs in the 'blending' of the legal personality of the wife into her husband's upon marriage, the privilege has survived for a variety of reasons. Many of these reasons again relate to the ideas of creating a safe forum and protecting loyalty in relationships. The marital privilege is now said to aim at ensuring peace in households or to provide the accused with a place in which to safely discuss his or her issues (see Manson).

The categories of privilege are not closed. Many decisions have attempted to recognize the social value of other relationships. The spiritual advisor-penitent (*R. v. Gruenke* [1991]) and therapist-client (*M. (A.) v. Ryan* [1997]) relationships have been analyzed along the lines defined by the traditional Wigmore (Wigmore, 1961, p. 2285) test. According to the test laid out by Wigmore, there are four requirements for a privilege to be recognized, for confidentiality to be protected in absolute or partial terms:

(1) the communication must originate in a confidence;
(2) the confidence must be essential to the relationship in which the communication arises;
(3) the relationship must be one that should be "sedulously fostered" in the public good;
(4) whether the interests served by protecting the communications from disclosure outweigh the interest in getting at the truth and disposing correctly of the litigation.

There is nothing particularly objectionable in the Wigmore test, which is consistent with the presumption that everyone ought to be obliged to participate in the enterprise of justice. However, it appears very demanding in some respects. One may question, for example, the second requirement that confidentiality be "essential" to the relationship as opposed to simply expected. It could be that the parent–child relationship does not require confidence to exist, but it just works better if there is trust. As discussed earlier, the failure to abide by requests of confidentiality in communications may not lead to the demise of the entire relationship but to a more general sense of untrustworthiness. The third criterion is equally problematic if restricted only to professional relationships that are structured and organized by society. As mentioned earlier, the social need for sanctuaries is not limited to the need for professional psychotherapeutic help. In a way, the Wigmore test proposes a distinction between classes of relationships, irrespective of the particular strengths or weaknesses of the relationship in question. It has the potential of restricting the privilege to "status" relationships, determined either by reference to professional criteria or by marital status.

Law could continue to protect and respect the secrecy of the lawyer-client and husband-wife relationships as well as partially recognize the therapist-client relationship, but be totally unresponsive to friendships. Why such a hierarchy? Why is it that the protection of confidential communication is protected in certain types of human relationships and not in others? The hierarchy established by the law between human relationships that enjoy confidentiality protection and those that do not seems arbitrary; at once too narrow and too wide. Why is it that we ought to always feel secure in speaking openly to our lawyer or spouse, but not to our psychiatrist or mother? Is it because we think it is better to use the services of a lawyer rather than a psychiatrist or are we better advised to confide in a spouse rather than in a parent? In a society that seeks to assist relationships of support between individuals, we may wonder why some relationships of support are favored while others are not.

We may have to question further the hierarchical grading of relationships that lay claim to confidentiality in their communications. It is particularly appropriate to raise questions in a pluralist society where the presumptions of the past have become obsolete and where it is dangerous to predict with certainty what type of relationships are beneficial for citizens. It is not always the case that a defendant who does not know whether to plead guilty will seek the advice of his or her lawyer or wish to discuss matters with his or her spouse. The defendant may not be married or he or she may not have access to legal counseling. His or her psychological and emotional support mechanisms are perhaps more diversified: they may include a social worker, a sibling, an old friend, or a gay spouse. His or her need to reflect with someone else, to seek relief, to share anxiety, or reveal secrets has not changed. But the law will treat the secrets confided to a social worker very differently from those confided to a lawyer, or even those whispered in the ear of a sibling rather than a wife.

Right now, the law respects confidentiality only in certain human relationships. It does so mostly on the basis of marital status or professional status. This hierarchy of relationships may not truly reflect the way people really share their secrets, or the richness of their relationships, or the support that the fulfillment of their expectations of confidentiality provides them. The law must evolve to take into account how citizens valorize and utilize a larger variety of human relationships (see the proposals made by the Law Commission of Canada, 2001).

B. Balancing the Relationship Against the Search for the Truth and other Societal Values

Even if we were to value a wider range of relationships and their potential to enhance the development of healthy relationships, we would have to confront the fear that information that could "save" someone might not be disclosed. At times, the search for truth or the ability to protect children may require a balancing of interests. For example, most provincial legislation requires professionals to disclose when there are grounds to suspect abuse of children (for a fuller review of the different pieces of legislation, see Des Rosiers and Langevin, 1998). This is what the fourth requirement of the Wigmore test imagines.

However, a couple of points need to be made. First, we may want to modestly suggest that the way in which the criteria is applied lacks transparency. The search for truth is often assumed to have requirements that are rarely spelled out. Very few questions are asked about the alternatives for the other side to obtain the information or make his or her point. Second, arguments could be advanced to suggest that the loss of confidentiality in personal relationships ought to be valued as a more substantial loss. A multidisciplinary approach allows for a different quantification and a broader understanding of the psychological dimensions of losses. Such an approach may help when we attempt to balance the search for truth and the loss of a therapeutic or caring relationship or even the loss of friendship. Further studies need to be done to respond adequately to the bias inherent in a system built on the predominance of the value of the search for truth. The loss of trust and the resulting loss in healthy relationships and safe forums are perhaps too heavy a price to pay for a truth that could often be obtained by other means.

Furthermore, other questions must be asked with respect to the effects on participants of forced disclosure. What are we seeking to obtain when we compel people to divulge secrets? What are the costs to them of having the loyalty conflicts removed from their agency and administered by an appointed authority, no matter how thoughtful the judge might be? Have we adequately explored the reasons why participants in the judicial system refuse to participate? Is it due to the perceived negative effects of the adversarial process? Is it the fear of surrendering to a strange legal system that is often incomprehensible? Is it the desire to protect other persons, their reputation, and their sentiments? We must ask ourselves whether the justice system in simply compelling disclosure prevents a more thorough analysis of the reasons behind the apparent reluctance of some witnesses to come forward. We should also study the reasons why victims and potential plaintiffs may forego their legal remedy because they value the safe haven that they have. In searching for the truth, we may have lost the search for justice.

Finally, it is almost impossible to engage in a meaningful discussion of the balancing of interests without reflecting on the ways in which the adversarial process may not always present the best way to resolve disputes. Earlier I argued that communities are legitimate places of governance and dispute resolution. A reflection on human agency and the need to foster community decision-making could also prove helpful in this context. It might be advisable to valorize the citizen's prerogative to speak or not, to participate in the justice system or not, and to make the hard moral choices this often implies. It may require rethinking the way in which the decision to recognize a partial or a full privilege may need to be done in a more transparent way and with better participation of the people involved.

We also ought to remember that the claims for privilege and protection of confidential information in front of a judge constitute a very small fraction of the instances where trust in relationships is balanced against other goods in our society. In our day-to-day lives, we constantly weigh trust, confidentiality, and the support for safe havens against other social imperatives. The examples listed earlier in this paper are often resolved in a variety of ways: through the integration of legal or ethical norms (the family law lawyer, therapist, or psychologist) or even spiritual and cultural norms (priest, possibly the publisher). At times, we do our own balancing of the Wigmore test and engage in self-reflection: Will she forgive me if I tell? Am I right to repeat this? How can I act with integrity in the circumstances? Should I confront him about his sexual tourism behavior? We may react with love, empathy, and generosity to a disclosure and seek to build trust in the relationships and hope to resolve the conflicts through exchanges and discussions. We may hope to convince the person that he or she should come forward and disclose. We may hope to help the person realize that there is courage in telling. I may want to convince my daughter that she can tell her dad about her crush on the neighbor's son and that he will not laugh at her. We may also offer support when disclosure brings pain, that is, when her father does laugh and she is crushed. We may discuss how and when disclosures should be made. It is through this constant balancing and reshaping that law is renewed and remodeled and that new ideas about appropriate behavior become tested, developed, and eventually advocated.

5. Conclusion

Official law has probably minimized the importance of confidentiality in relationships and devalued the richness of human relationships through the hierarchical grading of them. Our society should continue to question the legal distinctions established between human relationships. Are they still appropriate? Do they reflect the values of our pluralist society?

This chapter has sought to examine why a relationship approach is necessary to law reform and to apply the insights of such an approach to the issue of confidentiality. It concludes by suggesting that we ought to move beyond the "status" analysis of relationships toward a more functional analysis of the interests at play. Is the relationship one that generated expressed or implicit expectations of confidentiality? Is the relationship one in which such expectations were appropriately respected? Would the relationship be damaged through disclosure? Is disclosure really necessary considering the damage to the capacity to trust in relationships?

The chapter also suggests that the analysis of confidentiality cannot be fully done without an examination of other issues relating to the adversarial process itself and the ways in which it responds to the citizens' needs to participate in the justice system and to be heard fully and respectfully. There will always be times when the protection of a confidential relationship will be assessed to be less important than other societal goods such as the pursuit of the truth, the protection of children, or the safety of citizens. A process that values human agency may want to resist the temptation to exercise too quickly the power to overrule the need for trust and confidentiality in human relationships.

Acknowledgments

I want to thank my research assistant, Christine Duval, for her help in the gathering of materials for this paper. I am indebted to the work of Christine Koggel and Sue Campbell who have developed the idea of confidentiality as a relational concept. The paper is inspired from the work undertaken by the Law Commission of Canada but does not reflect the views of the Commissioners.

Note

[1] All quotations may be found in Eugene Ehrlich and Marshall De Bruhl, *The International Thesaurus of Citations*. New York: Harper Collins Publishers, 1996, p. 607.

Works Cited

Access to Information Act, R. S. C. 1985, c. A–1.

Bloom, Sandra. (1997) *Creating Sanctuary: Toward an Evolution of Sane Societies* (New York: Routledge).

Busby, Karen. (1997) "Discriminatory Uses of Personal Records in Sexual Violence Cases," *Canadian Journal of Women and the Law*, 9: pp. 148-177.

Campbell, Sue. (2002) "Dependence in Client-Therapist Relationships: A Relational Reading of *O'Connor* and *Mills*." In *Personal Relationships of Dependence and Interdependence in Law*, ed. Law Commission of Canada. Vancouver: University of British Columbia Press, pp. 3-39; also published in French by Commission du droit du Canada, dir. *Les rapports de dépendence et d'interdépendence*. Quebec: Presses de l'University Laval, 2002.

Des Rosiers, Nathalie. *Governance and the Citizen: The Research Agenda of the Law Commission of Canada*. Available online at:
URL = http://www.lcc.gc.ca/en/gc/speeches/s171100.asp.

———. (2000) "Rethinking or Reforming the Law: The Canadian Experience in Law Reform," speech delivered at the International Congress of Francophone Jurists, June. Available online at:
URL = http://www.lcc.gc.ca/en/pc/speeches/20000629.asp.

———. (2001) "Engaging Canadians in Law Reform," speech delivered to the Nova Scotia Legal Information Society, March. Available online at: URL = http://www.lcc.gc.ca/en/pc/speeches/20010403.asp.

Des Rosiers, Nathalie, and Louise Langevin. (1998) *L'indemnisation des victimes de violence sexuelle et conjugale*. (Cowansville: Les Éditions Yvon Blais), English translation, *Representing Victims of Sexual Violence*. (Toronto: Irwin, 2002): Chapter 2.

Finkelhor, David, and Angela Browne. (1985) "The Traumatic Impact of Child Sexual Abuse: A Conceptualization," *American Journal of Orthopsychiatry*, 55(4): pp. 530-541.

Govier, Trudy. (1998) *Dilemmas of Trust* (Montreal & Kingston: McGill-Queen's University Press).

Herman, J. (1992) *Trauma and Recovery* (New York, Basic Books).

Koggel, Christine M. (2000) "Confidentiality in Liberal Democracy: A Relational Approach," presented at Confidentiality & Society: Therapy, Ethics and the Law, Social Philosophical and Psychoanalytic Perspectives, Montreal, Canada, October; revised version in this volume, pp. 113 ff.

Lauzière, Lucie. (2002) "Dependence and Interdependence in the Lawyer-Client Relationship," in *Personal Relationships of Dependence and Interdependence in Law*, ed. Law Commission of Canada. Vancouver: University of British Columbia Press, pp. 40–56.

Law Commission of Canada. (1997) *The Act Respecting the Law*. R. S. C., c. L–6.7.

———. (1998) *The Living Law*; First Annual Report (Ottawa: Law Commission of Canada). Available online at: URL = http://www.lcc.gc.ca/en/about/rapports/1997/vivant/e 1.pdf.

———. (2000) *Restoring Dignity: Responding to Child Abuse in Canadian Institutions*. Available online at: URL = http://www.lcc.gc.ca/en/themes/mr/ica/2000/html/restore1.asp.

———. (2001) *Beyond Conjugality: Recognizing and Supporting Close Personal Adult Relationships*. Report to Parliament (Ottawa: Law Commission of Canada). Also available online at: URL = http://www.lcc.gc.ca/en/themes/pr/cpra/report.asp.

———, ed. (2002) *Personal Relationships of Dependence and Independence in Law*. Vancouver: University of British Columbia Press.

M. (A.) v. Ryan. [1997] 1 S. C. R. 157.

Macdonald, Roderick. (2002) *Law and Logos*, available online at: URL = http://www.lcc.gc.ca/en/pc/message/logo.asp.

Macklin, Audrey. (1993) "Law Reform Error: Retry or Abort?" *Dalhousie Law Journal*, 16: pp. 395–415.

Manson, Alan. "Spousal Testimony in Criminal Cases in Canada," published at URL = http://www.lcc.gc.ca/en/themes/pr/cpra/manson/manson.pdf.

Nehring, Cristina. (2002) "Last the Night: The Abiding Genius of Edna St. Vincent Millay," *Harper's Magazine*, 305(1826) (July): p. 79.

Personal Information Protection and Electronic Documents Act, S.C. 2000, c.5.

Privacy Act, R. S. C. 1985, c. P–21

R. v. Gruenke. [1991] 3 R. C. S. 263.

Sheehy, Elizabeth, Susan Boyd, and Josee Bouchard. *Canadian Feminist Literature on Law: An Annotated Bibliography (1989–1999)*. Special book issue of the *Canadian Journal of Women and the Law*, forthcoming.

Trammel v. U. S. [1980] 445 U. S. 40.

Wigmore, John Henry. (1961) *Wigmore on Evidence*, vol. 8, rev. John T. McNaughton (Boston: Little Brown), p. 2285.

Wolfe, David, Peter Jaffe, Jennifer Jetté, and Samantha Poisson. (2002) "Child Abuse in Community Institutions and Organizations: Improving Public and Professional Understanding," available from the offices of the Law Commission and to be published on the website of the Law Commission.

ABOUT THE CONTRIBUTORS

Andrew Brook is Professor of Philosophy and Cognitive Science and Director of the Institute of Interdisciplinary Studies at Carleton University in Ottawa, Canada. He is past-president of Canadian Philosophical Association and a member and past National Council member of the Canadian Psychoanalytic Society. He is the author of *Kant and the Mind*, co-author of *Knowledge and Mind: A Philosophical Introduction*; co-editor of *Dennett's Philosophy: A Comprehensive Assessment*; as well as numerous journal articles in the areas of Philosophy and Psychoanalysis.

Karen Busby is Professor of Law at the University of Manitoba. Much of her research and community work over the last twenty years has focused on sexual violence and the law. She has personal experience working on the "front line" as a sexual assault counselor. Her work on the discriminatory uses and effects on complainants and counselors of requests for personal records in sexual violence cases has been influential in judicial reasoning in Canada. Two of her articles, "Discriminatory Uses of Personal Records in Sexual Violence Cases" and "Third Party Records Cases Since *O'Connor*" were cited by the Canadian Supreme Court in its 1999 *Mills* decision.

Sue Campbell is Associate Professor of Philosophy and Women's Studies at Dalhousie University. She is the author of *Interpreting the Personal: Expression and the Formations of Feelings* (1997) and co-editor (with Susan Babbitt) of *Racism and Philosophy* (1999). She is currently working on a book on relational remembering.

Margaret Denike is Assistant Professor and Coordinator in the Program in Gender Equality and Social Justice at Nipissing University. She has a Ph.D. in Social and Political Thought with a concentration in Continental Philosophies of Semiotics, Hermeneutics, and the production of meaning. Formerly the President of the National Association of Women and the Law (NAWL), she is currently a member of the National Legal Committee of the Women's Legal Education and Action Fund (LEAF) and a member of the Advisory Council to the Law Commission of Canada. In addition to contemporary work in feminist and legal social activism, she has spent the past several years researching and writing on the European Witch Craze, and on the social and legal conditions making possible such regimes of persecution.

Nathalie Des Rosiers is President of the Law Commission of Canada. She is a Professor of Law on leave from the Faculty of Law, Common Law, at the

University of Ottawa. From 1987 to 2000, Ms. Des Rosiers was a Faculty member at the Faculty of Law, University of Western Ontario. She is the author with Louise Langevin of "L'indemnisation des victimes de violence sexuelle et conjugale," published in 1998 by Les Éditions Yvon Blais.

Allannah Furlong, Ph. D., is a private practice Psychologist and Psychoanalyst (member of the Canadian Psychoanalytic Society and the International Psychoanalytical Association). She was co-chair of the 2000 conference, "Confidentiality & Society: Psychoanalysis, Ethics, and the Law" in Montreal. She is the author of several articles on technical and ethical issues concerning the treatment setting, including the topics of clinical reporting, payment, dossier access, and "counter-transference translation." Her current research is into the auto-theorizing function of memory.

R. D. Hinshelwood, M. D., is a Member of the British Psychoanalytical Society and Professor in the Centre for Psychoanalytic Studies, University of Essex, UK. He founded the *British Journal of Psychotherapy* in 1984 and more recently the journal, *Psychoanalysis and History*. He published A *Dictionary of Kleinian Thought* in 1989, and *Clinical Klein* in 1994, followed in 1997 by *Therapy and Coercion: Does Psychoanalysis Differ from Brainwashing?* His most recent work, consecrated to a psychoanalytic understanding of organizations, includes *Thinking about Institutions*.

Christine Koggel is Associate Professor of Philosophy at Bryn Mawr College. Her main areas of teaching and research are moral and political theory, practical ethics, and feminist theory. She is the author of *Perspectives on Equality: Constructing a Relational Theory* (Rowman & Littlefield, 1998); editor of *Moral Issues in Global Perspective* (Broadview 1999); and co-editor (with Wesley Cragg) of the fourth edition (McGraw-Hill Ryerson, 1997) and the fifth edition (McGraw-Hill Ryerson, forthcoming in 2003) of *Contemporary Moral Issues*.

Charles Levin, Ph. D., is a member of the Canadian Psychoanalytic Society (CPS) in full time practice in Montreal. He is President of the Quebec English Branch of the CPS and Adjunct Professor, Graduate Program in Art History and Communication Studies, McGill University. He was co-chair of the Conference: "Confidentiality & Society: Psychotherapy, Ethics and the Law", held in Montreal, 13–15 October 2000. His publications include *Jean Baudrillard: A Study in Cultural Metaphysics* (London: Prentice Hall, 1995).

Jacques Mauger, M.D., is a member of the Canadian Psychoanalytic Society and Institute and the Association des médecins psychiatres du Québec. Of his numerous publications, two recent ones, "Pratiques de mémoire, pratiques de répétition, L'avenir d'une illusion" and the monograph "Pure culture..." are part of an on-going meditation on the meta-psychological and clinical implications of the trans-individual foundations of human identity and unconscious conflict. He is considered one of Canada's leading psychoanalytic theorists.

Paul W. Mosher, M. D., is a Psychoanalyst in private practice in Albany, New York. He is a former Chairman of the Joint Committee on Confidentiality of the American Psychoanalytic Association and is currently a consultant to that Committee. He is also that organization's Allied Professional Organization Representative to the American Psychiatric Association Committee on Confidentiality. Dr. Mosher coordinated the preparation of the amici curiae brief submitted to the United States Supreme Court by a consortium of United States psychoanalytic organizations in *Jaffee v. Redmond* and has lectured and written on the *Jaffee* case and the HHS Privacy Rule. He also maintains a WWW site devoted to the *Jaffee* privilege at URL = http://jaffee-redmond.org. Dr. Mosher is a councilor-at-Large of the American Psychoanalytic Association.

Christine Ury, D. Ps, is a member of the Canadian Psychoanalytic Society (CPS) in full-time practice in Montreal. She is Director of the Individual Psychotherapy Training Program at the Argyle Institute of Human Relations. Her psychoanalytic publications include "The Shadow of Object Love: Reconstructing Freud's Theory of PreOedipal Guilt" in *Psychoanalytic Quarterly.*

Michael Yeo is a philosopher who specializes in ethics and values in health and social policy. He has lectured and published extensively on a range of topics, including health privacy, resource allocation, and professional ethics. Yeo is currently an Adjunct Professor in the Faculty of Medicine at the University of Ottawa and, for 2002/2003, Visiting Professor at Carleton University. Michael also consults to professions and organizations on issues of ethics and values

Index

Prepared by Richard T. Hull

Hyphenated numbers indicate a range of pages on each of which the term appears; "ff." indicates that the term appears in a chapter title.

VIBS

The **Value Inquiry Book Series** is co-sponsored by:

Adler School of Professional Psychology
American Indian Philosophy Association
American Maritain Association
American Society for Value Inquiry
Association for Process Philosophy of Education
Canadian Society for Philosophical Practice
Center for Bioethics, University of Turku
Center for Professional and Applied Ethics, University of North Carolina at Charlotte
Center for Research in Cognitive Science, Autonomous University of Barcelona
Centre for Applied Ethics, Hong Kong Baptist University
Centre for Cultural Research, Aarhus University
Centre for Professional Ethics, University of Central Lancashire
Centre for the Study of Philosophy and Religion, University College of Cape Breton
Centro de Estudos em Filosofia Americana
College of Education and Allied Professions, Bowling Green State University
College of Liberal Arts, Rochester Institute of Technology
Concerned Philosophers for Peace
Conference of Philosophical Societies
Department of Moral and Social Philosophy, University of Helsinki
Gannon University
Gilson Society
The Haitian Studies Association
Ikeda University
Institute of Philosophy of the High Council of Scientific Research, Spain
International Academy of Philosophy of the Principality of Liechtenstein
International Association of Bioethics
International Center for the Arts, Humanities, and Value Inquiry
International Society for Universal Dialogue
Natural Law Society
Personalist Discussion Group
Philosophical Society of Finland
Philosophy Born of Struggle Association
Philosophy Seminar, University of Mainz
Pragmatism Archive
R.S. Hartman Institute for Formal and Applied Axiology
Research Institute, Lakeridge Health Corporation
Russian Philosophical Society
Society for Iberian and Latin-American Thought
Society for the Philosophic Study of Genocide and the Holocaust
Society for the Philosophy of Sex and Love
Yves R. Simon Institute

Titles Published

1. Noel Balzer, *The Human Being as a Logical Thinker*

2. Archie J. Bahm, *Axiology: The Science of Values*

3. H. P. P. (Hennie) Lötter, *Justice for an Unjust Society*

4. H. G. Callaway, *Context for Meaning and Analysis: A Critical Study in the Philosophy of Language*

5. Benjamin S. Llamzon, *A Humane Case for Moral Intuition*

6. James R. Watson, *Between Auschwitz and Tradition: Postmodern Reflections on the Task of Thinking.* A volume in **Holocaust and Genocide Studies**

7. Robert S. Hartman, *Freedom to Live: The Robert Hartman Story, edited by Arthur R. Ellis.* A volume in **Hartman Institute Axiology Studies**

8. Archie J. Bahm, *Ethics: The Science of Oughtness*

9. George David Miller, *An Idiosyncratic Ethics; Or, the Lauramachean Ethics*

10. Joseph P. DeMarco, *A Coherence Theory in Ethics*

11. Frank G. Forrest, *Valuemetrics: The Science of Personal and Professional Ethics.* A volume in **Hartman Institute Axiology Studies**

12. William Gerber, *The Meaning of Life: Insights of the World's Great Thinkers*

13. Richard T. Hull, Editor, *A Quarter Century of Value Inquiry: Presidential Addresses of the American Society for Value Inquiry.* A volume in **Histories and Addresses of Philosophical Societies**

14. William Gerber, *Nuggets of Wisdom from Great Jewish Thinkers: From Biblical Times to the Present*

15. Sidney Axinn, *The Logic of Hope: Extensions of Kant's View of Religion*

16. Messay Kebede, *Meaning and Development*

17. Amihud Gilead, *The Platonic Odyssey: A Philosophical-Literary Inquiry*

into the Phaedo

18. Necip Fikri Alican, *Mill's Principle of Utility: A Defense of John Stuart Mill's Notorious Proof.* A volume in **Universal Justice**

19. Michael H. Mitias, Editor, *Philosophy and Architecture.*

20. Roger T. Simonds, *Rational Individualism: The Perennial Philosophy of Legal Interpretation.* A volume in **Natural Law Studies**

21. William Pencak, *The Conflict of Law and Justice in the Icelandic Sagas*

22. Samuel M. Natale and Brian M. Rothschild, Editors, *Values, Work, Education: The Meanings of Work*

23. N. Georgopoulos and Michael Heim, Editors, *Being Human in the Ultimate: Studies in the Thought of John M. Anderson*

24. Robert Wesson and Patricia A. Williams, Editors, *Evolution and Human Values*

25. Wim J. van der Steen, *Facts, Values, and Methodology: A New Approach to Ethics*

26. Avi Sagi and Daniel Statman, *Religion and Morality*

27. Albert William Levi, *The High Road of Humanity: The Seven Ethical Ages of Western Man*, Edited by Donald Phillip Verene and Molly Black Verene

28. Samuel M. Natale and Brian M. Rothschild, Editors, *Work Values: Education, Organization, and Religious Concerns*

29. Laurence F. Bove and Laura Duhan Kaplan, Editors, From the Eye of the Storm: Regional Conflicts and the Philosophy of Peace. A volume in **Philosophy of Peace**

30. Robin Attfield, *Value, Obligation, and Meta-Ethics*

31. William Gerber, *The Deepest Questions You Can Ask About God: As Answered by the World's Great Thinkers*

32. Daniel Statman, *Moral Dilemmas*

33. Rem B. Edwards, Editor, *Formal Axiology and Its Critics*. A volume in **Hartman Institute Axiology Studies**

34. George David Miller and Conrad P. Pritscher, *On Education and Values: In Praise of Pariahs and Nomads*. A volume in **Philosophy of Education**

35. Paul S. Penner, *Altruistic Behavior: An Inquiry into Motivation*

36. Corbin Fowler, *Morality for Moderns*

37. Giambattista Vico, The Art of Rhetoric (Institutiones Oratoriae, 1711–1741), from the definitive Latin text and notes, Italian commentary and introduction by Giuliano Crifò. Translated and Edited by Giorgio A. Pinton and Arthur W. Shippee. A volume in **Values in Italian Philosophy**

38. W. H. Werkmeister, *Martin Heidegger on the Way*. Edited by Richard T. Hull. A volume in **Werkmeister Studies**

39. Phillip Stambovsky, *Myth and the Limits of Reason*

40. Samantha Brennan, Tracy Isaacs, and Michael Milde, Editors, *A Question of Values: New Canadian Perspectives in Ethics and Political Philosophy*

41. Peter A. Redpath, *Cartesian Nightmare: An Introduction to Transcendental Sophistry*. A volume in **Studies in the History of Western Philosophy**

42. Clark Butler, *History as the Story of Freedom: Philosophy in Intercultural Context*, with responses by sixteen scholars

43. Dennis Rohatyn, *Philosophy History Sophistry*

44. Leon Shaskolsky Sheleff, *Social Cohesion and Legal Coercion: A Critique of Weber, Durkheim, and Marx*. Afterword by Virginia Black

45. Alan Soble, Editor, *Sex, Love, and Friendship: Studies of the Society for the Philosophy of Sex and Love, 1977–1992.* A volume **in Histories and Addresses of Philosophical Societies**

46. Peter A. Redpath, Wisdom's Odyssey: From Philosophy to Transcendental *Sophistry*. A volume in **Studies in the History of Western Philosophy**

47. Albert A. Anderson, *Universal Justice: A Dialectical Approach.* A volume in **Universal Justice**

48. Pio Colonnello, *The Philosophy of José Gaos*. Translated from Italian by Peter Cocozzella. Edited by Myra Moss. Introduction by Giovanni Gullace. A volume in **Values in Italian Philosophy**

49. Laura Duhan Kaplan and Laurence F. Bove, Editors, *Philosophical Perspectives on Power and Domination: Theories and Practices.* A volume in **Philosophy of Peace**

50. Gregory F. Mellema, *Collective Responsibility*

51. Josef Seifert, *What Is Life? The Originality, Irreducibility, and Value of Life.* A volume in **Central-European Value Studies**

52. William Gerber, *Anatomy of What We Value Most*

53. Armando Molina, *Our Ways: Values and Character*, Edited by Rem B. Edwards. A volume in **Hartman Institute Axiology Studies**

54. Kathleen J. Wininger, *Nietzsche's Reclamation of Philosophy.* A volume in **Central-European Value Studies**

55. Thomas Magnell, Editor, *Explorations of Value*

56. HPP (Hennie) Lötter, *Injustice, Violence, and Peace: The Case of South Africa.* A volume in **Philosophy of Peace**

57. Lennart Nordenfelt, *Talking About Health: A Philosophical Dialogue.* A volume in **Nordic Value Studies**

58. Jon Mills and Janusz A. Polanowski, *The Ontology of Prejudice.* A volume in **Philosophy and Psychology**

59. Leena Vilkka, *The Intrinsic Value of Nature*

60. Palmer Talbutt, Jr., Rough Dialectics: *Sorokin's Philosophy of Value*, with contributions by Lawrence T. Nichols and Pitirim A. Sorokin

61. C. L. Sheng, *A Utilitarian General Theory of Value*

62. George David Miller, *Negotiating Toward Truth: The Extinction of Teachers and Students*. Epilogue by Mark Roelof Eleveld.
A volume in **Philosophy of Education**

63. William Gerber, *Love, Poetry, and Immortality: Luminous Insights of the World's Great Thinkers*

64. Dane R. Gordon, Editor, *Philosophy in Post-Communist Europe*.
A volume in **Post-Communist European Thought**

65. Dane R. Gordon and Józef Niznik, Editors, *Criticism and Defense of Rationality in Contemporary Philosophy*.
A volume in **Post-Communist European Thought**

66. John R. Shook, *Pragmatism: An Annotated Bibliography, 1898-1940*. With contributions by E. Paul Colella, Lesley Friedman, Frank X. Ryan, and Ignas K. Skrupskelis

67. Lansana Keita, *The Human Project and the Temptations of Science*

68. Michael M. Kazanjian, *Phenomenology and Education: Cosmology, Co-Being, and Core Curriculum*. A volume in **Philosophy of Education**

69. James W. Vice, *The Reopening of the American Mind: On Skepticism and Constitutionalism*

70. Sarah Bishop Merrill, *Defining Personhood: Toward the Ethics of Quality in Clinical Care*

71. Dane R. Gordon, *Philosophy and Vision*

72. Alan Milchman and Alan Rosenberg, Editors, *Postmodernism and the Holocaust*. A volume in **Holocaust and Genocide Studies**

73. Peter A. Redpath, *Masquerade of the Dream Walkers: Prophetic Theology from the Cartesians to Hegel*. A volume in **Studies in the History of Western**

Philosophy

74. Malcolm D. Evans, *Whitehead and Philosophy of Education: The Seamless Coat of Learning*. A volume in **Philosophy of Education**

75. Warren E. Steinkraus, *Taking Religious Claims Seriously: A Philosophy of Religion*, edited by Michael H. Mitias. A volume in **Universal Justice**

76. Thomas Magnell, Editor, *Values and Education*

77. Kenneth A. Bryson, *Persons and Immortality*.
A volume in **Natural Law Studies**

78. Steven V. Hicks, *International Law and the Possibility of a Just World Order: An Essay on Hegel's Universalism*. A volume in **Universal Justice**

79. E. F. Kaelin, *Texts on Texts and Textuality: A Phenomenology of Literary Art*, Edited by Ellen J. Burns

80. Amihud Gilead, Saving Possibilities: A Study in Philosophical Psychology. *A volume in Philosophy and Psychology*

81. André Mineau, *The Making of the Holocaust: Ideology and Ethics in the Systems Perspective*. A volume in **Holocaust and Genocide Studies**

82. Howard P. Kainz, *Politically Incorrect Dialogues: Topics Not Discussed in Polite Circles*

83. Veikko Launis, Juhani Pietarinen, and Juha Räikkä, Editors, *Genes and Morality: New Essays*. A volume in **Nordic Value Studies**

84. Steven Schroeder, *The Metaphysics of Cooperation: A Study of F. D. Maurice*

85. Caroline Joan ("Kay") S. Picart, *Thomas Mann and Friedrich Nietzsche: Eroticism, Death, Music, and Laughter*.
A volume in **Central-European Value Studies**

86. G. John M. Abbarno, Editor, *The Ethics of Homelessness: Philosophical Perspectives*

87. James Giles, Editor, *French Existentialism: Consciousness, Ethics, and Relations with Others*. A volume in **Nordic Value Studies**

88. Deane Curtin and Robert Litke, Editors, *Institutional Violence*. A volume in **Philosophy of Peace**

89. Yuval Lurie, *Cultural Beings: Reading the Philosophers of Genesis*

90. Sandra A. Wawrytko, Editor, *The Problem of Evil: An Intercultural Exploration*. A volume in **Philosophy and Psychology**

91. Gary J. Acquaviva, *Values, Violence, and Our Future*. volume in **Hartman Institute Axiology Studies**

92. Michael R. Rhodes, *Coercion: A Nonevaluative Approach*

93. Jacques Kriel, *Matter, Mind, and Medicine: Transforming the Clinical Method*

94. Haim Gordon, *Dwelling Poetically: Educational Challenges in Heidegger's Thinking on Poetry*. A volume in **Philosophy of Education**

95. Ludwig Grünberg, *The Mystery of Values: Studies in Axiology*, edited by Cornelia Grünberg and Laura Grünberg

96. Gerhold K. Becker, Editor, *The Moral Status of Persons: Perspectives on Bioethics*. A volume in **Studies in Applied Ethics**

97. Roxanne Claire Farrar, *Sartrean Dialectics: A Method for Critical Discourse on Aesthetic Experience*

98. Ugo Spirito, *Memoirs of the Twentieth Century*. Translated from Italian and edited by Anthony G. Costantini. A volume in **Values in Italian Philosophy**

99. Steven Schroeder, *Between Freedom and Necessity: An Essay on the Place of Value*

100. Foster N. Walker, *Enjoyment and the Activity of Mind: Dialogues on Whitehead and Education*. A volume in **Philosophy of Education**

101. Avi Sagi, Kierkegaard, *Religion, and Existence: The Voyage of the Self*. Translated from Hebrew by Batya Stein

102. Bennie R. Crockett, Jr., Editor, *Addresses of the Mississippi Philosophical Association*. A volume in **Histories and Addresses of Philosophical Societies**

103. Paul van Dijk, *Anthropology in the Age of Technology: The Philosophical Contribution of Günther Anders*

104. Giambattista Vico, *Universal Right*. Translated from Latin and Edited by Giorgio Pinton and Margaret Diehl. A volume in **Values in Italian Philosophy**

105. Judith Presler and Sally J. Scholz, Editors, *Peacemaking: Lessons from the Past, Visions for the Future*. A volume in **Philosophy of Peace**

106. Dennis Bonnette, *Origin of the Human Species*. A volume in **Studies in the History of Western Philosophy**

107. Phyllis Chiasson, *Peirce's Pragmatism: The Design for Thinking*. A volume in **Studies in Pragmatism and Values**

108. Dan Stone, Editor, *Theoretical Interpretations of the Hol*ocaust. A volume in **Holocaust and Genocide Studies**

109. Raymond Angelo Belliotti, *What Is the Meaning of Human Life?*

110. Lennart Nordenfelt, *Health, Science, and Ordinary Language*, with Contributions by George Khushf and K. W. M. Fulford

111. Daryl Koehn, *Local Insights, Global Ethics for Business*. A volume in **Studies in Applied Ethics**

112. Matti Häyry and Tuija Takala, Editors, *The Future of Value Inquiry*. A volume in **Nordic Value Studies**

113. Conrad P. Pritscher, *Quantum Learning: Beyond Duality*

114. Thomas M. Dicken and Rem B. Edwards, *Dialogues on Values and Centers of Value: Old Friends, New Thoughts*. A volume in **Hartman Institute Axiology Studies**

115. Rem B. Edwards, *What Caused the Big Bang?* A volume in **Philosophy and Religion**

116. Jon Mills, Editor, *A Pedagogy of Becoming*. A volume in **Philosophy of Education**

117. Robert T. Radford, *Cicero: A Study in the Origins of Republican Philosophy*. A volume in **Studies in the History of Western Philosophy**

118. Arleen L. F. Salles and María Julia Bertomeu, Editors, *Bioethics: Latin American Perspectives*. A volume in **Philosophy in Latin America**

119. Nicola Abbagnano, *The Human Project: The Year 2000*, with an Interview by Guiseppe Grieco. Translated from Italian by Bruno Martini and Nino Langiulli. Edited with an introduction by Nino Langiulli. A volume in **Studies in the History of Western Philosophy**

120. Daniel M. Haybron, Editor, *Earth's Abominations: Philosophical Studies of Evil*. A volume in **Personalist Studies**

121. Anna T. Challenger, *Philosophy and Art in Gurdjieff's Beelzebub: A Modern Sufi Odyssey*

122. George David Miller, *Peace, Value, and Wisdom: The Educational Philosophy of Daisaku Ikeda*. A volume in **Daisaku Ikeda Studies**

123. Haim Gordon and Rivca Gordon, *Sophistry and Twentieth-Century Art*

124. Thomas O Buford and Harold H. Oliver, Editors *Personalism Revisited: Its Proponents and Critics*. A volume in **Histories and Addresses of Philosophical Societies**

125. Avi Sagi, *Albert Camus and the Philosophy of the Absurd*. Translated from Hebrew by Batya Stein

126. Robert S. Hartman, *The Knowledge of Good: Critique of Axiologic l Reason*. Expanded translation from the Spanish by Robert S. Hartman. Edited by Arthur R. Ellis and Rem B. Edwards. A volume in **Hartman Institute Axiology Studies**

127. Alison Bailey and Paula J. Smithka, Editors. *Community, Diversity, and Difference: Implications for Peace*. A volume in **Philosophy of Peace**

128. Oscar Vilarroya, *The Dissolution of Mind: A Fable of How Experience Gives Rise to Cognition*. A volume in **Cognitive Science**

129. Paul Bube and Jefferey Geller, Editors, *Conversations with Pragmatism*. A volume in **Studies in Pragmatism and Values**

130. Richard Rumana, *Richard Rorty: An Annotated Bibliography of Secondary Literature*. A volume in **Studies in Pragmatism and Values**

131. Stephen Schneck, *Max Scheler's Acting Persons: New Perspectives*. A volume in **Personalist Studies**

132. Michael Kazanjian, *Learning Values Lifelong: From Inert Ideas to Wholes*. A volume in **Philosophy of Education**

133. Rudolph Alexander Kofi Cain: *Alain Leroy Locke: Race, Culture, and the Education of African American Adults.* A Volume in **African American Philosophy**

134. Werner J. Krieglstein, *Compassion: A New Philosophy of the Other.*

135. Robert N. Fisher, Daniel T. Primozic, Peter A. Day, and Joel A. Thompson, Editors, *Suffering, Death, and Identity*. A volume in **Personalist Studies**

136. Steven Schroeder, *Touching Philosophy, Sounding Religion, Placing Education.* A volume in **Philosophy of Education**

137. Guy Debrock, *Process Pragmatism: Essays on a Quiet Philosophical Revolution*. A volume in **Studies in Pragmatism and Values**

138. Lennart Nordenfelt and Per-Erik Liss, Editors, *Dimensions of Health and Health Promotion.*

139. Amihud Gilead, *Singularity and Other Possibilities: Panenmentalist Novelties.*

140. Samantha Mei-che Pang, *Nursing Ethics in Modern China: Conflicting Values and Competing Role Requirements*. A volume in **Studies in Applied Ethics**

141. Christine M. Koggel, Allannah Furlong, and Charles Levin, Editors, *Confidential Relationships: Psychoanalytic, Ethical, and Legal Contexts*. A volume in **Philosophy and Psychology**